Woodland creation for wildlife and people in a changing climate

Principles and practice

by

David Blakesley and Peter Buckley

Wildlife Landscapes
ECOLOGICAL PRACTITIONERS

Sponsored by

To Kik and Tone

Citation
For bibliographic purposes, this book should be referred to as
Blakesley, D and Buckley, GP. 2010. *Woodland Creation for Wildlife and People in a Changing Climate: principles and practice*. Pisces Publications, Newbury.

The rights of David Blakesley and Peter Buckley to be identified as the Authors of this work has been asserted by them in accordance with the Copyright, Designs and Patents Act 1988

Copyright © David Blakesley and Peter Buckley
Illustrations © Tharada Blakesley; photographs © David Blakesley, Wildlife Landscapes unless stated in the text

All rights reserved. No part of this publication may be reproduced in any form without prior permission of the authors

First published 2010

British-Library-in-Publication Data
A catalogue record for this book is available from the British Library

ISBN: 978-1-874357-44-5

Designed and published by Pisces Publications

Pisces Publications is the imprint of NatureBureau, 36 Kingfisher Court, Hambridge Road, Newbury, Berkshire RG14 5SJ

Printed by Information Press
Cover photographs by David Blakesley and Nigel Blake, rspb-images.com (willow warbler)

All reasonable efforts have been made by the authors to trace the copyright owners of the material quoted in this book and any images reproduced in this book. In the event that the authors or publishers are notified of any mistakes or omissions by copyright owners after publication of this book, the authors and the publishers will endeavour to rectify the position accordingly for any subsequent printing.

Dr David Blakesley CEnv, MIEEM (Wildlife Landscapes) is an ecological practitioner and writer, specialising in habitat restoration and wildlife surveys; david.blakesley@btinternet.com

Dr Peter Buckley MIEEM is an ex-academic and forest ecologist, specialising in habitat restoration and management; gp.buckley@yahoo.co.uk

Disclaimer
The information presented in this book on behalf of the authors is believed to be accurate and correct, but this cannot be guaranteed. Readers must take all appropriate steps to ensure health and safety of all users, and to follow their own health and safety policy. The authors issue this book without responsibility for accidents or damage as a result of its use or the implementation of any of the recommendations within this book.

CONTENTS

Foreword	vi
Messages of support	vii
Acknowledgements	viii
Introduction	ix
PART 1 GENERAL PRINCIPLES	1

Chapter 1
Native woodland in the British landscape — 2

- 1.1 Extent of native woodland in Britain — 2
- 1.2 Native woodland communities — 4
  - 1.2.1 Lowland beech and yew woodland — 6
  - 1.2.2 Lowland mixed deciduous woodland — 8
  - 1.2.3 Upland mixed ash woods — 8
  - 1.2.4 Upland oak woods — 8
  - 1.2.5 Upland birch woods — 10
  - 1.2.6 Native pinewoods — 11
  - 1.2.7 Wet woodlands — 11
  - 1.2.8 Wood pasture and parkland — 12
  - 1.2.9 Scrub communities — 13
- 1.3 A brief review of modern woodland creation in Britain — 14
- 1.4 New native woodland initiatives — 15
  - 1.4.1 Woodland creation in the future — 16

Chapter 2
Woodlands for wildlife — 18

- 2.1 Natural succession — 18
  - 2.1.1 Woodland succession — 19
  - 2.1.2 Woodland seed banks — 22
- 2.2 Woodland plants — 22
  - 2.2.1 Herbaceous plants — 22
  - 2.2.2 Shade-tolerant plants — 24
  - 2.2.3 Woodland specialist plants — 26
- 2.3 Woodland birds — 28
  - 2.3.1 Generalist and specialist species — 28
  - 2.3.2 Birds and woodland types — 29
  - 2.3.3 Birds of new native woodland — 30
  - 2.3.4 Woodland birds of conservation concern — 31
- 2.4 Woodland bats — 33
- 2.5 Woodland invertebrates — 34
  - 2.5.1 Invertebrate diversity in mature woodland — 34
  - 2.5.2 Butterflies of new native woodland — 37

Chapter 3
Woodlands for people — 41

- 3.1 Woodland and society — 41
  - 3.1.1 Recreation and accessibility — 41
  - 3.1.2 Health and well-being — 43
  - 3.1.3 Children and woodland — 45
  - 3.1.4 Involving people in woodland creation and management — 47
- 3.2 Ecosystem services — 49
  - 3.2.1 Regulating services — 49
  - 3.2.2 Provisioning services — 50

Chapter 4
Woodland creation in a changing climate   51

- 4.1 Britain – a changing climate   51
- 4.2 How climate change might affect woodland communities   51
  - 4.2.1 Community composition and plant dispersal   53
  - 4.2.2 Climate space for individual species   55
  - 4.2.3 The future for Britain's woodland including UK BAP priority habitats   56
- 4.3 Specifying sources of seeds of trees and shrubs   59
  - 4.3.1 Origin and provenance   59
  - 4.3.2 Gene flow and genetic diversity   60
  - 4.3.3 Regions of provenance and seed zones in Britain   60
  - 4.3.4 Consideration of seed sources in a changing climate   62
- 4.4 Coping strategies for climate change   63
  - 4.4.1 Ecological networks   63
  - 4.4.2 Woodland habitat networks   66

Chapter 5
Landscape planning for woodland creation   69

- 5.1 Landscape Character Assessment in the Britain   69
  - 5.1.1 Landscape character in England   69
  - 5.1.2 Landscape character in Wales   71
  - 5.1.3 Landscape character in Scotland   72
- 5.2 Siting new woods: the landscape context   73
  - 5.2.1 Planting strategies   73
  - 5.2.2 Buffering existing woods   74
  - 5.2.3 Habitat extension – adding to existing woods   74
  - 5.2.4 Increasing connectivity between woods   76
  - 5.2.5 Which strategy?   77
  - 5.2.6 General conclusions   78

PART 2 WOODLAND CREATION PRACTICE   79

Chapter 6
Planning a woodland creation project   80

- Introduction   80
- 6.1 Assessing landscape character   80
  - 6.1.1 Published information on local landscape character   80
  - 6.1.2 Undertaking a landscape evaluation   84
- 6.2 Biodiversity of the proposed woodland creation site and its environs   87
  - 6.2.1 European Protected Species   87
  - 6.2.2 Undertaking a Phase 1 habitat survey   88
  - 6.2.3 Wildlife surveys   90
- 6.3 Geology and soils of the proposed woodland creation site   94
  - 6.3.1 Published information on local geology and soils   94
  - 6.3.2 Commissioning a soil survey   95
- 6.4 Semi-natural 'reference' habitats in the local landscape   96
  - 6.4.1 Published information on potential reference sites   97
  - 6.4.2 Visiting reference sites   98
- 6.5 Reviewing ecological data   102
  - 6.5.1 Ecological assessment of Lamberhurst Farm – a worked example   103
- 6.6 Other landscape evaluation methods   104
  - 6.6.1 Ecological Site Classification   104
  - 6.6.2 Environmental Impact Assessment (Forestry)   104
- 6.7 Finding out about planting grants for new native woodland   105
  - 6.7.1 Forestry Commission grants   105
  - 6.7.2 Other planting grants   106

CONTENTS

Chapter 7
Designing a new wood and selecting species to plant   107

- 7.1 Designing a new wood   107
  - 7.1.1 Making use of natural regeneration   107
  - 7.1.2 Limitations of natural regeneration   109
  - 7.1.3 The value of open space in a woodland creation scheme   110
  - 7.1.4 Designing rides and glades   111
  - 7.1.5 Managing rides and glades   114
- 7.2 Selecting trees and shrubs   115
- 7.3 Sourcing seed of trees and shrubs   122
- 7.4 Planting patterns   123
  - 7.4.1 Designs for new native woodland   123
- 7.5 Creating plant communities in rides and open spaces   124
  - 7.5.1 Formulating seed mixes   127

Chapter 8
Establishing new native woodland   134

- 8.1 Planting trees and shrubs   134
  - 8.1.1 Planting stock   134
  - 8.1.2 Protection after planting   135
- 8.2 Direct seeding   137
- 8.3 Taking care of trees and shrubs after planting   139
  - 8.3.1 Weed control   140
  - 8.3.2 Replacing dead trees   143

Chapter 9
Post-establishment management   144

- 9.1 Post-establishment operations   144
  - 9.1.1 Respacing and cleaning   144
  - 9.1.2 Pruning young trees   144
  - 9.1.3 Thinning   146
  - 9.1.4 Coppicing and group felling   146
- 9.2 Providing additional resources for wildlife   147
  - 9.2.1 Deadwood   147
  - 9.2.2 Bat boxes   148
  - 9.2.3 Boxes for other mammals   148
  - 9.2.4 Bird nestboxes   148
  - 9.2.5 Woodland ponds   149
- 9.3 Introducing a woodland ground flora   150
  - 9.3.1 Arguments for and against introducing a woodland ground flora   150
  - 9.3.2 Procuring woodland plants   150
  - 9.3.3 Introducing woodland plants   152
- 9.4 Monitoring tree establishment and growth   153
- 9.5 Monitoring biodiversity change   153
  - 9.5.1 Monitoring ground flora   154
  - 9.5.2 Monitoring birds   154
  - 9.5.3 Monitoring mammals   155
  - 9.5.4 Monitoring butterflies   155

Glossary   157

List of species mentioned in the text   161

Acronyms   165

References   166

FOREWORD

You walk on a heath, over grassland, across a bog... but you walk *through* a wood. It encloses you, envelopes you and shelters you. And not only you: woodlands' relative complexity, their 'spatial heterogeneity', their strata and multitude of surfaces provide for a greater number of possibilities, niches, for a far greater range of wildlife than out on the 'flatlands'. That's why we are so concerned about conserving woodlands; they are our most biodiverse terrestrial habitat. A pity, then, that they have, and continue to be, felled... but don't dismay, nature is tenacious, it doesn't give up, it is designed to recover and given the chance of a helping hand, it will.

I recall sitting in my O Level Biology class and being told that if we left an arable field alone for 90 years it would become oak woodland. The process was called 'succession' and as explained it made sense. But it seemed a long time to wait to get back to a native habitat that in truth wouldn't be a really good piece of woodland anyway. Well, that lesson was taught long ago and today those processes are not only better understood, but better managed too. And that is the essential key to this book's remarkable potential – through measured, tried and tested research we now know how to 'build' better woodlands and it doesn't take a lifetime. If the guidance and advice provided by the authors were applied, then the whole process can be optimised for a great range of species, from the first seedling: so the eventual and dynamic climax would be ensured to be maximally productive too.

So don't be frightened by the concept, making woodland is not the stuff of ages, it's the stuff of gardens, school grounds, road verges and the wider countryside. By using this passionately driven and comprehensive guide to plan the development of canopy layers, shrubs, herbs, clearings, glades and rides, to organise species lists and design landscape strategies you, yes you, can create prosperous and rich communities of life, and frankly – what could be a finer ambition?

Chris Packham
New Forest
2010

MESSAGES OF SUPPORT

The Woodland Trust

The Woodland Trust is the UK's largest woodland conservation charity. Our vision is of a UK rich in native woods and trees, yet currently we are one of the least wooded countries in Europe. For many years, the Woodland Trust has worked hard to tackle this by designing and planting our own new native woods with wildlife in mind, usually close to where people live and with free public access. We're passionate about protecting the wonderful wildlife to be found in the UK's woods, and we want to share that passion with others by inspiring them to get out into the woods too. Increasingly, we are now encouraging others to plant trees and create native woods on their own land, so that together we can create new, more wooded landscapes that will benefit humans and wildlife alike.

Sian Atkinson
Conservation Team Leader, Woodland Trust

The Eden Project

At Eden we have been pleased to work with the authors over many years as leading practitioners of woodland creation and restoration in the UK and globally.

Their book is fantastically timely. There has never been such a need to repair some of the damage and help the recovery of natural systems. By supporting the restoration of ecosystem services and species movements restoration is now accepted as a critical complement to the traditional palette of nature conservation and a vitally important approach for the 21st century.

Tony Kendle
Director of the Eden Foundation

The RSPB

There are many valid reasons why new woodlands are needed in the landscape. However, if they are to help to meet the challenges that biodiversity and people will face in the coming decades, they will need to be designed and implemented with great care.

The RSPB supports this handbook as a major contribution to ensuring that new woodland will provide quality space for wildlife to adapt to the environmental changes we face today and into the foreseeable future, and for us to enjoy.

Nigel Symes
Land Management Advisor

ACKNOWLEDGEMENTS

We must start by expressing our sincere gratitude to the Woodland Trust, the Eden Project, and the Royal Society for the Protection of Birds (RSPB) for their sponsorship of this book, and in particular John Tucker, Nicola Strazzullo, Sian Atkinson, Tony Kendle and Nigel Symes. Without their backing and support, this book would not have been possible.

Many people have helped us by providing advice, information or discussing ideas. We would especially like to thank David Anning (RSPB), Philip Ashmole (Borders Forest Trust), Pam Berry (Oxford University Centre for the Environment), Paul Bowyer (Oxford University Centre for the Environment), Ewan Calcott (Forestry Commission), Steve Coldrick (Forestry Commission), Laura Dunne (Bat Conservation Trust), Andrea Faber Taylor (University of Illinois), Jonathan Harding (Forestry Commission), Bruce Jackson (Countryside Council for Wales), Jim Latham (Countryside Council for Wales), Dave Leech (British Trust for Ornithology), Colin Morris (Vincent Wildlife Trust), James Newmarch (East Sussex County Council), Gordon Patterson (Forestry Commission Scotland), Steve Scott (Forestry Commission), Clive Steward (Woodland Trust), Ruth Swetnam (University of Cambridge), Kevin Watts (Forest Research) and Pete Wilson (RSPB). We would like to thank Neil Hipps (East Malling Research) for allowing us to draw on material gathered as part of a European Union Interreg IIIA project, co-sponsored by the Highways Agency.

The book has benefitted greatly from being critically read by Nigel Symes (RSPB), with whom we were able to discuss many key aspects of the subject matter. Keith Kirby (Natural England) commented constructively on whole chapters, and also provided original material on the siting of new woods in a landscape context. Many others gave valuable insights on sections of the book, including Sian Atkinson (Woodland Trust), Nicola Banister (Landscape Archaeologist), John Briggs (Countryside Council for Wales), Paul Bright (Royal Holloway, University of London), Laura Campbell (Scottish Natural Heritage), Dan Hoare (Butterfly Conservation), David Hill (University of Sussex), Liz O'Brien (Forest Research) and Richard Smithers (Woodland Trust). Any errors that remain are firmly our responsibility.

We are indebted to Peter and Barbara Creed (Pisces Publications) for the design and layout of the book and thank those who have provided additional photographs and material for maps and figures, all of whom are acknowledged individually in the captions. Finally, we are both grateful for the support and understanding of our families during the writing of this book.

David Blakesley and Peter Buckley

INTRODUCTION

The British landscape is greatly enriched by its forests, woodland and trees, which in turn provide valuable habitats for wildlife and a wide range of benefits for society. Ancient, semi-natural woodlands are particularly rich in biodiversity, their complex ecosystems ensuring that each is in some way unique. Mature trees and an overhead canopy epitomises woodland for many people, but woodland encompasses a wider range of habitats, including structurally diverse edges, rides and glades which may support communities more typical of meadows, wetlands or heathlands. These open habitats should be considered as integral components of new native woodland creation schemes and be included in the development of woodland habitat networks.

The area of woodland in Britain has declined dramatically since man first started to clear the 'wildwood' six thousand years ago. Although probably in excess of 80% of Britain's land was forested at one time, this had declined to just 5% by the early part of the twentieth century. More recently, large areas of native woodland have been further fragmented through agriculture, urban development or replanting with conifers, a process which continues to threaten woodland margins and scrub, habitats which are extremely important to wildlife in our highly managed landscapes. In contrast, although once intensively managed, over the past few decades many ancient woods have lost much of their structural diversity through neglect. Climate change represents a new threat, with accumulating scientific evidence suggesting that woodland ecosystems are already being affected. Ancient woods are now recognised as a vital resource for wildlife in the Government's UK Biodiversity Action Plan. However, the survival of many woodland species may come to depend on measures to expand their habitat or improve its quality. The fragmented distribution of native woodland means that new woods must be created on a significant scale in order to maintain species populations and facilitate the dispersal of woodland plants and animals through the landscape. Creating ecological or habitat networks, and buffering small isolated woods to make existing populations more resilient, is becoming more important.

Although there has been a modest increase in woodland cover over the past 90 years, Britain still has one of the lowest areas of woodland in Europe. Commercial, mainly non-native conifer plantations account for much of this increase, but have less wildlife potential than native woodland. In order to achieve significant new native woodland creation and develop woodland habitat networks, it is important to engage people and communities. People need to be aware not only of the conservation issues surrounding native woodland and the threats of climate change, but also the way in which woodland can enrich their own lives and benefit their communities. Much work has been undertaken over the past 15 years to understand the range of ways in which people engage with, enjoy, use and help to conserve woodlands. This has focused on issues such as the ecosystem services and other important contributions that woodland and trees can make to people's physical health, and their psychological and social well-being. The educational value of woodland has also become apparent.

Bluebells and wood anemones, pictured here along the edge of ancient woodland, are beginning to colonise the new woodland in the background.

Wildlife of new native woodland

New native woodland has been planted under various woodland grant schemes implemented both before and since the introduction of the Forestry Commission's pivotal Broadleaves Policy Review of 1985, which advocated 'the greater use of broadleaved woodlands generally for conservation, recreation, sport and landscape'. Many were designed to complement local landscape character and provide valuable habitat for its wildlife. Managed appropriately, they have the potential to make a significant contribution to conservation by supporting a rich variety of woodland flora and fauna, while contributing to broader habitat networks. For example, investigations by the authors in new native woodland in South East England have found birds of conservation concern such as turtle dove, nightingale, willow warbler and bullfinch; declining wider countryside butterflies such as small copper and small heath; and plants characteristic of ancient woodland such as bluebell and ramsons.

Open habitats in woodlands are becoming increasingly important in a wider countryside context too, with the loss of large areas of unimproved grassland, wetland and heathland. Rides and glades in new native woodland can support such communities, and act as stepping stones to facilitate the movement of species through often inhospitable agricultural landscapes. Even small fragments of open habitat in new native woodland can be important in their own right, supporting not just plants, but also a rich diversity of invertebrates.

Scope of the guide

This guide considers the many environmental issues of the day which contribute to the success of woodland creation initiatives in Britain, and how they might feature in forward planning. This will require an understanding of the local landscape and the habitats which it supports, the needs of local people, the crucial issue of climate change and the critical role that new woodlands can play in supporting the movement of wildlife across fragmented landscapes. In Part 1, we consider the principles and issues underlying woodland creation projects, such as the relevance of different woodland community types, the trajectory of natural succession, and the wildlife that may colonise new woods, including birds, bats, insects and plants. We also consider the ecosystem services provided by new woodland for people, the threat of climate change, coping strategies to mitigate the loss of climate space for individual species, and the planning of woodland habitat networks and planting strategies.

Part 2 provides more practical information for anyone carrying out woodland creation schemes, from the planning and selection of optimum sites, sourcing seeds and selecting tree species to woodland design, layout and management. It is aimed particularly at woodland creation on former agricultural, urban or industrial land and is intended as a guide to woodland owners, private landowners, national and local conservation organisations, foresters, consultants, planners, local authorities and community groups.

LEFT **Small heath, a UK Biodiversity Action Plan priority species which can be found in new woodland rides.**

RIGHT **Lords-and-ladies is a plant which often colonises new native woodland.**

INTRODUCTION

Tall herbs along the edge of a new woodland ride are very attractive to a diverse range of invertebrates.

New native woodland at the thicket stage.

PART 1
GENERAL PRINCIPLES

1 NATIVE WOODLAND IN THE BRITISH LANDSCAPE

1.1 Extent of native woodland in Britain

The UK is one of the least forested nations in the European Union, with only 2.84 million ha or c.12% of tree cover compared with an average of 44% in the 27 EU countries (Figure 1.1). Woodland covered only about 5% of Britain at the beginning of the 20th century, at a time when there was little government interest in forestry. Since then it has more than doubled through the growth of state sector forests, government planting incentives to the private sector, non-government organisations and conservation charities. Two-thirds of the woodland area of the UK has now been established through deliberate planting, compared with 86% in Ireland, 63% in Denmark, 41% in Belgium and 13% in France (FAO, 2006).

Forest expansion policies date back to the First World War, when the loss of almost one-third of the standing timber volume was the stimulus for the formation in 1919 of the Forestry Commission. Their remit was to grow a 'strategic reserve' of woodland in case of future emergencies, but also to offset the heavy dependency of the country on imports of industrial timber, especially conifers. Besides emphasising forest productivity, government policies over the last three decades have increasingly recognised other, non-timber benefits such as public recreation, urban renewal, biodiversity conservation and carbon sequestration. In particular, the 1985 Wildlife and Countryside (Amendment) Act introduced a new Broadleaves Policy with nature conservation as a key aim, modifying the traditional commercial orientation of forestry incentive schemes.

From 1919 until the mid-1980s the new forests replaced heaths, moors, upland and lowland grassland, bogs and sand dunes – habitats that today are recognised by Biodiversity Action Plans as valuable in their own right for wildlife conservation. Land of low agricultural value that was available at the time was leased or purchased, with the centres of expansion in the uplands and mountains of southern and western Scotland, the Borders, Wales and the North Yorkshire Moors. Lowland heaths and unproductive grasslands in Norfolk, Suffolk, Dorset and the High Weald were also targeted. Because of the poor quality of this land, conifers were planted as they grew well on, or tolerated such sites, invariably out-yielding broadleaved species; and they were the type of timber that the market demanded. As a result, conifers are the dominant forest type today, particularly in Scotland and Wales, accounting for nearly half of Britain's woodland cover. In contrast, lowland England remains predominantly broadleaved, with a significant area still present as old coppice woodlands, predating 20th century expansion (Figure 1.2). In addition, the Forestry Commission's *National Inventory of Woodland and Trees* (Forestry Commission, 2003a) identified a significant population of 123 million non-woodland trees in the wider landscape, of which over 70% were in England, present as individuals, linear features and groups.

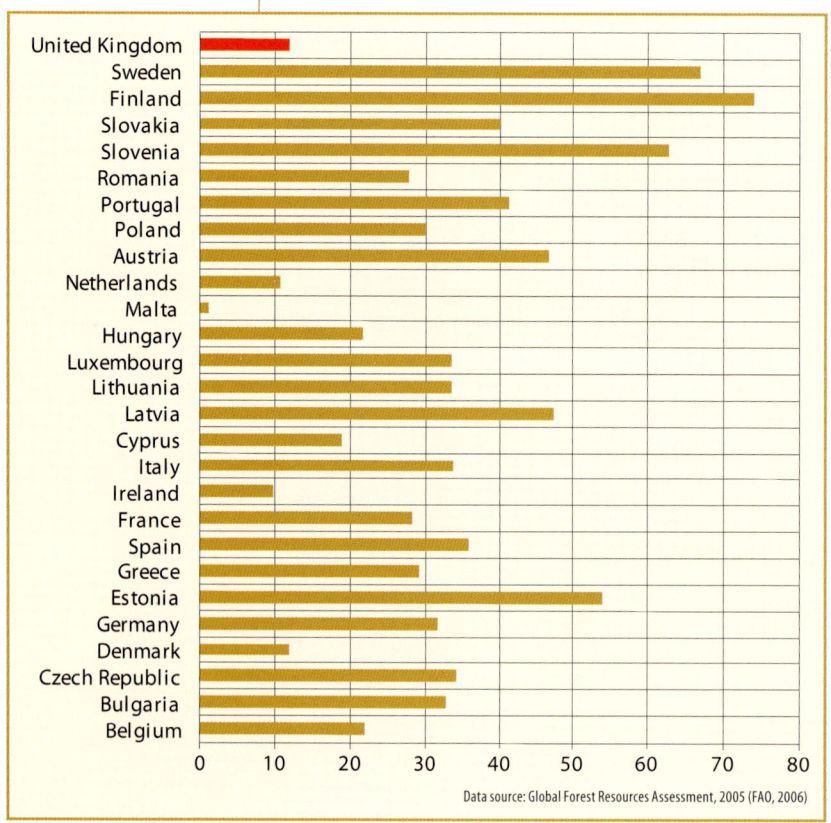

Figure 1.1 Forest cover (%) in the 27 EU member states.

Data source: Global Forest Resources Assessment, 2005 (FAO, 2006)

The species composition of forests and woodlands reflects their history. Relatively few tree species are suitable for productive plantation forestry and many of these are introduced, exotic species, used in both the public and private forestry sectors. Sitka spruce was first used as a major afforestation species in the 1920s and now dominates British forestry in the uplands, occupying approximately 28% of the entire forest area – greater than that covered by native

PART ONE GENERAL PRINCIPLES – NATIVE WOODLAND IN THE BRITISH LANDSCAPE

broadleaves. The native Scots pine is the next most important – traditionally grown on light, free-draining soils, especially by private estates in central and eastern Scotland. Lodgepole pine is another upland species favoured by the Forestry Commission, grown on peaty soils, while Corsican pine was preferred on poor soils in the lowlands. Most of the broadleaves grown commercially are native; of the five main species, oak is most important (and was the dominant species in England before Scots pine and Sitka spruce), with a large bias towards private estates: beech and oak are the only significant species in Forestry Commission ownership. Birch is next in importance, especially in Scotland, followed by ash and sycamore and other broadleaves such as poplar, elm and sweet chestnut (Figure 1.3).

The private sector also controls considerable areas of long-established woodland of relatively high conservation value, consisting mainly of broadleaved coppices and naturally regenerated high forest categories, which form unique stand types such as the lime coppices in North Essex and South Suffolk, the hornbeam woods of the Weald and the pinewoods of the Scottish Highlands. Since 1930 the remaining fragments of ancient, semi-natural woodland have suffered greatly – in England about half survives (Spencer and Kirby, 1992) – 7% having been lost through direct clearance (mostly agricultural), and 38% converted to plantations (often coniferous, with the largest woods usually converted). Concern over the loss and fragmentation of ancient woodland led to the commissioning of an Ancient Woodland Inventory, a survey carried out between 1981–91 by the Nature Conservancy Council (now comprising Natural England, the Countryside Council for Wales and Scottish Natural Heritage), using maps, historic documents and field surveys to locate such woodlands and record losses over time. This produced easily accessible maps and gave the first estimates of the remaining native woodland resource.

Altogether, about 20% of the woodland cover in Britain and c.60% of its broadleaved area is ancient in origin (550,000 ha, defined as having been in continuous woodland cover for at least 400 years). Of this, some 325,800 ha are ancient, semi-natural – i.e. consisting of largely intact canopies of native species that have not been replanted (Pryor and Smith, 2002). These are predominantly broadleaved in character, but include nearly 18,000 ha of native, Caledonian pinewoods in the Scottish Highlands (Jones, 1999). The balance is made up of plantations on ancient woodland sites (PAWS) (224,100 ha), where the original canopy species were felled and

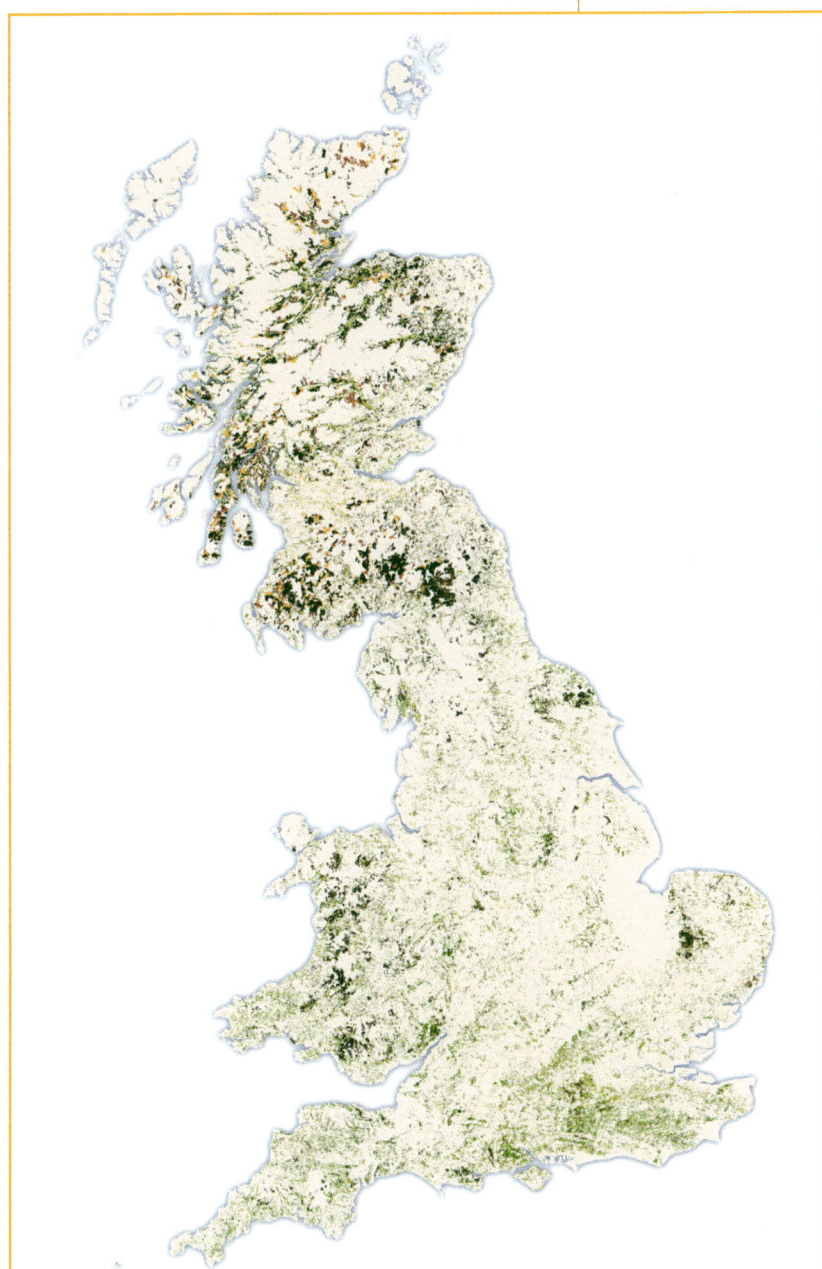

Figure 1.2 Distribution of woodland over 2 ha by forest type; conifer areas in dark green; broadleaved woodland in pale green. (Source: Forestry Commission, 2003a; Crown copyright, reproduced with the kind permission of the Forestry Commission). © Crown copyright and/or database right. All rights reserved. Licence number 100049759.

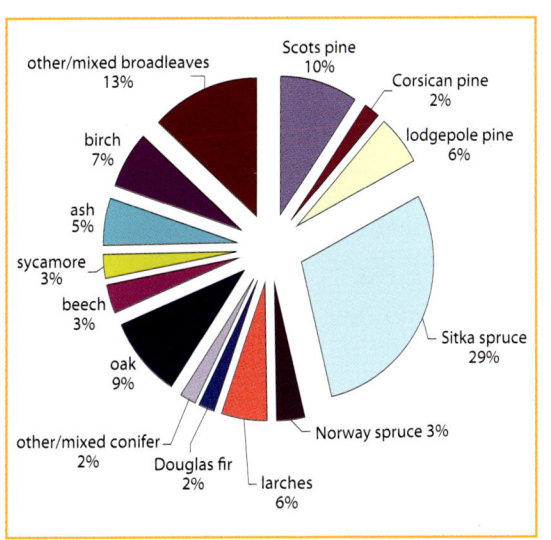

Figure 1.3 Proportion of the total woodland area by principal tree species, Great Britain. (After Forestry Commission, 2003a).

LEFT **Plantations of larch, spruce and pine on a Welsh hillside.**

RIGHT **An ancient hornbeam wood with ash on the Sussex High Weald.**

Figure 1.4 **Proportions of woodland according to their conservation status, showing the extent of ancient, semi-natural woodland; plantations on ancient sites; recent, semi-natural; and recent plantations.**

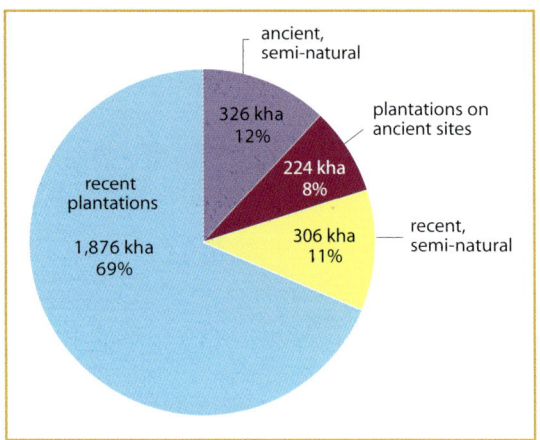

replaced with plantations of spruce, pine or occasionally broadleaved species (Figure 1.4). Current government policies now favour the restoration of such areas to native woodland by removing non-native trees and encouraging natural regeneration and replanting.

The distribution of these ancient woodland sites is very patchy and sparse in some counties but the majority of the area, about 62%, is concentrated in southern England with only 27% in Scotland and 11% in Wales. In some well-wooded lowland counties, particularly in those regions described by Oliver Rackham as 'ancient countryside' (Rackham, 1986), the proportion of ancient woodland cover can be high – 77% of the woodland area in Kent – compared with the 'planned countryside', resulting from the agricultural enclosures, of parts of the East Midlands. Unfortunately the vast majority of ancient woods are relatively small and scattered: in England and Wales, some 83% are 20 ha or less in area[1] and only 500 woods extend to more than 100 ha. About half are unmanaged and only about 10% are currently in traditional coppice management (Peterken, 2000a).

In addition to ancient woodland, a further 305,500 ha are also semi-natural, but of more recent origin (i.e. post-1600), mainly the result of the scrubbing over of abandoned heaths, moors and grasslands. Some of these older sites have assumed a mature woodland character and developed some of the features and biodiversity interest of ancient woodlands. The balance is made up by modern plantations, ranging from the large blocks of conifers in the uplands to the small woodlands planted on less productive farmland in lowland England over the past 25 years. Considering all these different categories in terms of conservation priorities, semi-natural ancient woodlands will usually tend to rank highest, followed by plantations on ancient sites, recent, semi-natural woods and 20th century plantations (Kirby, 1993). The disproportion of the different types illustrates not only the size of the challenge for woodland conservation, but also future opportunities to diversify the whole of the forestry sector for the benefit of wildlife.

1.2 Native woodland communities

Whatever the scale of woodland creation, it is important that the species planted reflect those most likely to have grown on the site originally, or take account of more recent changes caused by agriculture or urban and industrial development. In Chapter 6 we recommend that species selection is guided by the semi-natural woodland communities present in the local landscape, so-called 'reference communities'. This section introduces the broad types of semi-natural woodland found in Britain today that might be used to guide species selection in new native woodlands.

The different types of semi-natural woods are a response to a range of factors – climate, soils and management, both past and present. At a regional and landscape scale, overriding climatic factors are: accumulated temperatures during the growing season, summer moisture deficits, oceanicity and windiness. Britain's position on the western seaboard of Europe is responsible for

---

1 The Ancient Woodland Inventory did not include all woods less than 2 ha in extent, so the actual proportion of small ancient woods is probably much higher than this.

PART ONE GENERAL PRINCIPLES – **NATIVE WOODLAND IN THE BRITISH LANDSCAPE**

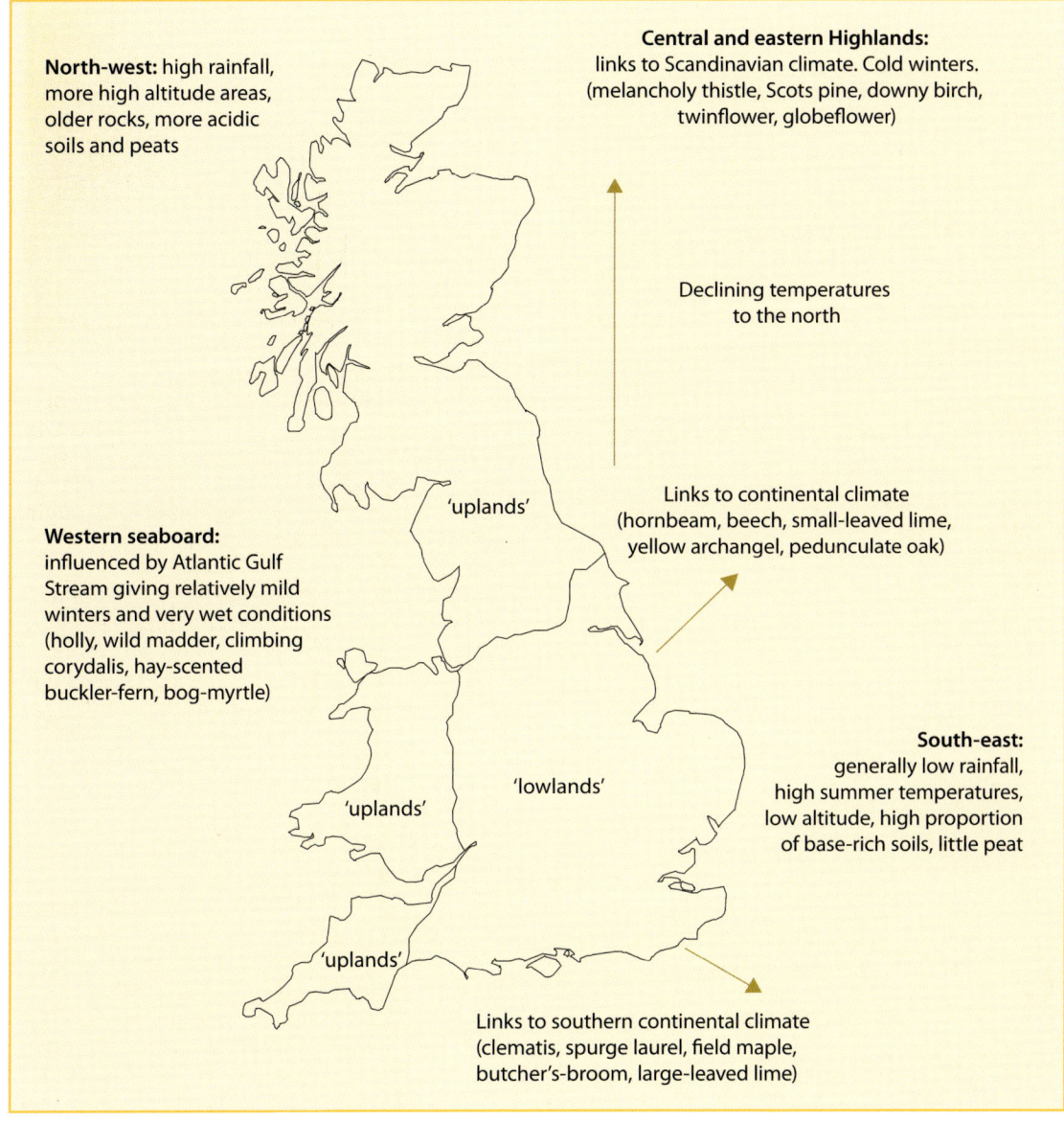

Figure 1.5 Broad patterns of environmental variation in Britain, showing the major climatic zones influencing forest communities. (Source Kirby, K.J., 1992; reproduced with the kind permission of Keith Kirby). © Crown copyright and/or database right. All rights reserved. Licence number 100049759.

the mild, oceanic climate which has a major influence on forest communities – for example in the west, ferns and Atlantic bryophytes thrive in the humid, shaded understoreys of oak, birch and ash woods. Cool, cloudy and moist conditions in the western uplands especially favour stands dominated by sessile oak, downy birch and hazel, with holly, rowan and bird cherry in places and a ground flora rich in mosses, liverworts and broad buckler, hay-scented buckler and hard-ferns. In the far north of Scotland, the exposed conditions, and salt spray near the coast, become limiting factors, reducing some stands of birch, oak and hazel to scrub woodland.

In contrast, parts of north eastern, central and eastern Britain are more continental in character, having wider annual temperature ranges, shorter growing seasons, lower relative humidity and more frequent frosts. Scandinavian boreal elements are manifest in the Caledonian pinewoods in Scotland, where the heathy and bryophyte-rich understoreys of pine, birch and common juniper stands include specialities such as twinflower, creeping lady's-tresses and lesser twayblade. Continental influences are also present in woods of oak, ash, hornbeam and beech in the south east lowlands, in which many species, including field maple, dogwood, spindle and herbs such as yellow archangel and wood spurge are also found in parts of mainland Europe which experience warm summers (Figure 1.5).

Variation in woodland character within these climatic zones is strongly influenced by geology, soil type and hydrology, giving rise to the range of communities described below. Several classifications have previously been used to describe British woodland vegetation types, all of which have their merits. Here we introduce the National Vegetation Classification (NVC) which has become widely adopted by ecological practitioners, describing not only woodland, but all vegetation types in Britain (Box 1.1).

> **Box 1.1 The National Vegetation Classification**
>
> The National Vegetation Classification (NVC) (Rodwell, 1991) is the most widely used classification system in Britain, describing 25 main woodland communities, most of which have two or more associated sub-communities. It includes 18 true woodland types: six have mainly northern distributions, while 11 are more common in the south (Figure 1.6a). A further seven scrub communities describe two high-altitude and five lowland successional types. Apart from obvious climatic divisions, major soil types can be used to further group the communities, based on wetness, fertility, and acidity. The NVC woodland types are not evenly sized; some are relatively scarce, such as W3 bay willow–bottle sedge woodland, with less than 200 ha recorded, whereas there are 113,000 ha of W10 oakwoods (Figure 1.6b). A useful key for identifying NVC communities is provided by Hall *et al.*, (2004).

Figure 1.6 Summary of National Vegetation Classification woodland communities, showing a) the main communities in relation to soil type and regional distribution in Britain (after Whitbread and Kirby, 1992; Thompson *et al.*, 2003; and b) the relative extent of each community in Britain (Cooke, 1992).

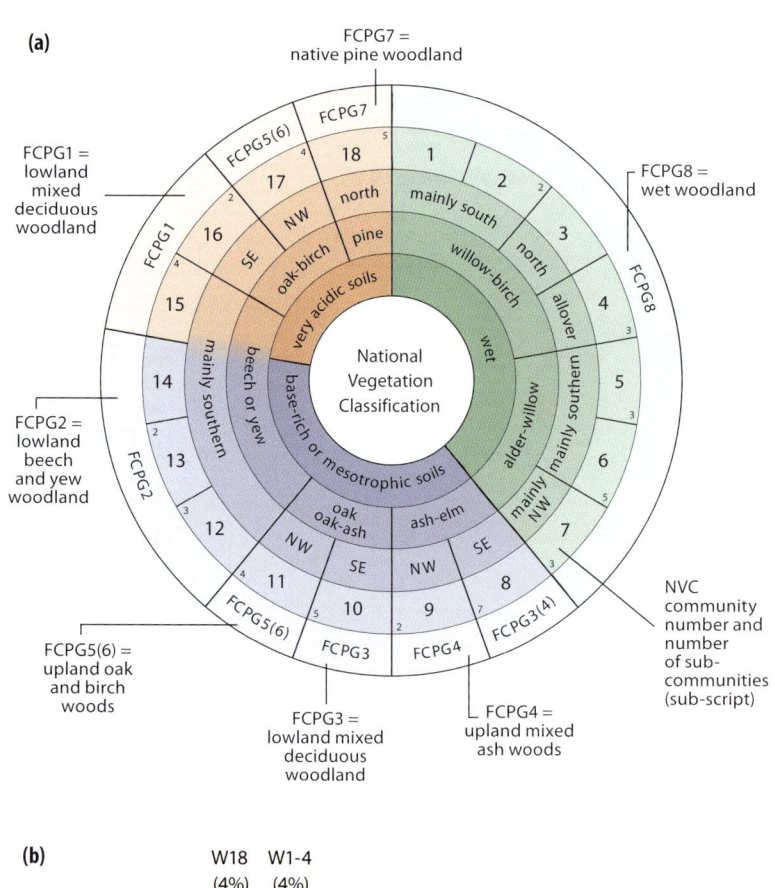

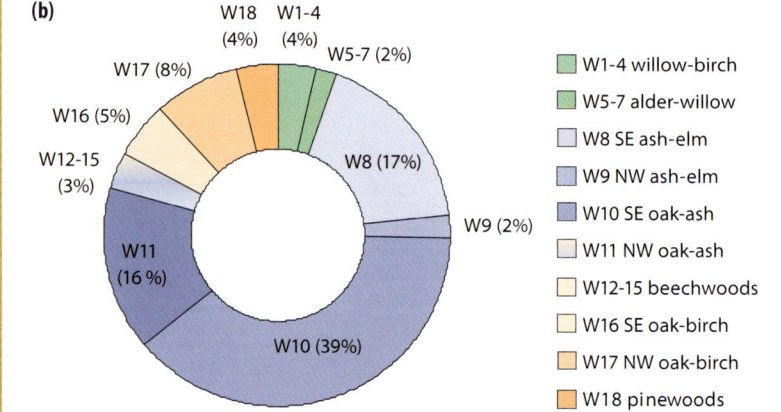

At a hierarchical level above the National Vegetation Classification, the 1992 EU Habitats and Species Directive recognises the conservation status of a range of key woodland and other habitat types across Europe, listed in Annex 1 of the Directive. These are based on broad habitat classifications called the *Coordination of Information on the Environment* (CORINE; Devillers *et al.*, 1991), and its successor the *European Nature Information System* (EUNIS, 2007), although present coverage is uneven and interpretation of the woodland types can vary markedly between countries (Rodwell and Dring, 2001). Special Areas of Conservation (SAC sites) have been proposed for woodlands in these categories and they form part of the European conservation network called Natura 2000, designed to capture a proportion of each of the habitats in the various member states.

The UK Biodiversity Action Plan identifies a number of woodland priority habitats (Government Report, 1995; Joint Nature Conservation Committee, 2007a). Affinities between these habitat types and other classifications e.g. NVC and European, are shown in Table 1.1. Individual communities are described for the priority BAP habitats in detail below:

1.2.1 Lowland beech and yew woodland (NVC: W12-15)

Three community types are distinguished by the constant presence of beech in the canopy, which can tolerate a range of soil conditions ranging from calcareous to acidic. There are c.30,000 ha of all ancient and recent woodland of this woodland type in South East England, comprising calcareous, neutral-basic and acid types.

Calcareous beech and yew woodland (W12) forms perhaps 40% of the overall woodland category. These high forest stands occur mainly on chalk or limestone soils in the South East, within the natural range of beech, but also as a more restricted distribution in North West England. They are dominated by beech, ash, sycamore, yew, holly and whitebeam, with oak less common than in other beech wood types. Uncommon understorey species include box, coralroot bitter-cress and bird's-nest orchid.

On neutral to slightly acidic and usually heavier soils, a further 45% of beech woodland habitat contains a higher proportion of oaks, often merging into typical oak forest communities. Bramble is a characteristic component of the ground vegetation, with rarities such as violet helleborine sometimes present, forming beech-bramble woodland (W14). Holly and yew are occasionally present in the shrub layer.

Acidic beech woodland (W15) has a much wider distribution than either of the previous types, but covers a smaller area (15%), occurring on well drained sands and gravels. Low pH (3.5 to 4.5) encourages an acid ground flora with frequent wavy hair-grass, and oak is common in the canopy, with holly and sometimes yew in the shrub layer. This type also occurs on several lowland wood pasture sites, also UK Biodiversity Action Plan habitats, in England.

Yew woodland (W13) occurs on thin, dry, humus-rich soils of chalk escarpments in southern Britain and the Carboniferous and Magnesian limestones of central and northern Britain, here usually associated with upland ash woods. Yew sometimes occurs on more acidic soils in the North West where they merge into sessile oak woods.

Calcareous beech and yew woodland with box at Box Hill in Surrey (NVC W12).

Table 1.1 Key woodland habitats recognised by the Biodiversity Action Plan (BAP), showing priority types and associated woodland communities described in the National Vegetation Classification (NVC) and their European equivalents (after Hall *et al.*, 2004)

BAP Priority Habitat	Description	Woodland type	NVC types	CORINE classification	EUNIS classification	% of total European SAC area[1]
Lowland beech and yew woodland	Mesophilous beech forests on brown calcareous mull soils	Woodruff – beech (*Asperula-Fagetum*) forest	W12, W14	41.12, 41.13	G1.63, G1.62	1
	Distinctive oceanic form of beech/oak forest, on nutrient-poor, acid brown earths	Beech forest with holly and yew	W14, W15	41.12, 41.16	G1.62, G1.66	3
	Atlantic yew woodland, unique to Britain and Ireland, usually on calcareous soils	Yew woodland of the British Isles	W13	42.A71	G3.9	100
Lowland mixed deciduous woodland	Oak-hornbeam woods on damp, relatively fertile soils where beech is disadvantaged	Sub-Atlantic and middle European oak-hornbeam woodlands	W10a-d	41.23, 41.24	G1.A13, G1.A14	1
	Ash-oak-hazel woodland on moderately base-rich soils	Lime – maple – sycamore (*Tilio-Acerion*) forests	W8a-d	41.32	G1.A22	
	Pedunculate oak woodland on lowland, impoverished acid soils	Old acidophilous oak woods on sandy plains	W16a	41.51, 41.52	G1.81, G1.82	15
Upland mixed ash woods	Ash woodland on base-rich soils and flushes on humid, shady slopes	Mixed species, lime – maple – sycamore (*Tilio-Acerion*) ravine forests in northern Britain, with occasional yew	W8e-g, W9, W13	41.31, 41.32, 41.41, 42	G1.A21, G1.A22, G1.A41	3
Upland oak woods	Atlantic, bryophyte-rich, sessile oak woodland on acid soils outside the range of beech	Old oak woods with holly and hard fern	W10e, W11, W16b, W17	41.53, 41.52	G1.83, G1.82	90
Upland birch woods[2]	Stands dominated by birch species with rowan, willows, juniper and aspen	Downy and silver birch, often associated with sessile oak, on poor, acidic soils and peats	W10e, W11, W17, W4a-b	41.53, 41.52	G1.83, G1.82	
Native pine woodlands	Distinctive western outlier of the boreal, heathy Scots pinewoods of northern Europe	Caledonian pinewoods with birch, juniper, willow and bird cherry on leached, podzolic or drier, peaty soils.	W18, W4b-c	42.51, 44.A2	G3.41, G1.51, G3.D	100
Wet woodland	Fragments of riverine woodland containing willow, alder and ash	Residual alluvial forest	W5-W7 W1-W3	44.31 44.13, 44.92	G1.211 G1.111, F9.2	1
	Birch-dominated woodland in wet Atlantic zone on acid, peaty soils	Bog woodland	W4c		G1.51	2
Wood pasture and parkland	Parks with veteran, pollarded trees and semi-natural grassland or heathland	Historic sites with open-grown trees over pasture on a range of different soil types	W10, W14, W15, W16	41.23, 41.24, 41.1, 41.16, 41.51, 41.52	G1.62, G1.66 G1.A13-14, G1.81, G1.82	

1 Based on the British proportion of the total area of each woodland type present in candidate Special Areas of Conservation (SACs) in EU member states in 2000 (Rodwell and Dring, 2001).
2 In England and Wales birch woods are not separated out in the UK Biodiversity Action Plan but are treated as a component of the oakwood mosaic.

1.2.2 Lowland mixed deciduous woodland (NVC: W8, W10, W16)

This is a very broad category of ash and oak woods that form a continuum from base-rich to more acid, but always relatively fertile soils, covering c.250,000 ha in the country as a whole. Most have a history of coppice management and are small-scale, typical of the enclosed landscapes of parts of lowland England. The main vegetation types on base-rich soils are dominated by ash and field maple with dog's mercury (W8), with sub-communities of other canopy and sub-canopy species, including hazel, hawthorn, blackthorn, dogwood, goat willow and grey willow.

On more acid soils, mainstay species with a wide tolerance of soil types, such as pedunculate oak, hazel, hawthorn, bluebell and bramble continue, but the lime-demanding species become less frequent as soil acidity increases and species like birch and wavy hair-grass come to dominate. Both species of oak may be present in W10 communities, with birch and a range of other species such as hornbeam, small-leaved lime and sweet chestnut, while ash is much less frequent. Sub-communities of this type are fairly widespread over the lowlands of England and Wales, but those characterised by wood anemone are much commoner in South East England and those with abundant ivy have a distinctly western bias.

On very impoverished, often sandy, acidic soils in the South East, pedunculate oak predominates, but with abundant silver birch and few other associates such as rowan, holly, alder buckthorn and aspen (W16). The field layer is species-poor and often dominated by bracken, wavy hair-grass and ericaceous species such as heather and bilberry. This type of lowland, acid oak woodland represents the northern and western range of 'old oak woods on sandy plains' in Europe.

All three types – W8, W10 and W16 – form mosaics with other woodland types, in particular with lowland beech and yew woodland. However, many have lost their semi-natural character and diversity of canopy species as a result of conversion to sweet chestnut or pure hornbeam coppice in the past, or more recently to conifer plantations of pine or spruce.

1.2.3 Upland mixed ash woods (NVC: W9, W8)

This woodland type is the northern and western equivalent of similar communities occurring on base-rich soils and flushes within lowland, mixed deciduous woodland. The cooler, wetter conditions allow a greater development and variety of ferns and bryophytes in the field layer, but under heavy grazing a grassy sward develops. Ash and hazel are the dominant canopy species, with rowan, downy birch and occasional oak, elm and sycamore. Where grazing is less of a factor, the field layers can be very species-rich, with constants such as wood sorrel, violets, dog's mercury, bluebell and herb Robert.

The main community (W9) replaces the lowland ash woods in this situation, but three W8 sub-communities, containing abundant herb Robert, ramsons or wood sage, respectively, are also essentially upland types. Together, these upland ash woods make up c.40,000–50,000 ha, distributed over much of northern Britain, upland Wales and Scotland where suitable calcareous substrates occur.

1.2.4 Upland oak woods (NVC: W11, W17, W16, W10)

Upland oak wood communities have a western, Atlantic distribution throughout northern England and the south west peninsula, Wales and Scotland that distinguishes them from similar stands in other parts of northern Europe. This oceanic influence is responsible for the prominence of sub-Atlantic species such as holly, honeysuckle, climbing corydalis and heath bedstraw, as well as a very rich flora of bryophytes, ferns and lichens. The three related communities have ground floras characterised by wood-sorrel (W11), wavy hair-grass (sub-community W16b) and greater fork-moss (W17). The upland fringe of a variant of W10, characterised by sycamore and wood sorrel, also contributes to the total area of around 70,000–100,000 ha.

Most upland oak woods occur on relatively poor, acid soils, often with strongly leached horizons and accumulated layers of humus. The dominant canopy trees are sessile oak (although sometimes pedunculate oak is also present) and downy and silver birch, with less frequent rowan and hazel. Grasses are frequent in the field layer, including sweet vernal-grass, creeping soft-grass and wavy hair-grass. Vernal herbs such as bluebell and wood anemone are present, the latter being commoner in more 'continental' sub-communities in north east Scotland. On the thinnest soils and most exposed sites, birch predominates over a heathy vegetation.

PART ONE GENERAL PRINCIPLES – **NATIVE WOODLAND IN THE BRITISH LANDSCAPE**

LEFT **Lowland oakwood in South East England (NVC W10).**

RIGHT **Transition from an NVC W10 to W8 community, with ash stems becoming more frequent in the canopy.**

BOTTOM **Upland mixed ash woodland in limestone country at Cheedale, Derbyshire, corresponding to NVC types W9a and 9b. The canopy is dominated by ash, with hazel and rowan underscrub and occasional wych elm in the valleys. On the rocky ledges and screes, scrub yew and rock whitebeam represent patches of W13 woodland.**

Upland oak wood at Yarner Wood National Nature Reserve, Devon. The sessile oak and birch canopy is derived from abandoned coppice, with rowan and holly frequent in the understorey and a heathy field layer of bilberry and heather (NVC W17d).

Beech-wavy hair-grass woodland community in Cornwall. Oak is as common as beech in the canopy; hairy wood-rush and bilberry may be found in the field layer (NVC W15c).

1.2.5 Upland birch woods (NVC: W4)

The upland birch woods form part of the continuum between upland oak woods and open moorland, with the addition of downy birch and purple moor-grass (W4). On the poorer, acidic and often peaty soils in this range, downy and silver birch become dominant at the expense of oak, with occasional rowan, willows, juniper and aspen. Sub-communities of this type on drier sites are characterised by species such as broad buckler-fern, honeysuckle and bramble (W4a), with common rush (W4b) and bog-mosses (W4c) becoming progressively frequent on wetter and peaty sites. At the interface with the upland oak communities, the field layers often consist of heather and bilberry, giving way to bracken and wavy hair-grass on richer soils.

Birch woods are essentially transient communities, invading moorland after burning or the cessation of grazing and forming stands under which a grass-herb vegetation can develop, but reverting later when the trees senesce. About 15,000–20,000 ha exist, mainly in Scotland.

PART ONE GENERAL PRINCIPLES – **NATIVE WOODLAND IN THE BRITISH LANDSCAPE**

1.2.6 Native pinewoods (NVC: W18)

Like the birch woods, pinewoods are regarded as successional communities, developing after major disturbances such as fire and storms, albeit over sometimes very long intervals, but often with a structure heavily modified by previous felling practices.

The 18,000 ha of Caledonian pinewoods are virtually confined to the Grampian region and the North West Highlands of Scotland and are best developed on acidic, podzolic soils and drier peats. The main canopy species is Scots pine, although its distribution is often discontinuous and patchy in older or damaged stands, with occasional birches, rowan and juniper. Field layers are rich in bulky, acid-loving mosses and ericaceous species such as heather, bilberry and cowberry, with the proportion of mosses and purple moor-grass increasing in the wetter, western stands. In very wet areas, pine tends to grow poorly and is replaced by downy birch, creating a mosaic of the wetter upland birch wood sub-communities (W4b and W4c) among pine stands. Grass cover also increases in stands heavily grazed by deer and sheep. Impoverished versions of the main vegetation type may also be found in plantations of conifers in south western Scotland and Cumbria.

1.2.7 Wet woodlands (NVC: W1–W7)

Wet woodlands occur on seasonally waterlogged soils along river valleys, in floodplains and on fens, mires and bogs. Alder, birch and willows are the predominant species, merging into oak, ash or beech communities in drier conditions, such as valley slopes. The communities dominated by willows tend to occur on the most permanently wet sites, colonising the edges of standing open water, or in mires where the succession is checked by a permanently high water table. One community characterised by grey willow and marsh bedstraw (W1) occurs mainly on mineral soils and has a somewhat western, coastal distribution, while the grey willow with downy birch and common reed woodland (W2) develops on fen peat, especially in East Anglia. A third type, bay willow with bottle sedge (W3) is a continental basin mire type, restricted to northern Britain.

In moderately base-rich and more fertile conditions, several wet woodlands are dominated by alder stands, often previously coppiced. On organic fen peats, alder with greater tussock-sedge woodland (W5) predominates but where there is an accumulation of alluvium a nettle understorey (W6) can develop, with associates in its various sub-communities of grey or crack willow and downy birch. On less fertile, predominantly mineral soils where there is little peat accumulation, the characteristic community changes to alder with ash and yellow pimpernel woodland (W7). A further type of wet or bog woodland (W4c), mentioned above in connection

Scots pine woodland at Abernethy Forest (NVC W18).

Wet woodland in South East England, with marsh marigold, wood sorrel and bluebell under a canopy of coppiced alder and birch (NVC W6).

with the native pinewoods, can develop in moderately acidic conditions on deep peats from wet heath and mires.

Compared with the rest of Europe, wet woodlands are poorly represented in Britain due to the extensive drainage work for land improvement and river canalisation. However, a crude estimate of the total wet woodland area in the UK is c.50,000–70,000 ha, of which perhaps 25,000–30,000 ha is of older origin. In conservation terms, these are important for their floristic variety and relict plant species of formerly open wetlands such as marsh fern; the deadwood habitats on wet substrates also support many localised invertebrates.

1.2.8 Wood pasture and parkland

Wood pasture and parkland habitats are sites distinguished by their structure of large, open-grown and often pollarded trees, scattered over a matrix of unimproved, grazed grasslands or

Mixed deciduous woodland on acidic soils in a parkland landscape at Knole Park, Kent, where mature and veteran trees include oak, beech, sweet chestnut and field maple (NVC W10).

heathlands. Many are ancient sites, originating as managed medieval wood pastures or commons, or as pre-19th century landscape parks. The veteran trees they contain are important habitats in their own right, while in vegetation terms they may represent several communities of both open and woodland character. Typically, these are closely allied with lowland beech and yew (W14, W15) and mixed deciduous woodland (W10, W16) communities, together with the corresponding non-woodland vegetation communities in open areas. In the uplands, examples may be found in mixed ash (W9) and oak woods (W17); and although grazing is a regular feature of upland oak and birch woods, they may not exhibit the classical structure of lowland wood pastures and are therefore not categorised as such.

A key feature of wood pasture and parkland is the distinctive saproxylic fauna (living in rotten wood, water-filled cavities on live trees, and sap runs) and epiphytic flora associated with the ancient trees, which are also important for hole-nesting birds and bats. They are important in southern England, where they are relatively abundant, and are of national and European importance. Notable examples are the New Forest, Windsor Great Park, Staverton Park, Savernake, Epping and Hainault Forests and Moccas Park. Earlier estimates suggested that there were 10,000–20,000 ha of this type of habitat surviving, but it is now recognised to be much more abundant and widespread. For example, only a few sites have been identified in the Uplands but wood pastures such as Glenamara Park (Cumbria) and Glen Finglas in the Trossachs are seen as a typical component of the former pastoral landscape.

1.2.9 Scrub communities (NVC: W19–W24)

Scrub is a complex habitat: some types are temporary, seral stages in a successional series from open ground to mature woodland, while others are more stable in their own right. The conservation value of scrub can be remarkably high, but it is frequently under-rated (Day *et al.*, 2003). Five scrub types and two under-scrub communities are recognised. The most common types in lowland Britain are hawthorn with ivy (W21), bramble with Yorkshire-fog (W24) and blackthorn with bramble (W22). Bramble-Yorkshire-fog scrub, which frequently occurs on abandoned farmland, often develops into hawthorn-ivy scrub on neutral or base-rich soils, and gorse-bramble scrub (W23) on acid soils. On deeper, moist and richer neutral soils, blackthorn scrub may dominate. A mosaic may develop with patches of hawthorn and blackthorn scrub, interspersed with bramble-Yorkshire-fog.

Two other types of scrub are largely confined to mountainous parts of northern Britain. These are juniper heath (W19), which occurs in the eastern and central Scottish Highlands and in more isolated stands on hills south to the Lake District; while high-altitude stands of dwarf willows, such as downy willow (W20), are located mainly in the southern and central Highlands.

Hawthorn-ivy scrub (NVC W21) on the South Downs dip slope, requiring careful management to maintain the proportion of unimproved chalk grassland.

1.3 A brief review of modern woodland creation in Britain

For many decades private landowners in Britain have received support from the State (the Forestry Commission) for planting and managing new woodland areas. This section presents a brief review of woodland grant schemes and how woodland creation schemes are being supported by Government today.

Grants for replanting and afforestation were first made available to the private sector after the First World War, but complex regulations at the time led to a relatively modest uptake and it was only after 1945 that they began to have a significant impact: up to that point new planting was led by the State. Immediately after the Second World War more attractive Dedication Schemes offered financial assistance to landowners who undertook to dedicate areas of their land to timber production 'in perpetuity', followed shortly by an Approved Woodlands scheme which allowed owners to plant land without dedication, but for less money.

The 1950s to the mid-1980s were boom years for the expansion of the forest estate. In the early 1970s, the planting rate exceeded 40,000 ha per year, almost equally divided between private landowners and the Forestry Commission (Figure 1.7a). Most of this afforestation took place on hill-farms in the uplands where conifers made up the bulk, except for a few amenity fringes. Replanting of traditional, broadleaved woodland in the lowlands with conifers also accelerated during this period, leading to the losses of ancient woodland described earlier. However, confidence of the private sector was briefly dented by a Treasury cost-benefit review of forestry policy in 1972, when a new Dedication Scheme (Basis III) was introduced: this removed the previous 'perpetuity' covenant and maintenance grants, and obliged grant recipients to discuss arrangements for public access. At the same time changes in Estate Duty, introduced in 1975 as Capital Transfer Tax, threatened to prevent tax-free transfers of woods between owners. An ever-faithful barometer of forestry policy, planting rates by the private sector fell by two-thirds over five years following the 1972 review.

Planting recovered in the 1980s, when a more favourable tax regime encouraged planting by forestry companies and wealthy private investors, outstripping the State as the main engine of upland afforestation. A new Forestry Grant Scheme was introduced in 1981, removing annual management grants but substantially increasing establishment payments, effectively maintaining rates of conifer planting. However, concerns that had long been growing amongst environmentalists about the impact of these new conifer blocks, both on the landscape and on upland wildlife habitats, now began to be reflected in Government policy. In 1985, the Broadleaved Woodland Policy and an accompanying grant scheme met with some success on better land in the lowlands. Another signal was the removal of tax loopholes in the 1988 budget, taking forestry out of Income and Corporation Tax, so that tree planting costs could no longer be offset against other income. Once again this led to a loss of confidence and a rapid shift from coniferous to broadleaved planting (Figure 1.7b).

To compensate for the loss of tax concessions, the Woodland Grant Scheme (WGS) was introduced in 1988, replacing previous schemes. The new arrangements were also accompanied by the launch of the Farm Woodland Scheme (FWS) and later in 1992 by the Farm Woodland Premium Scheme (FWPS), jointly managed by the Forestry Commission and the Ministry of Agriculture, Fisheries and Food. These differed from their predecessors in that, besides receiving planting grants, annual payments were made

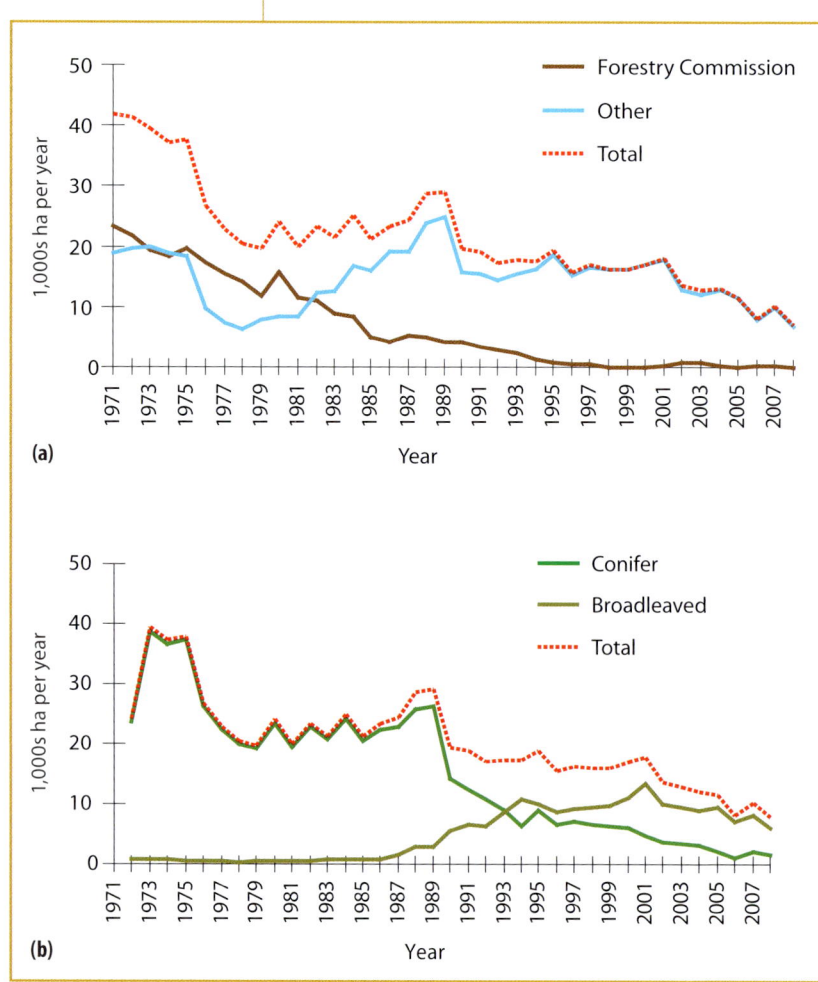

Figure 1.7 Changes in the rate of new woodland planting in Great Britain over the period 1971–2008: a) planting rates by the state and other private and public sectors; b) the proportion of conifer to broadleaved trees planted. Source: Forestry Commission, 2009a.

to farmers planting on improved agricultural land, in compensation for the income forgone. At its inception the scheme had broad aims: diverting land from agricultural production, boosting rural employment, contributing to farm income and encouraging a greater interest in timber production on farms. Enhancing the landscape, providing new habitats and increasing biodiversity gradually assumed greater importance that was reflected in later Woodland Grant Scheme amendments and by the introduction of Woodland Improvement Grants (1995 and 1996) and various Challenge Funds (1996).

Another target area for forest expansion in the lowlands was on the fringe of major conurbations. Forest recreation had been a major policy issue since 1970, when it was recognised as a primary non-timber benefit. The principle of allowing public access to forests was by then well established in State forests and further encouraged in grant-aid schemes with private forest owners, but eligible woodlands were usually located far from urban centres. To compensate, a Forests for the Community programme was launched in 1989 by the Countryside Commission (now part of Natural England) and the Forestry Commission in England, when 12 'lead' community forest areas were designated on the urban fringe or derelict land, to be built up over 25 years. This was followed soon afterwards by the designation of a new National Forest in the Midlands, the combined target of both initiatives representing a 10% expansion of England's woodland cover. The National Forest has increased in woodland cover from 6% to 18% since 1991, similar to the overall performance in other community forests. The introduction in 1992 of Community Woodland Supplements to augment establishment grants offered by the Woodland Grant Scheme was designed to stimulate these developments.

For more than a decade after the introduction of the Woodland Grant and Farm Woodland Schemes the private sector responded positively, planting an average of c.20,000 ha per year on less profitable corners of their land and to a lesser extent in urban situations, so that in 1993 the area of new broadleaved planting exceeded that of conifers for the first time since 1920. These new woodlands were remarkably uniform in character: more than 75% consisted of broadleaved mixtures (oak, ash, beech and wild cherry being particularly common), planted intimately or in segregated groups. Some had 'edge-mixes' of shrubs planted along the margins and, in the bigger planting blocks, broad rides were left, reflecting grant scheme rules that allowed for 20% open space and 10% shrub planting. Block sizes were also small and fragmented. A study of participants entering the FWPS in Kent and East Sussex over a three-year period between 1992 and 1995 found that new planting areas averaged 4.3 ha per holding, dispersed as several smaller individual blocks (mean 1.7 ha). The uptake was greatest on larger holdings where there was spare land of average agricultural quality (Fraser and Buckley, 2000).

In contrast, the new woodland funded by Community Woodland supplements in peri-urban situations, accounted for only about a third of all new grant-aided planting in the first 10 years following their introduction. Although most schemes fell within the 12 Community and National Forests, many local schemes developed rapidly around smaller settlements. In Scotland alone, about 3,000 ha of community woods, mainly concentrated around urban areas of the Central Belt, were planted in 368 separate schemes between 1990 and 2002 (Scottish Natural Heritage, 2004).

Since 2003, when the Forestry Commission separated into the three country agencies, reviews of the WGS in England, Scotland and Wales have led to the institution of separate, regional grant schemes operating in each country, replacing both the WGS and the FWPS. With more precisely targeted objectives operating than previously, new planting rates have recently declined to less than 8,000 ha per year.

1.4 New native woodland initiatives

The fashion for establishing new native woodlands might be said to have begun in the late 1980s, when the impacts of the Broadleaved Woodland Policy, new planting incentives and revised fiscal measures began to shift forestry 'down the hill' on to better agricultural land in the lowlands and into community forests surrounding urban areas. Although predominantly broadleaved, these early plantings were often poorly conceived in terms of their structure, limited species composition and location, and so fell well short of fulfilling their biodiversity potential. Recently there has been a strong emphasis on expanding and linking networks of semi-natural woods; restoring ancient woods planted with non-native conifers; using local provenance seed (though there is some debate about this now because of the need to widen the genetic base in the face of climate change – see Chapter 4); and planting mixtures to resemble semi-natural woodland communities described in the National Vegetation Classification (Rodwell and Patterson, 1994).

A diverse wood planted in the early 1990s.

Many native woodland schemes were initiated in Scotland, where much effort has been focused on the restoration of the native pinewoods and riparian woodland. One of the first was the establishment of forest enclosures in the National Nature Reserve on Rùm in the Inner Hebrides, where the planting of native Scots pine, alder and birch was carried from the late 1950s (Stiven and Smith, 2005). A nursery was set up which sourced material from remnant woodlands on the island, but also from the Western Highlands and elsewhere where local supplies were lacking. More recent examples include the restoration and expansion of Atlantic oak and pine woodlands around Loch Katrine in the Loch Lomond and the Trossachs National Park, where the Forestry Commission, the Woodland Trust and the Royal Society for the Protection of Birds have large estates. Other major schemes operate in Speyside, the Glen Affric pinewoods and the Sunart oakwoods, and in many urban community forest schemes that are also committed to using native species.

An interesting example of new native woodland creation is the 650 ha Carrifran 'wildwood' project in the Southern Uplands of Scotland that began in 2000, centred on a denuded moorland valley. Here the original forest vegetation could only be interpreted from pollen preserved in peat cores, but a few natural woodland relicts remained, mainly on inaccessible crags and along streamsides. The management plan (Newton and Ashmole, 1999) divided regions of the valley into compartments where new planting was based on the prevailing soil conditions and corresponding to NVC communities such as juniper scrub (W19), oak-birch woodland (W17 and W4) and upland broadleaved woodland (W7 and W9) (Figure 7.5).

The National Forest, a major reforestation initiative in central England, began in the early 1990s and extends over a project area of more than 500 km^2. Like the other Community Forests in England starting around the same time, it has multiple objectives in servicing public access, recreation and biodiversity aims: the current planting rates of 500 ha per year contribute to the overall target of 16,000 ha (The National Forest Company (NFC), 2005). The NFC operates a local provenance policy that promotes the use of broadleaf stock from within the Forest area or other UK sources, and operates a local Biodiversity Action Plan in which the planting pattern and composition is in sympathy with the local, semi-natural woodlands.

1.4.1 Woodland creation in the future

There is plenty of scope for continuing the expansion of new native woods. Woodland creation rates in the UK during the first decade of the 21st century fell to under 10,000 ha per year, although more than 80% of those new plantings were broadleaved. This was well short of aspirational targets suggested in the UK Biodiversity Action Plan (an average of nearly 20,000 ha per year over 25–50 years), and the Woodland Trust's vision of a doubling of native woodland cover by 2050 (equivalent to 25,000 ha per year: Woodland Trust, 2009a). Together with the restoration of plantations on ancient woodland sites, this will require an enormous and sustained effort. However, as this review has already shown, Government support for planting is subject to constant revision and change. Indeed, in 2009, the Government announced a target of 10,000 ha of new woodland planting every year for 15 years, as part of its UK Low Carbon Transition Plan (HM Government, 2009). This was followed by an independent steering group assessment, commissioned by the Forestry Commission, of the UK's trees and woodlands to mitigate and adapt to our changing climate (Read *et al.*, 2009), forming part of the UK's response to the Intergovernmental Panel on Climate Change (IPCC) report of 2007. One finding of the group was that:

> *Woodlands planted since 1990, coupled to an enhanced woodland creation programme of 23,200 ha per year... over the next 40 years, could, by the 2050s, be delivering, on an annual basis, emissions abatement equivalent to 10% of total GHG emissions at that time. Such a programme would represent a 4% change in land cover and would bring UK forest area to 16% ...*

More recently, the Read Report was endorsed in Defra's *Climate Change Plan 2010* (Defra, 2010) which indicated that the Government would like to see a major increase in the level of new woodland planting to help to mitigate climate change. Planting an additional 10,000 ha of sustainably managed woodland each year for the next 15 years is projected to absorb 50 $MtCO_2e$ by 2050, and the wood produced could reduce UK emissions by a further 37 $MtCO_2e$. The Climate Change Plan also highlighted the need for adaptive measures in the forestry sector to be appropriate to both current and future climatic conditions, reflect the needs of wildlife, and the services provided by woodlands for people.

2 WOODLANDS FOR WILDLIFE

A basic appreciation of woodland ecology is helpful for anyone planning to create new native woodland for wildlife and people. In particular, familiarity with existing, semi–natural woods can provide clues for practitioners when choosing trees and shrubs for planting; deciding on a woodland layout and design; and selecting appropriate techniques for management. At the same time, an understanding of the wildlife associated with semi-natural, ancient woods and their habitat requirements will help to manage expectations about which plants and animals may colonise, or might be encouraged to do so. This chapter discusses the aspects of ecology relevant to creating new native woodland and introduces some of the key groups of species that will use this new habitat, including birds, bats, invertebrates and plants. These groups represent the more visible elements of the woodland flora and fauna, and clearly illustrate the potential conservation value of new native woodland.

2.1 Natural succession

As woodland is the so-called 'climax' vegetation cover over most of Britain, given the circumstances and the availability of seed sources, new woodland will colonise open ground in a process called natural succession. This is essentially a series of developments in ecosystem structure and composition over time, known as seral stages, which eventually result in a relatively stable, mature ecosystem. Succession from a bare substrate (including quarries), fresh water or sand dunes – which have not supported an ecological community before – to woodland, is termed primary succession. Sand dunes are among the best examples, in areas where creeping willow dominates, forming low, scrubby growth. Good examples can be seen along the Sefton coast, and at Braunton Burrows in Devon, where there are also transitional stages between willow and more mature scrub vegetation. Primary succession, starting with open fresh water, can also lead eventually to mature woodland. Succession on cleared land such as lowland arable farmland or upland heather moorland, where a soil layer has already formed, is called secondary succession.

Each seral stage is accompanied by different communities of plants and animals; increasing biomass; and usually an increase in species richness. Britain's temperate climate usually leads to deciduous forest, except in the Highland zone of northern Britain, where Scots pine and common juniper woodland can develop. Recognisable stages in the development of deciduous forest include:

- establishment of saplings prior to canopy closure
- closed canopy thickets, leading to heavy shading of the field layer
- maturing trees, with canopy gaps allowing some tree and shrub regeneration
- mature woodland with relatively little deadwood
- older growth, with some very large, mature trees, standing/fallen dead trees and cohorts of younger age classes present.

BELOW **An example of primary succession, with scrub dominated by broom, gorse and willow developing on shingle at Dungeness, Kent.**

Succession or regeneration within mature woodland usually involves colonisation of relatively small areas created by natural disturbances through windthrow, disease, etc. or artificially through small group felling or coppicing. Rarely, these disturbances are much more widespread and catastrophic, caused by major windstorms, fire, flooding or disease epidemics, but also large-scale logging. In the boreal zone of the North East Highlands, very infrequent fires are considered part of the natural disturbance regime within the Scots pine, birch and common juniper forests. More commonly, when a large tree or group of trees falls, saplings will regenerate quickly from seed and root-suckers in the immediate vicinity, as well as from coppice shoots arising from broken or fallen stems. Advanced regeneration may already be present in the understorey, ready to take advantage of any break in the canopy. The ground vegetation will also respond rapidly through invasion by species of open spaces, vegetative reproduction of species already present and the germination of woodland herbs from the local (short-lived) seed bank. Saplings act as bird perches, increasing the number of bird-dispersed seed whilst adjacent maturing trees produce seed to fill the gaps directly. Eventually, canopy closure brings about natural thinning (the stem exclusion stage), which results in even-aged stands which cast a heavy shade. After 50 years or so, the vigour of the canopy declines and light begins to penetrate to the understorey. This allows a secondary flush of saplings to reach for new light gaps, so diversifying the canopy (Oliver, 1981). There are many sites around the country which provide excellent examples of regeneration after disturbance, for example Larkey Valley Wood in the Stour Valley (Kent), Lady Park Wood in the Forest of Dean (Peterken and Mountford, 1995) and Denny Wood in the New Forest (Mountford *et al.*, 1999).

Where plantations on ancient woodland sites (PAWS) have been cleared for woodland restoration, regeneration may follow a pattern similar to that which occurs following a catastrophic disturbance in ancient woodland. Success will ultimately depend on how badly damaged the site was following clearance and the introduction of plantation species, to what extent the original flora and fauna have persisted and how restoration is carried out.

2.1.1 Woodland succession

The majority of 'new' woodland which has developed in Britain has come about through secondary succession or deliberate planting, but woods that are known to have been planted or regenerated before 1600 AD can also be classed as ancient woodland. Good examples are Monks Wood in Cambridgeshire and Swithland Wood in Leicestershire, where the remains of extensive medieval ridge-and-furrow are clearly visible on the forest floor.

Any new woodland that is allowed to develop naturally on former grazing or arable land is secondary succession (see Box 2.1). This will follow a different course to regeneration in gaps in ancient woodland, as the suite of colonising species is often restricted and the sites isolated from sources of colonisers. Studies of the biodiversity of older regenerated woods can help us to understand more about natural succession on cleared land, and the likely future development of woodland established today. We must, of course, take into account the features of the landscape when these woods were developing, and how this might have differed quite dramatically from what we see today. In the past, woodland succession may have taken place on semi-natural habitats such as heathland, marshland and unimproved grassland, whereas now such land is likely to be protected. There may have been considerable movement of farm traffic and domestic animals between the developing woodland and semi-natural areas which acted as dispersers of woodland plants. For example, relic woodland habitat such as hedgerows may have continued to support small populations

Small-gap regeneration of birch at Scords Wood, Kent following the storm of 1987 (right), and with a surviving beech tree (left).

> **Box 2.1 Land abandonment and woodland development**
>
> The classic long-term colonisation experiment at Broadbalk Wilderness, Rothamsted on ex-arable loamy brown earths, abandoned in 1833, went through a phase of weeds, followed by false oat-grass grassland and scrub, reaching a thicket stage only after 30 years (Brenchley and Adam, 1915; Tansley, 1939). In a companion plot, Geescroft, on heavier clay soils, Yorkshire-fog and tufted hair-grass grassland established first, and the invasion of shrubs and trees was even slower. After 70 years, the Geescroft woodland consisted largely of ash, oak and small-leaved elm (Harmer *et al*., 2001). There are many other examples of secondary succession across the British Isles, although none as well recorded as the Rothamsted plots. These include birchwood regeneration on southern English heathland, the ashwoods of Derbyshire, beech woodland in the Chilterns, carr woodland in the Fens, the Caledonian pine forest and even woody colonisation of urban and industrial sites in the West Midlands (Hodge and Harmer, 1996).
>
> Harmer, *et al*., (2001) analysed all records for the Broadbalk and Geescroft Wilderness, including recent observations of their own made in 1995 and 1998. Of 100 herbs and 20 grasses recorded in Broadbalk over the study period, only 20 remained in 1995. Five of these were initially present, the rest being shade-tolerant plants which subsequently colonised. Bluebell and lesser celandine were among eight species which colonised within 50 years or so. In Geescroft, 30 species of grasses and herbs were found in 1998, the most frequent being bluebell and ground-ivy. In both woods, many of the shade-tolerant species were still restricted to the margins. Harmer comments that the flora now is typical of many small woods on abandoned farmland in eastern England: it was most diverse just before canopy closure.
>
> What is particularly interesting about both woods is that there has been a substantial turnover of shade-tolerant species since canopy closure, which limits overall colonisation. At Broadbalk for example, 13 shade species have died out, six from the initial flora of the site and seven early colonists, including normally aggressive colonists such as hogweed, bracken, sanicle and sweet violet. Other shade-tolerant plants which colonised the adjacent meadow at Broadbalk, notably barren strawberry and goldilocks buttercup, failed to colonise the wood. In the woodlands of Lincolnshire, Peterken (2000b) found that the number of specialist ancient woodland 'indicator' plants in 273 recent (post 1600) woods ranged from none to 22: 21 such woods contained 10 or more indicators, which exceeded six of the ancient woods investigated. He concluded that the 'relatively' rich woodland vascular flora in these woods was due to their close proximity to ancient woodland, which offers further encouragement and guidance to practitioners of woodland creation.
>
> An interesting study carried out by Peterken (1981) on the composition of ash-maple woodland in Cambridgeshire on calcareous boulder clay compared woodland of different ages: from recent woodland planted in the last 100 years or so, through to the undisturbed ancient woodland of Hayley Wood. The more recent woods were recognisably related to ash-maple woodland, the youngest of which held a mixture of rapid colonists including ash, hawthorn, wayfaring-tree and elder. However, field maple and Midland hawthorn only appeared in woods planted in the 17–18th centuries, whilst oak and hazel were only present in ancient woodland and woods more than 500 years old.

of woodland plants, and some shade-tolerant species such as primrose and wood anemone may have survived in hay meadows. These habitats are much rarer in modern agricultural landscapes.

The early stages of lowland woodland succession on abandoned agricultural land may occur quite quickly or last for several decades, with considerable variation from site to site. There are unlikely to be any remnants of a woodland seed bank or ground vegetation and the soil profile will have been altered considerably after years of fertiliser application and drainage. Factors limiting woodland regeneration include:

- the absence of a buried, viable seed bank of woodland plants
- limited tree seed sources or absence of nearby suckering species
- poor seed dispersal within fragmented agricultural landscapes
- unsuitable microclimates or soil conditions for colonising woodland plants
- dominance by highly competitive herbaceous weeds
- browsing by deer or domestic animals.

At some point however, an ex-agricultural site is likely to be colonised by light, windblown pioneers such as birches and willows, and bird-dispersed hawthorn. Ash and sycamore have heavier seeds, and at most will only be dispersed a few hundred metres. Oak and beech, whose seed can be distributed several kilometres by birds such as Eurasian jays, can also be early colonisers.

It is often suggested that new woodland can be created simply by fencing off an area and letting it regenerate naturally. In practice, however, the process can be unpredictable, slow and incomplete, as a number of studies have shown: for example in a study of 46 sites of unmanaged urban and industrial sites in community forests in the West Midlands, Hodge and Harmer (1996) found that only 19% of the surveyed area had sufficient regeneration to form a closed woodland canopy after varying intervals of 10–42 years. Regenerating species included ash, birch, goat willow and hawthorn, but in general the species diversity was low, limited by the paucity of nearby seed sources. Compared with abandoned agricultural land in close proximity to hedgerows or mature woodland edges, this situation may represent a worst-case scenario for successful regeneration.

PART ONE GENERAL PRINCIPLES – **WOODLANDS FOR WILDLIFE**

The distance from a woodland edge where adequate regeneration might reasonably be expected to occur is relatively narrow for most species (Table 2.1) and rarely exceeds 100 m for light-seeded or winged-seeded trees such as birch, willow, ash, field maple and Scots pine; whereas 20 m may be more typical for heavy-seeded species such as oak, beech and hazel. Fleshy-fruited species like hawthorn, yew and rowan can also be dispersed by birds and heavier seeds by small mammals, often resulting in scattered, patchy distributions, but occasionally in long-distance transfers. In practical terms, regeneration success is a combination of distance and ground conditions on which the seed rain falls. Most Scots pine seed falls within 3–4 tree heights (100 m) of the adjacent stand; artificial scarification, disturbing surface vegetation and litter, allows the seed contact with mineral soil which increases establishment success. The same effect would be achieved by natural disturbances such as burning or windthrow.

Ash-maple woodland succession (NVC W8): an example

On neutral soils, pioneer woodland will pass through a scrubby stage, usually dominated by hawthorn, bramble and blackthorn; on wet soils the pioneers are likely to be alders,

Table 2.1 Maximum colonisation distances at which colonisation can be reasonably expected to occur, and dispersal modes of native British trees (after Harmer, 1999a)

	Distance (m)	Dispersal*
Alder	20	W
Ash	50–100	W
Aspen	100–200	W
Beech	20	G, M
Birches	100–200	W
Crab apple	20	G, M
Elms	50–100	W
Field maple	50–100	W
Hazel	20	G, M
Holly		G, B
Hornbeam	50–100	W, M
Limes	50–100	W
Oaks	20	G, B, M
Rowan		G, B
Scots pine	100–200	W
Common whitebeam		G, B
Wild cherry		G, B, M
Willows	100–200	W
Yew		G, B

* G = gravity; W = wind; B = birds; M = mammals

Secondary succession comprising predominately willow scrub on ex-arable land at Havering Park Farm, Essex: in 2006 when cropping ceased (top) and three years later (bottom).

Figure 2.1 Succession from grassland to W8 woodland, through bramble-Yorkshire-fog underscrub, and hawthorn-ivy scrub communities (not to scale).

birches and willows; and on light, acid soils birches, gorse and broom are probable precursors. Over very long periods of time, these woodlands may gradually come to resemble the semi-natural woodland communities described in Section 1.2. Quite diverse grassland communities, such as abandoned neutral or chalk grassland on well-drained soils, may converge into ash-field maple (W8) woodland (Rodwell, 1991); while less base-rich soils may develop into oak-bracken-bramble (W10) woodland. Wetter, heavier soils and rush-pastures in southern England are also commonly invaded by ash-maple woodland, or there may be an intervening seral scrub stage, usually resulting in a hawthorn-ivy scrub (W21). Bramble-Yorkshire-fog underscrub (W24) often forms a fringe between grassland and scrub and also survives along the edge of woodland, usually with a false oat-grass ground layer (Figure 2.1). Such examples can be useful when designing new woodlands (see Chapter 7), but they are also a reminder that one can be too precious when prescribing species mixes for ex-agricultural sites.

2.1.2 Woodland seed banks

In ancient woodland, the seed bank mostly consists of light-demanding, early successional species, so there is often a poor correlation between the seed bank and the actual ground vegetation, especially where there has been a long interval without disturbance (Van Calster, *et al.*, 2008). These light-demanding species are usually not able to establish large populations in a stressful, shady woodland environment, unless light gaps are formed through natural disturbances or felling. Such an opportunity allows seed to germinate and replenish the seed bank. In contrast, many shade-tolerant, ancient woodland species produce only small numbers of short-lived seeds, which do not become incorporated into the seed bank for any length of time: less than a third of ancient woodland species in England have persistent seed banks, but these include species such as wood-sedge, broad-leaved willowherb and wood spurge. Studies in Belgium have shown that as new woodland ages beyond 50 years, the number of true forest species in the seed bank tends to increase, but reaches only low densities (Hermy, *et al.*, 1999).

In recent woods, even after 50 years, there may still be a sizeable density of early successional species in the seed bank. Consequently soil disturbance should be avoided in such habitat (Bossuyt, *et al.*, 2002), although it is generally believed that if forests remain undisturbed for 50 years or more, most of these seeds will begin to lose their viability, and the seed bank will decline steadily thereafter (Brown and Warr, 1992; Buckley *et al.*, 1997). However, there is no early replacement with ancient woodland plants: even after 100 years or more, these may still be undetectable in the seed bank, irrespective of the proximity of ancient woodland, although large-seeded forest species may disperse across short distances (Bossuyt, *et al.*, 2002).

2.2 Woodland plants

2.2.1 Herbaceous plants

If you walk through ancient woodland, you are likely to find a range of plants which tolerate shade. Some of these are woodland specialists, and may only be found in ancient woods. Other shade-tolerant plants are cosmopolitan, commoner in the wider landscape, along hedgerows and in younger woods. Rides and glades support another group of plants which require sunlight. These communities may closely resemble those present in meadows, heathland or marshland. This section introduces the different woodland plant communities, considers natural dispersal mechanisms, and hence the likelihood that they will develop naturally in new native woodland.

Plants of woodland open spaces

Woods and meadows are usually considered as distinct ecological communities, and treated as such by ecologists and other professionals. Traditional 'hay meadows' are not continuously grazed and allowed to grow, flower and set seed during the summer months before cutting for hay.

Historically this was the case in many woodland open spaces, which were essentially extensions of open meadows. In prehistoric forests, meadow-like grassland may have been present in relatively small areas, rather like the rides and margins of woodland today (Peterken, 2009).

The vegetation of open areas in ancient and recent woods is characterised by a mixture of woodland edge species and species of open habitats such as grassland and heathland. In a study of 362 ancient and recent woods in central Lincolnshire, Peterken and Francis (1999) found that 60% of all woodland species were strongly associated with open space. This amounted to 264 species, with a similar level of diversity in the combined open spaces of both categories of woods surveyed. Although most of the rare and specialist plants of semi-natural grassland, heathland and mires were absent, healthy populations of formerly common grassland species were found. Many species characteristic of neutral meadow communities are equally widespread in ancient woodlands today, including herbs such as meadowsweet, meadow buttercup and tormentil; and grasses such as sweet vernal-grass, creeping bent and rough meadow-grass. Conversely, so-called 'woodland' species such as common twayblade, wood anemone and early-purple orchid can also be found in meadows; bluebells are frequent in meadows and along roadside verges in south west England. In many of the intensively farmed areas of Britain such as the East Midlands and East Anglia, many of the best examples of natural 'meadows' are now to be found in rides of both ancient and more recent woods.

Many new woodlands include substantial areas of open ground, so there is an opportunity here to encourage the regeneration of diverse plant communities to support diminishing non-woodland habitats in the wider landscape (Table 2.2). However, in recent years almost all new native woodland in the lowlands has been planted on ex-arable land or improved pasture with little intrinsic conservation value. Without intervention, the vegetation communities which develop naturally are likely to be species-poor, depending on the soil type. However, in the semi-natural landscape of the uplands there remains considerable scope for expanding woodlands. A study by Good, *et al.*, (1997) examined the potential for establishing new woodland areas in four National Parks (Northumberland, the Lake District, Dartmoor and the Peak District) and one Area of Outstanding Natural Beauty (the Shropshire Hills). Land between 200 and 600 m was considered, provided that it did not include scrub, woodland, deep peat, or areas of heathland and moorland

LEFT **Yorkshire-fog, an early colonist of woodland open spaces.**

RIGHT **Silverweed is an early colonist of bare ground in new woodland.**

LEFT **Oxeye daisy and kidney vetch (with nectaring small blue butterfly) are potential colonists of woodland open space across much of Britain.**

RIGHT **Wild teasel frequently colonises woodland open space in southern and central England, here being visited by a spotted longhorn beetle.**

greater than 5 ha; whereas land cover such as grass heath, moorland grass, bracken, cultivated land and semi-natural vegetation less than 5 ha in extent was considered potentially suitable. The overall conclusion was that about 18% of the study area (out of a total of c.900 km^2) could support new woodland without damaging, and indeed complementing, conservation interests. While not all of this land would be available, it illustrates the potential for expanding upland woodland habitats proposed in Biodiversity Action Plans, especially if well targeted through forest habitat networks.

2.2.2 Shade-tolerant plants

Several highly mobile, shade-tolerant species can quickly colonise new woodland. They usually have very effective dispersal mechanisms (e.g. light, hooked or feathered seeds or berries) and are common and widespread, particularly in old hedges, established wood margins and disturbed ground (Peterken, 1981). They include species such as lords-and-ladies, common nettle, hogweed, bramble, cow parsley and tall grasses such as false oat-grass and cock's-foot (Table 2.3). However, very few specialist ancient woodland species will colonise at this early stage and the intimate mixes of species which typify ancient woodland will take very much longer.

Table 2.2 Examples of potential colonists of open ground in lowland new native woodland, most of which also occur in partial shade; all have Ellenberg light scores of 7 or higher (plants of generally well lit places) (Hill *et al.*, 1999)

Annual meadow-grass	Greater plantain
Bristly oxtongue	Hoary ragwort
Cock's-foot	Hoary willowherb
Common bird's-foot-trefoil	Hogweed
Common couch	Lesser stitchwort
Common fleabane	Marsh thistle
Common knapweed	Meadow buttercup
Common mouse-ear	Meadow vetchling
Common ragwort	Perennial rye-grass
Common vetch	Perforate St John's-wort
Compact rush	Red clover
Creeping bent	Ribwort plantain
Creeping cinquefoil	Rough meadow-grass
Creeping thistle	Selfheal
Curled dock	Smooth meadow-grass
Cut-leaved crane's-bill	Soft-rush
Dandelion	Thyme-leaved speedwell
False oat-grass	Tufted vetch
Field horsetail	White clover
Glaucous sedge	Wild angelica
Great willowherb	Wood dock
Greater bird's-foot-trefoil	Yorkshire-fog

Faster colonising woodland plants include hedge woundwort (right), broad buckler-fern (top left) and red campion (bottom left).

PART ONE GENERAL PRINCIPLES – **WOODLANDS FOR WILDLIFE**

Colonisation of new woods by shade-tolerant plants

Woodland plants likely to colonise new woodlands include those with efficient dispersal mechanisms, some shade tolerance and an ability to thrive and compete on fertile soils with elevated levels of phosphate and other nutrients (Table 2.3). In agricultural soils acidification is usually countered by liming, and although calcium and magnesium will be leached from the surface layers over time, increased phosphate from fertilisation can persist for many decades as it is largely immobile in the soil. Most agricultural soils are also characterised by low organic matter, poor soil structure and compacted layers. A few studies have tried to relate changes in the chemical and physical characteristics of the soil to the ability of forest species to germinate and establish. These indicate that while the combination of light conditions prior to canopy closure and fertile soils represents a major barrier to colonisation by some ancient woodland species (de Keersmaeker *et al.*, 2004; Honnay *et al.*, 1999), the competition from vigorous, fast colonising grasses and tall herbs is more likely to be inhibiting than soil conditions *per se* (Hipps *et al.*, 2005). Once canopy closure has taken place, the competitive advantage of these vigorous species is much reduced, allowing opportunities for colonisation by woodland species. Older woods that exhibit some diversity of shade flora may have been planted close to ancient woodland habitat or old hedgerows. Care must be exercised when predicting natural colonisation rates based on studies of the ground flora in older planted woods, because source populations may have been destroyed.

Table 2.3 Potential colonists of lowland new native woodland, including shade-tolerant species typically found in woodland margins, hedges and waste ground; and several species characteristic of ancient woodland communities

Species occurring in partial shade	Ellenberg light score	Faster colonising woodland species	Ellenberg light score
Annual meadow-grass	7	Black bryony	6
Bittersweet	7	Bramble	6
Broad-leaved dock	7	Broad buckler-fern	5
Cleavers	6	Broad-leaved willowherb	6
Cock's-foot	7	Common nettle	6
Common chickweed	7	Common twayblade	6
Common hemp-nettle	7	Dewberry	7
Cow parsley	6	Enchanter's-nightshade	4
Creeping cinquefoil	7	False brome	6
Dandelion	7	Giant fescue	5
False oat-grass	7	Ground-ivy	6
Field forget-me-not	7	Hairy-brome	6
Garlic mustard	5	Hedge woundwort	6
Ground-elder	6	Herb-Robert	5
Hogweed	7	Honeysuckle	5
Ivy-leaved speedwell	6	Ivy	4
Lesser burdock	6	Lords-and-ladies	4
Nipplewort	6	Male-fern	5
Rosebay willowherb	6	Narrow buckler-fern	6
Spear thistle	7	Raspberry	6
Upright hedge-parsley	7	Red campion	5
White bryony	7	Sanicle	4
White dead-nettle	7	Sweet violet	5
		Three-nerved sandwort	4
		Wood avens	4
		Wood dock	5

Ellenberg light scores (based on values recalibrated for the British situation (Hill *et al.*, 1999):
1. Plants in deep shade
2. Between 1 and 3
3. Shade plants
4. Between 3 and 5
5. Semi-shade plants
6. Between 5 and 7
7. Generally well lit places
8. Between 7 and 9
9. Full light plants.

Box 2.2 Pioneering work on introducing woodland ground flora

'Ecological' plantations, comprising mixtures of native species, became a popular feature in landscape design of urban areas such as Warrington New Town, Milton Keynes, Wolverhampton and St Helens, as well as on waste and derelict land, roadsides and in other major infrastructure schemes. Because the spread of woodland understorey plants into new sites can be very slow, several schemes artificially introduced them as the canopy developed. Later, as various community and National Forest planting initiatives developed in the 1990s, further opportunities arose to diversify the new woodlands in order to make them more attractive. One example was the Woodland Wildflowers Project (2001–2005), a partnership initiative for the 12 Community Forests, in which understorey plants were collected, propagated and introduced into both newly created and existing woodlands. Various recommendations have been reported in the literature regarding ground preparation methods, species choice, sowing rates, soil manipulation, weed control, and optimal shade levels for woodland flora introductions (Buckley and Knight, 1989; Francis *et al.*, 1992; Cohn *et al.*, 2000). Typical priority species were bluebell, primrose and greater stitchwort, together with other common woodland plants such as lesser celandine, wood avens, wood anemone, hedge woundwort and red campion.

A re-evaluation of woodland wildflower seeding at five main sites in north west England found the greatest success under predominantly closed canopy with intermediate disturbance levels created by thinning (Scott, 2004). The least successful sites had little canopy cover and suffered strong competition from ruderal species. Subjects showing the best establishment were cosmopolitan, relatively competitive species tolerant of disturbance, such as herb-Robert, primrose, red campion, wood avens and hedge woundwort. At Milton Keynes, 14 years after their initial introduction, most species had survived well and developed their own populations of multi-aged cohorts. Several slow-growing woodland interior species (bluebell, woodruff, bugle, yellow archangel and sweet violet) had increased their cover, while that of some of the woodland marginals had decreased. Spread into new areas was limited, apart from three marginal species (wood avens, garlic mustard and red campion) and bluebell (Francis and Morton, 2001).

2.2.3 Woodland specialist plants

The first modern reference to ancient woodland plants or 'indicator species' in Britain was Peterken's studies of Lincolnshire woods (Peterken, 1974), since when regional lists have been prepared by Natural England and other conservation agencies to aid the identification and designation of ancient woods (Peterken, 2000b; Rose, 1999; 2006; Crawford, 2009). Although there are many exceptions, characteristics of such species include:

- poor dispersal ability
- low fecundity
- production of few, relatively large seeds, often not forming long-term seed banks
- limited ability to compete with other species in open conditions
- tolerant of shade and low nutrient levels
- vegetative propagation through expansion and fragmentation of the plant by bulbs, rhizomes, stolons or suckers.

In the last case, species that expand readily through vegetative propagation can only colonise new woodland if they are already present, or through (sometimes rare) seed dispersal. In some cases vegetative expansion may help the initial colonisation phase, particularly if it is difficult for seedlings to readily establish. In tree-fall gaps in established woodlands, for example, wood anemone relies on vegetative persistence to survive. In these more stressful environments, seedling survival is likely to be poor.

Woodland floral diversity is strongly influenced by parent soil type. Calcareous brown earth soils such as those found on the lower slopes of the North Downs, contain large numbers of ancient woodland plants. In contrast, woodlands on the acidic sands and clays of the nearby Weald of Kent and Sussex, have a much lower diversity. Not all these ancient woodland plants are entirely restricted to ancient woodland and may also be found in more recent woodland or even outside woodland altogether, particularly adjacent to ancient woodland: wood spurge for example can grow outside woodland on chalky soils. It is also important to remember that ancient woodland plants in one region may not be 'indicators' in another. For example, golden-rod, wood club-rush and marsh violet are all indicators of ancient woodland in the South East, but not in East Anglia; chickweed wintergreen and creeping lady's tresses are indicators in parts of Scotland, but less common south of the border (Crawford, 2009).

Because of the relative immobility of many ancient woodland plants, it is worthwhile incorporating existing species-rich hedgerows and adjacent ancient woodland into new planting designs. Other habitats which may host woodland flora include ditches, old lanes, stream banks and riparian woodland. Such an approach may lead to colonisation of a new wood by several ancient woodland species. The main issues that govern whether a species is able to colonise a wood successfully are a) dispersal, and b) establishment, which can only take place if the habitat is suitable (Verheyen and Hermy, 2001; Box 2.3). Species such as oxlip and yellow archangel may be limited by both of these factors; or establishment may be the main factor, as in the case of herb Paris and Solomon's seal. Even introducing these species artificially into new woodland might be problematic. However, species limited mainly by dispersal, such as wood anemone and bluebell; or by neither factor, e.g. wood avens, lesser celandine, ground-ivy, ground-elder, bugle, moschatel and wood-sorrel, represent a group which may respond positively, albeit very slowly to introduction.

> **Box 2.3 Dispersal of ancient woodland plants**
>
> Hermy *et al.*, (1999) identified 132 ancient forest species (equivalent to ancient woodland indicator species in Britain and with similar characteristics), constituting 21% of the European forest flora. They considered that 24% were relatively weak dispersers, relying on ants; 27% were animal or bird-dispersed; 25% by wind; 7% by gravity; 3% by water; and 14% had unknown dispersal mechanisms. Compared to wind-dispersal, relatively few studies have modelled animal dispersal, so the efficiency of seed dissemination in the fur of herbivores, for example, is not well understood. Distance from ancient forest source populations is significant: a decrease in cover of forest plant colonists occurs with increasing distance. Species which are ingested by birds or animals may be dispersed over greater distances than species relying on wind or ants (Matlack, 1994). Experimental introduction of ancient woodland plants into relatively young woodlands have tended to prove successful (e.g. Francis and Morton, 2001), suggesting that dispersal-limitation is usually more important than recruitment- (germination and establishment) limitation. Nevertheless, these woods must have sufficient undisturbed core areas suitable for establishment. A species may establish small colonies in discrete parts of a wood, which may be defined by quite sharp edges.

PART ONE GENERAL PRINCIPLES – **WOODLANDS FOR WILDLIFE**

LEFT **Pendulous sedge is an ancient woodland plant which has been recorded in new native woodland.**

CENTRE **Bluebells occur sporadically in new native woodland planted adjacent to ancient woodland.**

RIGHT **Colonisation of new native woodland by yellow archangel is limited by seed dispersal.**

LEFT **White helleborine colonising new native woodland planted on chalk.**

RIGHT **Ramsons may be found along the edge of new native woodland planted within a few metres of a source population.**

Herb-Paris (left) and wild daffodil (right) are ancient woodland plants unlikely to colonise new woods.

LEFT **Dog's mercury is a plant of ancient woodland which may colonise new woods.**

RIGHT **Bastard balm is an indicator of ancient woodland in South West England.**

Surveys by the authors in young woodlands in southern England have identified a range of woodland plants, many of which are ancient woodland species. These include moschatel, pendulous sedge, remote sedge, pignut, enchanter's-nightshade, bluebell, three-nerved sandwort, common spotted-orchid, black bryony, dog's mercury, yellow archangel and wood speedwell.

2.3 Woodland birds

Structurally diverse, mature woodland supports a rich diversity of birds in Britain, often at high population densities, compared with less structured habitats such as grasslands. However, the well-described decline in woodland management has contributed to a parallel decline in some woodland species.

The abundance of birds breeding in woodland is influenced by the availability of food, particularly invertebrates, during spring and summer, and by suitable nest sites. Other factors determining potential population size include the quality of wintering habitat, both for resident and migrant species and, in the latter case, the hazards they face during migration.

The availability of food depends on the diversity of the wood, because some 'specialist' birds often occupy only very specific habitats. Marsh tits, for example, forage very largely in the understorey and not in the canopy, so will not be present where an understorey is lacking or does not provide food, especially if dominated by non-native shrubs like laurel or rhododendron. Similarly, birds often have specific requirements for nest sites; an over-grazed wood will not support birds like leaf warblers or woodcock that need a structured field layer to nest in.

2.3.1 Generalist and specialist species

Woodland birds fall into two broad categories; generalists are those species that can utilise a range of habitats like gardens, hedgerows and parks as well as woods and include bullfinch, dunnock and blackcap. The specialists are usually only found in woodland habitats, e.g. marsh tit, pied flycatcher and lesser spotted woodpecker. They have particular requirements of their habitat and so can be vulnerable to changes in the woodland condition. Research suggests that the generalist species are faring well in woodland whereas some of the specialists have undergone severe declines.

There is also some emerging evidence that increasing woodland isolation in the increasingly intensively managed countryside is a factor explaining the decline of specialists such as hawfinch, marsh tit and lesser spotted woodpecker. New woodland, if strategically located, can

The woodcock is a bird of mature broadleaved and coniferous woodland with a substantial field layer, which has suffered significant declines in recent years.

Stanley Porter (rspb-images.com)

benefit these species by helping them to navigate through an otherwise 'hostile' landscape. New native woodland that is designed or naturally develops a range of features, including a dense understorey, should also support a number of specialists of early woodland and scrub communities. Willow tit, one of the rarest and most precarious of woodland birds, depends on this habitat in wet conditions; other declining birds like willow warbler, nightingale and garden warbler can also occur at good densities.

2.3.2 Birds and woodland types

Well-structured, native broadleaved woodland generally supports rich bird communities, varying according to rainfall, soil type and fertility. Similarly, the assemblage of species utilising new woodlands in the lowlands is influenced by its character; on poor acidic soils the succession is typically dominated by birch with a bracken field layer, which is favoured by willow warblers and later by lesser redpoll. Where soils are more base-rich and retain more moisture, species like hawthorn and ash are early colonists, and here common whitethroat and garden warbler are typical, followed later by nightingale and bullfinch. In wetter conditions with willow, alder and birch, reed buntings and willow warbler colonise the early stages, and the developing thicket supports willow tit and nightingale.

On poorer soils in the wet climate of western and northern Britain, upland broadleaved woodland types can paradoxically occur at sea-level, and usually have a relatively simple structure. Predominantly mature, with a closed canopy and relatively low abundance of understorey, they support a characteristic bird community with pied flycatcher, common redstart and wood warbler. Tree pipit and several other woodland specialists including both lesser and great spotted woodpecker, spotted flycatcher, marsh tit and Eurasian jay also occur.

These upland woods are typically dominated by oak, but where soils are richer, ash is important and where soils or climate limit the oak, birch woodland occurs. Such variations influence the bird community to some extent, particularly where birch woodland gives out to moorland; here tree pipit, lesser redpoll, common redstart and willow warbler are often common, and this habitat is important for black grouse. New broadleaved woodland in the uplands also has the potential to attract willow warbler, tree pipit and even black grouse in the pre-canopy closure stages, and lesser redpoll in the thicket.

Native pinewoods in the Scottish Highlands support a particularly distinctive woodland bird community that includes capercaillie, crested tit, Scottish and parrot crossbills; where birch and other deciduous species occur, black grouse, redwing, lesser redpoll, spotted flycatcher, willow warbler, common crossbill and siskin may be found.

The bullfinch utilises a wide range of habitats including new woodland thickets.

2.3.3 Birds of new native woodland

Woodland creation provides opportunities for a number of strongly declining woodland birds characteristic of young woodland, such as tree pipit, willow warbler and garden warbler. The species benefiting from new woodlands will vary depending on a) the type of new woodland created; b) the stage of growth; and c) their distribution in the country.

The bird communities using new woodland will change as the canopy develops. Initial colonists will be species of open habitats, which endure until the developing trees and shrubs form scrub, when open-scrub birds colonise. As thickets develop, species such as willow warbler can occur at high densities. Eventually the woodland will develop mature structures, displacing the bird communities of young woodland. Under some management regimes, it is possible to maintain good populations of a number of woodland birds in Britain through coppice management or by providing scrub along rides and the woodland edge. The high volume of foliage in sheltered conditions gives rise to an abundance of invertebrates besides providing good cover for nesting. New woodland which retains such a variety of features is likely to provide the optimum opportunity for bird diversity.

Many birds using young woodland are able to exploit a range of woodland types – for instance bullfinch and song thrush are often abundant in young upland conifer stands and in young deciduous woodland. However, some conservation priority species, like the willow tit which favours younger wet woodland, will vacate once it begins to mature or dry out.

The diet of many of woodland bird species expands in late summer and early autumn to exploit the production of seeds and fruits at a time when bird numbers are dramatically increased by juveniles and when their nutritional needs are increased – either to survive the winter or to undertake long, often trans-Saharan migrations. The composition of scrub and trees in new woodland is potentially valuable, as a high proportion of fruit- and seed-bearing species will improve the quality of foraging for breeding, migrating and wintering birds. The bird community in winter is different to that in the breeding season; summer migrants leave and winter visitors arrive. Meanwhile other species of farmland and upland habitats will move in to exploit fleshy fruiting shrubs in well designed new woodland, and dense scrub and trees may also host large numbers of roosting birds at this time of year, such as thrushes, finches and starlings.

A number of species will use young woodland incidentally, rather than as part of their main habitat. Birds of open habitats such as skylark, meadow pipit and grey partridge will use clearings and open space in woodland, including areas prior to canopy development. However, although nightjar and woodlark may occupy new woodland on light soils up to the point of canopy closure, sites suitable for these species should not be densely planted as this could compromise the conservation of rare and vulnerable species. Other birds which use new woodland mainly occupy more mature woodland: resident species such as hawfinch, marsh tit and lesser spotted woodpecker need to move through the countryside to find new habitats if they are not to decline further. Young woodlands can provide a distribution network, particularly in an open landscape.

LEFT **The spotted flycatcher, which has suffered significant declines in recent years, may feed in new native woodland.**

RIGHT **The willow warbler is a strongly declining species which breeds in new native woodland with good structural diversity.**

OPPOSITE **Willow tit, which is now one of the rarest woodland birds in Britain favours early woodland and scrub communities in wet conditions.**

2.3.4 Woodland birds of conservation concern

Many of the bird species which utilise new native broadleaved woodland are of conservation concern (Table 2.4), mostly due to declining populations. The majority are species that will both nest and feed within closed canopy scrub and woodland (Fuller, 1995); although some are unlikely to breed in the absence of mature trees, such as kestrel and green woodpecker; or other features (such as rotten stumps for willow tit). Some, like the turtle dove will feed mainly in more open country.

The Wild Bird Indicator is part of the Government's Quality of Life approach first introduced in 1999. It is monitored annually using standard methods to assess change over time. Thirty-three species of woodland birds are included in the Wild Bird Indicator, and although there has been an overall decline in this assemblage, it masks a more complex picture of increases in some species and dramatic declines in others. Several mature woodland specialists have declined significantly, such as woodcock, lesser spotted woodpecker, pied flycatcher, spotted flycatcher and wood warbler. The causes still require further investigation but a simplification in woodland structure may be responsible, driven by excessive deer browsing, a broad scale decline in management, or a general maturation of successional woodland, or a combination of all of these. In general the 'specialist' species have fared twice as badly as the 'generalists'.

Some generalist birds of new native woodland and scrub, and those of open canopy woodland have also exhibited rapid declines, including turtle dove, cuckoo, tree pipit, willow warbler, willow tit, starling, lesser redpoll and yellowhammer. Although the causes of some species' declines are unknown, many would benefit from appropriately designed and managed new native woodland. In addition, nightingale has shown a marked range contraction over the past 20 years, and although the overall population decline has been just 8% there has been a large-scale abandonment of woodland habitats. These declines in selected species are also detected in other monitoring, such as the Repeat Woodland Bird Survey, which assessed woodland bird population change in over 450 broadleaved woods throughout Britain over a 20-year period (Amar et al., 2006).

The list of Birds of Conservation Concern (BoCC) (Gregory et al., 2002) is a non-statutory approach to classifying breeding and wintering British birds depending on their conservation status. Red-Listed birds are of the highest concern, Amber moderate and Green of low conservation concern. These lists are periodically reviewed to take account of recent trends and issues.

Table 2.4 Priority bird species, their conservation status and use of new native broadleaved woodland and scrub.

	Nesting	Feeding	Conservation status	
			BoCC	UK BAP priority
Hen harrier*			Red	
Montagu's harrier*			Amber	
Merlin*			Amber	
Black grouse			Red	
Woodcock			Amber	
Turtle dove			Red	✓
Cuckoo			Red	✓
Barn owl			Amber	
Short-eared owl*			Amber	
Green woodpecker			Amber	
Nightjar*			Red	
Woodlark*			Amber	✓
Tree pipit*			Red	✓
Whinchat*			Amber	
Dunnock			Amber	✓
Nightingale			Amber	
Song thrush			Red	✓
Mistle thrush			Amber	
Fieldfare			Red	
Redwing			Red	
Ring ouzel			Red	✓
Grasshopper warbler*			Red	✓
Common whitethroat*			Amber	
Willow warbler			Amber	
Spotted flycatcher			Red	✓
Willow tit			Red	✓
Starling*			Red	✓
Tree sparrow			Red	✓
House sparrow			Red	✓
Lesser redpoll			Red	✓
Linnet*			Red	✓
Twite*			Red	✓
Bullfinch			Amber	✓
Cirl bunting*			Red	✓
Reed bunting*			Amber	✓
Yellowhammer*			Red	✓

* Birds which nest or feed primarily in open canopy woodland/scrub including young broadleaved and conifer plantations, which may use new native woodland before canopy closure

David Kjaer

The categories are derived objectively, as follows:

Red List criteria:

- globally threatened species (IUCN listing)
- historic population decline during 1800–1995
- rapid decline in UK breeding population (> 50%) over the last 25 years
- rapid contraction in UK breeding range (> 50%) over the last 25 years.

Amber-listed species (medium conservation concern) criteria:

- historic population decline during 1800–1995, but recovering; population has more than doubled over the last 25 years
- moderate decline in UK breeding population (25–49%) over the last 25 years
- moderate contraction in UK breeding range (25–49%) over the last 25 years
- moderate decline in UK non-breeding population (25–49%) over the last 25 years
- species with unfavourable conservation status in Europe.

A significant number of the woodland birds that breed or feed in young new native broadleaved woodland are Red or Amber-listed (Tables 2.4 and 2.5).

Table 2.5 Other conservation priority birds that will benefit in time as new woodland matures

	Conservation status	
	BoCC	UK BAP priority
Red kite	Amber	
Honey buzzard	Amber	
Osprey	Amber	
Goshawk		
Woodcock	Amber	
Capercaillie*	Red	✓
Black grouse	Red	✓
Stock dove	Amber	
Lesser spotted woodpecker	Red	✓
Common redstart	Amber	
Wood warbler	Red	✓
Firecrest	Amber	
Spotted flycatcher	Red	✓
Pied flycatcher	Amber	
Marsh tit	Red	✓
Crested tit*	Amber	
Golden oriole	Red	
Tree sparrow	Red	✓
Lesser redpoll	Red	✓
Scottish crossbill*	Amber	✓
Hawfinch	Red	✓

* breeding restricted to conifer or mixed forest and plantations in Scotland

The UK Biodiversity Action Plan (BAP) priority list includes birds for which the UK has international importance that have undergone large declines, including those that are endemic species or races. Most Red-listed woodland birds and some Amber-listed species are included on the UK BAP priority list. Of the 59 UK BAP priority bird species, 25 are associated with young woodlands.

LEFT **The whinchat is a bird of conservation concern which prefers open scrub.**

RIGHT **Nightingales, which have undergone a significant range contraction in recent years, may be found in the dense understorey of new native woodland.**

2.4 Woodland bats

More than 30% of the native terrestrial mammal fauna of the British Isles are bats (16 species) and all of them regularly use woodlands and trees (Table 2.6). Most of these have suffered significant declines in the last 100 years or so (Stebbings, 1988; Hutson, 1993; Harris et al., 1995), due in part to agricultural intensification resulting in habitat loss, including roost sites (Hutson, 1993). All species and their roosts are protected by legislation and are listed on the EU Habitats Directive Annex IV (species in need of particularly strict protection) of which four (including Bechsteins's bat and the barbastelle) are given additional protection under Annex II. Seven of the British bats are UK BAP priority species, including Bechstein's bat and the barbastelle, which are both on the IUCN Red List of Near Threatened Species.

Many bats have a close association with woodlands, particularly riparian woodland, and avoid arable land. Hedgerows and riparian woodland provide for both foraging and commuting between roosting and feeding areas. Mature woodland with a wide age range of trees, a diverse canopy structure, good quality rides, open spaces and woodland edges provides good habitat for many bats, although the edges and open areas mostly encourage the commoner species. Acoustic lure studies have shown that a clear association also exists between a well-developed understorey and the diversity of woodland bat species (Hill and Greenaway, 2008).

A landscape which includes mature woodland, together with a mosaic of hedgerows, riparian woodland, scrub, unimproved grassland areas, ponds and rivers (both slow- and fast-flowing) would suit the feeding and commuting activities of all the British bats (Box 2.4). All of these habitats provide insect food in abundance, which is one of the major factors governing the

> **Box 2.4 Bats recorded in new native woodland**
>
> Studies in Suffolk and the Vale of York found that bats made widespread use of farm woodlands (Pottie et al., 1997; Central Science Laboratory, 2000; 2003). In the Vale of York, nine species were putatively identified in farm woodlands. The majority of bats recorded were pipistrelle species, which made greater use of farm woods than adjacent arable land. Noctule and several unidentified *Myotis* species (probably Natterer's, Daubenton's and Brandt's bats) were also widespread, and detected in both farm woodland and arable land. Whiskered bats were found foraging preferentially in farm woods and both Leisler's and brown long-eared bats were also recorded in one or two farm woods. More mature farm woodlands are likely to be particularly suitable for brown long-eared bat (Central Science Laboratory, 2003).
>
> Few other studies of bats have been undertaken in new native woodland, so further work is required to establish how this habitat can be best designed for bats. However, enough is already known about bat ecology to confirm the importance of location in facilitating movement, and the value of woodland edges, rides and open space for feeding. The presence of permanent surface water either on site or nearby, such as a pond or stream, is also very important (David Hill, pers com).

Table 2.6 British bats; their status, foraging habitat and food

Species	Status and distribution	Commuting/foraging habitat	Food
Greater horseshoe bat*	South Wales and the South West, rare	Forages in deciduous woodland and pasture	Predominantly beetles and moths
Lesser horseshoe bat*	South Wales, Welsh borders and the South West, rare	Forages in deciduous woodland and pasture	Flies and small moths
Bechstein's bat*	Very rare	Forages in mature woodland with good three-dimensional structure	Moths, flies and spiders
Natterer's bat	Widespread	Forages in woodland, wet woodland, linear woods, woodland edge, open grassland, over water; commutes/forages along hedgerows	Wide range of insects and spiders
Daubenton's bat	Widespread	Forages along riparian woodland, over water, other woodland at certain times of year	Insects with aquatic larvae
Whiskered bat	Widespread	Predominately aerial hawkers in riparian habitats, woodland, woodland edge, open rides	Moths, spiders and wide range of other insects
Brandt's bat	Widespread, scarce	Believed to be similar to whiskered bat	Moths, spiders and wide range of other insects
Serotine	Mainly South East England, scarce	Forages in pasture, lowland parkland, woodland edge, hedgerows	Beetles, moths and other insects
Noctule*	England and Wales, frequent	Forages in wide range of habitats, including woodland edge/glades	Beetles, flies, moths
Leisler's bat	England, rare	Forages in wide range of habitats, including woodland edge/glades, over woodland canopy	Flies and other small insects
Common pipistrelle	Widespread, common	Forages in wide range of habitats, including woodland edge, hedgerows, open ground	Flies and other insects
Soprano pipistrelle*	Widespread, common	Forages in wide range of habitats, including woodland edges, open ground, riverside/lakeside vegetation	Flies and other insects
Nathusius' pipistrelle	Not known	Lowland woods and parks	Flies
Brown long-eared bat*	Widespread, common	Gleans from foliage/other surfaces, favours woodland, woodland edge, parkland; commutes along linear features	Moths
Grey long-eared bat	South West England, very rare	Gleans from foliage/other surfaces, favours woodland, woodland edge	Moths
The barbastelle*	Widespread, very rare	Forages in woodland canopy, woodland edge, orchards	Moths

* UK BAP priority species. Source: Bat Conservation Trust and Altringham (2003)

suitability of a habitat for foraging bats. Such a landscape may once have been commonplace, but is less so today. Consequently, the creation of new native woodland could provide important foraging habitat for bats and make a substantial contribution to bat conservation in the wider landscape.

2.5 Woodland invertebrates

2.5.1 Invertebrate diversity in mature woodland

Woodland has the richest invertebrate fauna of any British habitat, due to its complex structure, diversity of niches and the relative stability of the mature state. Ancient woodland also provides historical continuity, which is especially important to species requiring rare and specialised niches (Table 2.7), or which have only limited powers of dispersal. Most insect groups are represented in British woodland by a large number of species. Some trees and shrubs, such as hawthorns, cherries, willows, birches and oaks, can support very high numbers of insects, exceeding 350 species in each case. In contrast, 30 species or less have been recorded on wild service-tree, spindle, ivy and box, illustrating the value of different trees and shrubs to feeding invertebrates. In addition there are also invertebrates closely associated with herbivores including predators, parasitoids, cleptoparasites and mutualists. Further information on the interactions between invertebrate herbivores and their host plants can be obtained from the comprehensive *Database of British Insects and their Foodplants* (Smith and Roy, 2008).

Some invertebrates specialise in woodland at different stages of succession, including shrubby woodland edges and patches of tall herbs in rides and glades. These areas provide opportunities for:

- nectaring and pollen collection (e.g. social and solitary bees)
- feeding on plant sap (e.g. tree aphids)
- leaf-eating (e.g. leaf miners and leaf rollers)
- stem-nesting (e.g. solitary wasps)
- nest construction (e.g. leaf-cutter bees)
- structural support (e.g. spiders)
- shelter (e.g. specialist woodland butterflies)
- foraging and hunting (e.g. ants and dragonflies).

How important are new woods for invertebrates?

New woods do not have the diversity of structure or age necessary to provide the full range of habitat niches required by all invertebrates (Table 2.7). This may be alleviated to some extent through planting close to ancient woodland, hedgerows, or even by incorporating large remnant trees. The proximity of ancient woodland is far more important for invertebrate colonisation than for colonisation by birds.

Speckled wood butterflies favour damper situations in woodland rides and glades, and often frequent new woods.

Invertebrates associated with deadwood are diverse, and exceptionally important for conservation (Kirby, P., 1992). Whilst the more specialised species are very unlikely to benefit from new woodland, the retention of dead trees, thinnings and brash might attract some commoner saproxylic species such as hoverflies and longhorn beetles, especially if there is ancient woodland nearby. After the canopy closes, stem exclusion resulting from competition for light can provide supplies of larger dead material. New woodlands which are isolated from ancient woodland are most likely to develop an invertebrate fauna more characteristic of the wider countryside.

Rides, open spaces and traditionally managed coppice offer a diverse habitat which is important for many woodland invertebrates. Coppice in particular can

LEFT Male bumblebee (*Bombus lapidarius*) nectaring on common knapweed in a woodland ride.

RIGHT Southern wood ant nests are threatened by overgrowth of rides and glades in ancient woodland.

Table 2.7 **Invertebrate habitat in woodland with features found in new woodland emboldened (largely based on Elton, 1966)**

	Habitat	Microhabitat	Species and use
Trees and shrubs	**Living wood**		Wood borers
	Decaying wood	Rot holes	Saproxylic species and cover
		Heart rot	Saproxylic species
		Cavities	Saproxylic species and cover
	Bark	**Surface**	Predators and perches
	Damaged bark	Surface	Cover
		Loose	Saproxylic species and cover
		Sap runs	Specialists
	Foliage	**Canopy**	Food
		Understorey	Food
		Climbers	Food, cover, hibernation
	Flowers		Nectar
	Roots	**Living**	Gall causers
		Decaying	Saproxylic species
Woodland edge/rides	**Foliage**		Food and perches
	Flowers		Nectar
Herbs	**Foliage**		Food and perches etc.
	Flowers		Nectar
	Roots		Food
Bryophytes			Cover
Fungi	**Soil**	**Mycelium and fruiting bodies**	Specialist mycophagous species
	Deadwood fungi	Mycelium and fruiting bodies	Specialist saproxylic species
Litter	**Leaves**		Saprophages and cover
	Deadwood	**Branches**	Saproxylic species
		Tree boles	Saproxylic species
Soil surface in rides	**Bare soil in sun**		Solitary bee nests
			Wasp nests
			Basking
Soil	**Soil particulate matter**		Specialist soil species
	Water	**Seepages**	Specialist species

LEFT **The golden-ringed dragonfly is a species of the west of Britain encountered over moorland and along woodland rides.**

RIGHT **Treble bar moths frequent woodland rides and other open habitats.**

LEFT **Hoverfly (*Volucella inanis*) nectaring on hemp-agrimony in a woodland ride.**

RIGHT **Common emerald moth in a lowland mixed deciduous woodland.**

LEFT **Six-spot burnet moth nectaring on wild marjoram in a woodland ride.**

CENTRE **Large skipper nectaring on creeping thistle in a woodland ride.**

RIGHT **The cream spot tiger moth is found in open woodland habitat.**

support a very rich invertebrate fauna attracted to young growth stages, although such management may only be appropriate to consider where new woodland is located within range of existing, invertebrate-rich coppice. Shrubs provide a home to many invertebrates, including those associated with lichens, algae and fungi found on their bark. Ward and Spalding (1993) report that over 2,000 invertebrates have been found on shrubs, of which about one third are genus-specific. In general terms, rides and open space are important to most woodland invertebrates at some point in their life cycle. Whilst the larvae of many woodland invertebrates feed in shady or damp conditions, adults require warm sunshine and clear flight lines to an abundant supply of flowers for nectaring. With the disappearance of flower-rich meadows, woodland rides have become important refuges for both sun loving plants and grassland invertebrate communities. Without careful management, even these island sanctuaries are under threat. Through the provision of wide rides and high quality woodland edge, new woodlands can make a significant contribution to invertebrate conservation, providing suitable management is undertaken.

Of all invertebrate groups, moths are likely to benefit quickly from new woodland creation, as the larvae of many species feed on trees, particularly native broadleaves. The larvae in turn provide a major food source for woodland birds and bats, forming a crucial part of the woodland ecosystem. While some moth species will benefit from open space in woodlands, many more are dependent upon mature trees, lichens, grasses, shrubs and even dead leaves. Planting a diverse range of trees and shrubs in new woodlands will greatly increase their value for moths. Moths will also benefit considerably from a diverse age structure.

2.5.2 Butterflies of new native woodland

Twenty-six wider countryside species may breed in the open spaces or edges of new native woodland in Britain (Table 2.8). Those which do not breed in colonies; brimstone, large white, small white, green-veined white, orange tip, holly blue, red admiral, painted lady, small tortoiseshell, peacock and comma, tend to range widely across the countryside, breeding in suitable habitat when they come across it. These species are amongst the most likely early visitors to new woodland, where they will effectively be using woodland edge habitats, such as glades and rides, rather than the trees themselves. In contrast, species which breed in discrete colonies tend to be more sedentary. Adults of some species will move between colonies within larger woodland blocks, and some will range several kilometres from their home colony in open grassland or woodland open space. Species which might colonise suitable habitat in new native woodland include small skipper, large skipper, small copper, brown argus, common blue, marbled white, gatekeeper, and meadow brown. In surveys of new native woodland in South East England between 2004–2009, the authors found all the closed population species listed in Table 2.8, with the exception of Scotch argus. Attracting most species, whether they breed in colonies or not, requires the presence of larval foodplants and a plentiful supply of nectar-rich flowers for the adults (see Chapter 7), preferably in a sheltered but sunny situation. For most butterflies this inevitably depends on the presence and management of open glades and rides (see Chapter 7), although speckled wood, ringlet and green-veined white may also occupy more shaded portions of the wood.

Wider countryside species, such as small copper and small heath have declined significantly in recent years and are confined to relatively small fragments of their former habitat. Bourn *et al.*, (2002) showed that it is as important to maintain high quality habitat on at least part of a site, as it is to maintain multiple contiguous sites within the landscape. This emphasises the value of creating high quality open spaces in new woodland, and supports the view that with appropriate management, a new wood could host significant breeding populations of many of the wider countryside butterfly species. By sowing a grassland and wildflower seed mix in the planned open spaces (see Chapter 7), a supply of larval food plants and a diversity of nectar sources can be quickly provided. New native woodland can also contribute to habitat networks designed to help butterfly populations at a landscape scale. Networks should help species to move between favourable habitats and might include unimproved grassland, woodland margins and open space, roadside verges, arable field margins and the open areas of new native woodland.

Can new woodlands help to conserve habitat specialist butterflies?

During the latter part of the 19th century, permanent rides were constructed in some heavily coppiced woodlands. Rides, glades and young coppice would have supported a diverse range of flora and fauna at this time, including both habitat specialist and wider countryside butterflies. Regular cutting and coppicing created a constant supply of open space and early successional growth for many woodland invertebrates. However, a reduction in the market for coppice products led to a decline in coppicing from the end of the 19th century, and by the late 20th century the practice had almost ceased in the broadleaved woodlands of southern England, having a severe affect on woodland ecosystems. It is perhaps the single most important element in the decline in the ranges of specialist woodland butterflies. The chequered skipper, for example, was still abundant in its East Midland stronghold as recently as the 1950s, but had disappeared completely from England by the mid 1970s due to cessation of coppicing and the shading of

The Scotch argus is still common and widespread in Scotland.
(Reproduced with the kind permission of Peter Eeles and Butterfly Conservation)

Table 2.8 Wider countryside butterflies which may occur in the rides and glades of new native woodland

	Range and population
Small skipper	Range expanding. Widespread and common. Distribution is probably limited by climate, rather than abundance of larval foodplants
Essex skipper	Range expanding. Colonies expanding within its range, possibly through increased use of roadside verges
Large skipper	Range expanding. Widespread and common. Distribution is probably limited by climate, rather than abundance of larval foodplants
Brimstone	Range expanding. Strong correlation between distribution of butterfly and its foodplant. Less abundant due to habitat destruction, despite expanding range. Planting buckthorn or alder buckthorn would benefit this species
Large white	Widespread and stable
Small white	Widespread and stable
Green-veined white	Widespread and stable
Orange tip	Range expanding, but less abundant due to decline in cuckooflower following drainage and grassland improvement. May do well in new woods if garlic mustard or cuckooflower are present, and left undisturbed during flowering
Purple hairstreak	Widespread and range expanding, requires presence of mature oaks
White-letter hairstreak [1,2]	Significant downward population trend following Dutch elm disease in the 1970s. May colonise rides and the shrubby edge of new native woodland planted with elms, particularly if they are associated with old woods or hedgerows where the butterfly already occurs
Small copper	Range stable, but has suffered considerable decline in numbers. Particularly susceptible to climate, and may be lost from woodlands in cool, wet summers, to be recolonised in later warm, dry summers
Brown argus	Range expanding due to set aside, following earlier declines following habitat loss. Long rotational ride management which encourages its annual foodplants to become established could benefit this species in new woodland
Common blue	Widespread and relatively stable. Has compensated to some extent for widespread habitat destruction by colonising new environments, though population has declined. New woods could benefit this species, providing areas of short swards are maintained in the rides and open spaces, especially if common bird's-foot-trefoil is present
Holly blue	Range expanding. More widespread within main distribution area. Open woodlands remain important for its populations, and it requires both holly and ivy to breed
Red admiral	Regular migrant. No threat, but still needs common nettle, which is less frequent than in the past
Painted lady	Regular migrant. Dependence on survival of suitable breeding areas outside Europe
Small tortoiseshell	Widespread, but has recently suffered a dramatic decline, particularly in the South East
Peacock	Range expanding. Widespread and common
Comma	Range expanding, including recent records in southern Scotland
Speckled wood	Range expanding. Recolonised much of former area over last 60 years, including new native woodland
Scotch Argus	Common and widespread in Scotland but declined in southern part of range. Sensitivity to grazing make woodland rides and young plantations important for this species
Marbled white	Range expanding, though many colonies lost throughout 20th century. Seems to be making use of patches of habitat in areas where grassland has decreased; new woodlands can provide good habitat for this species
Gatekeeper	Range expanding, though colonies lost through agricultural intensification, and loss of hedgerows and unimproved grassland. Even small woodlands could be colonised
Meadow brown	Range stable. Common and widespread, but declining through agricultural intensification. Benefits from smaller habitat fragments, such as rides in woodlands
Ringlet	Range expanding. Many colonies lost through loss of native grasses, drainage and overgrazing. Uncut areas in grassy rides in new woodland could be important for this species
Small heath [1,2]	Long term significant decrease. Many colonies lost through loss of native grasses to arable or improved grassland; now much less abundant locally, and causing considerable concern. New woodlands can provide good habitat for this species

[1] UK BAP priority species; [2] Red-listed species (Fox *et al.*, 2010). Data source: Asher *et al.*, (2001) and Fox *et al.*, (2006)

PART ONE GENERAL PRINCIPLES – **WOODLANDS FOR WILDLIFE**

LEFT **Green-veined white nectaring on small scabious in a woodland ride.**

RIGHT **Small skipper nectaring on thistle in a woodland ride.**

LEFT **Female Duke of Burgundy resting on a cowslip, the larval foodplant.**

RIGHT **Marbled white resting along the shrubby edge of in a woodland ride.**

Woodland open space maintained for small pearl-bordered fritillary in Park Corner Wood, East Sussex.

LEFT **Small pearl-bordered fritillary.**

RIGHT **Male heath fritillary nectaring in new woodland, recently planted on a site bordering ancient woodland in the Blean, Kent.**

39

rides. Other species which have also suffered major range losses include wood white, Duke of Burgundy, small pearl-bordered fritillary, pearl-bordered fritillary, high brown fritillary and heath fritillary. These species depend upon elements of the woodland ground flora such as dog-violets, vetches and common cow-wheat that are not easily established in new woodlands. The Blean forest complex, north of Canterbury in Kent, is the last stronghold of the heath fritillary in eastern England. Extinction of the butterfly here was averted by careful conservation management, involving ride widening and renewed management of sweet chestnut coppice. In contrast, species which utilise the shady conditions of mature woodland, such as purple hairstreak and silver-washed fritillary have remained largely stable in recent years.

Planting new native woodland will 'enrich' habitat mosaics, which may support existing colonies of habitat specialists and provide corridors through which butterflies might move from one suitable habitat to another. New woodland could also provide breeding habitat for some habitat specialists (Table 2.9). One example is the brown hairstreak, which has suffered from hedgerow removal and annual trimming of the blackthorn hedges on which it breeds. The adult butterflies rarely come to nectar, but cluster around large clumps of trees such as ash, where they feed upon honeydew produced by aphids. Colonies are dispersed over a wide area, requiring sympathetic management of the landscape rather than protection of a single wood. Butterfly Conservation and Natural England have produced information for landowners, detailing the brown hairstreak's requirement for untrimmed or layered hedgerows and woodland edges, which are focal points for a colony. Consequently, in areas where the butterfly occurs, blackthorn scrub associated with new woodland and woodland edges could well benefit it. This has been demonstrated recently by the successful colonisation of the M40 compensation area adjacent to Bernwood in Oxfordshire. Here, both brown and black hairstreak butterflies have successfully expanded their existing colonies into new hedgerow and grassland habitat.

Table 2.9 Habitat specialist butterflies found in mature woodland habitat and their potential to colonise new native woodland

	Species notes
Chequered skipper [1,2]	Range stable, but restricted to a small region of western Scotland. Requires open grassland dominated by purple moor-grass, favouring broadleaved woodland edges. Unlikely to benefit from woodland creation
Dingy skipper [1,2]	Range declining, partially due to shading in woods. Only likely to colonise new native woodland if adjacent to existing colonies and suitable open grassland habitat is created
Grizzled skipper [1,2]	Range and population declining, stronghold remains in southern England. Only likely to colonise new native woodland if adjacent to existing colonies, and suitable open grassland habitat is created
Wood white [1,2]	Shows rapid recent decline in distribution and population. New woodlands planted in its strongholds might be beneficial if rides and glades are managed sympathetically
Green hairstreak	Widespread and stable, but showing signs of decline, possibly due to shading. Requires short turf, or scrub in sunshine, and suitable ant colonies to bury the pupae
Brown hairstreak [1,2]	Range declining; loss of hedgerows and widespread mechanical cutting are major factors. In its strongholds, blackthorn scrub associated with new woodland, and new woodland edges could benefit this species
Black hairstreak [2]	Range stable, but still rare and vulnerable to changes in woodland management. Most likely to benefit from changes in mature woodland management
Duke of Burgundy [1,2]	In serious decline. Habitat can be restored in old woods; may colonise adjacent new woods with suitable sunny open spaces with plentiful cowslips and primroses
White admiral [1,2]	Significant recent population decreases and range decline suggests that this is an unlikely colonist of new woodland at present
Purple emperor [2]	Status possibly stable, but with cause for concern. New woodlands planted in its strongholds would be beneficial if they included plentiful willows along rides and woodland edges
Small pearl-bordered fritillary [1,2]	Widespread in western and northern Britain but declining in the south. New woods in the south might be beneficial if rides were created between the new woodland perimeter and an existing old-woodland edge
Pearl-bordered fritillary [1,2]	Continues to decline in England and Wales. New woods in south could serve as habitat linkages, facilitating movement between suitable existing habitat
High brown fritillary [1,2]	Localised and highly threatened following significant declines. Unlikely to benefit from woodland creation
Silver-washed fritillary [1,2]	Significant recent range expansion suggests this species could possibly colonise sympathetically managed new woodland
Heath fritillary*	Confined to a few sites in the South East and South West. Responding to active management in Bleak Woods, Kent where it may use new woods to move between sites

[1] UK BAP priority species; [2] Red-listed species (Fox *et al.*, 2010)

3 WOODLANDS FOR PEOPLE

3.1 Woodland and society

Woodland offers a diverse range of benefits to society, which have been the subject of considerable research efforts in recent years, with several detailed reviews published on the subject (e.g. Tabbush and O'Brien, 2003; O'Brien, 2005a; Nail, 2008). An exploration of the social and economic contribution of forestry in Scotland identified seven key themes outlining the wide range of benefits that people derive from woodlands including: 1) employment and volunteering; 2) contribution to the economy; 3) recreation and accessibility; 4) learning and education; 5) health and well-being; 6) culture and landscape; and 7) community capacity (Edwards *et al.*, 2008). This section considers some of the key issues relating to leisure, health, and participation; with special reference to children's education.

Dog walking is one of the most popular woodland pursuits.

3.1.1 Recreation and accessibility

People may engage with trees and woodlands at many different levels from enjoying the view of a tree from their window, walking or cycling in woodland, through to actively engaging with woodland creation through volunteering work. Woodland plays a key role in leisure and tourism activities in Britain, helping not only to boost people's health and well being, but also the economy. An *England Leisure Visits Survey* in 2005 showed that 700 million trips were made to the English countryside, accounting for 20% of all leisure visits (Natural England, 2006). Of these, some 170 million visits were made to woodland. Two-fifths of adults had made a trip to woodland within the previous year. Walking was found to be the most popular pastime in woodland, followed by cycling and then other hobbies. Around the same time, an *All Forests Visitor Monitoring Survey* commissioned by Forestry Commission Scotland (which reported in 2008) estimated that 8.7 million visits are made each year to the national forest estate in Scotland; 85% from Scotland and 10% from England. Of these, 84% of people had been to the forest before and 20% visited the forest every day. The most popular activities were dog walking, other walking, and cycling on way-marked tracks.

Existing, mature woodlands with good public access provide both social and environmental benefits for people and wildlife, but these may not exist in some areas. This raises the possibility

The Weald Woodfair is an annual event which attracts large numbers of visitors, both public and professional.

ABOVE **A well-worn path indicates that this woodland, which is surrounded by housing, is well used.**

BELOW **Suburban settlements often have good access to woodland.**

of planting new native woodland where there is little or no mature woodland, for example in close proximity to urban communities. Such woodlands may offer fewer benefits for wildlife in the shorter term, but could enhance the health and well-being of local communities. Creating new woodlands near to where people live also has the potential of involving a wider range of people in tree planting, maintaining or enjoying these spaces e.g. through 'Friends of' groups. A report by the Woodland Trust *'Space for People'* (Woodland Trust, 2004b) argued that accessible woods planted near centres of population, both urban and rural, would benefit society through improved health and well-being, and also enhance the landscape, increase local wildlife, and provide better air quality (Collinson, 2007).

The *Space for People* report concluded that a minimum of 77,000 ha of new woodland would be needed to allow most people in the UK to live near to accessible woodland. Based on wide-ranging surveys of public use and opinion of woodland, it proposed a 'Woodland Access Standard', suggesting that people should not live more than 500 m from at least one area of accessible woodland no less than 2 ha in size; and that there should be at least one area of accessible woodland of 20 ha or more within 4 km of their home. Currently only 16% of the population have access to woodlands within 500 m of their home. The report identified where new woodland is most needed to benefit people, and provided a basis for local decision makers to plan for accessible woodland provision, targeting public money where it was most needed. It also recognised that a core element of the plan should be to increase people's understanding and enjoyment of woods.

PART ONE GENERAL PRINCIPLES – **WOODLANDS FOR PEOPLE**

3.1.2 Health and well-being

Woodland and trees can make a distinct and important contribution to people's physical health, psychological well-being and social well-being. Woodland and other natural habitats make people feel better in themselves, and there is much evidence to support this (e.g. Pretty *et al.*, 2005). This 'feel-good' factor can result from visiting mature woodland, but in urban environments, the presence of street trees alone may give the desired effect. Experiencing woodland and trees is encouraged by health organisations, as well as countryside agencies and conservation organisations. Public health is a very important element of Government Policy in the UK. It is estimated that each year, physical inactivity costs over £8 billion, and the total cost of mental healthcare in England alone is £41.8 billion (Bird, 2004; 2007a). The Government's *Choosing Health White Paper* (Department of Health, 2004) indicated that many of the underlying determinants of inequalities in health are environmental, including access to green spaces. However, the positive link between nature and health is rarely reflected in healthcare or education policies, planning guidelines or economic strategies (Bird, 2007b).

Bird watching is a popular woodland activity.

Physical activity

Physical inactivity may contribute to major illnesses such as heart disease, diabetes and some types of cancer. Obesity is another symptom of inactivity which is growing rapidly, both in adults and children, and can itself lead to other health problems. One of the key benefits of woodland is the opportunity it provides for health improvements through physical activity and exercise. Activity in woods and green spaces may benefit people's health by reducing the risk of physical as well as psychological illness. Walking is one of the best solutions, which together with enjoyment of nature – which is seriously underestimated – is cheap (Bird, 2007b).

In many cases, visits to woodland *per se* will not be undertaken primarily for 'healthy exercise': nevertheless, this may be a benefit which comes naturally with the activity, such as bird watching or cycling. Exercise might be encouraged through signed walks for less active pursuits such as picnicking, where picnic tables may be located further from car parks. Various initiatives have been set up to motivate and encourage people to become more physically active, and to maintain this activity throughout their lives. The British Trust for Conservation Volunteers (BTCV) has a scheme called the 'Green Gym', designed to provide aerobic exercise for conservation work parties. Similarly, the British Heart Foundation and Natural England have a 'Walking the Way to Health' scheme, introduced in 2000 to promote health and fitness through exercise in the

LEFT **A high-wire forest adventure course in the tree tops of a mature plantation.**

RIGHT **Mountain bikes for hire in Bedgebury Forest – cycling in woodland is increasing in popularity.**

The canopy walk at the Royal Botanic Gardens, Kew gives people the opportunity to walk through and experience the high forest canopy.

Autumn colour attracts many visitors to woodland and parkland estates.

countryside. The Forestry Commission also launched an 'Active Woods' campaign, supported by the British Heart Foundation in 2005, which aims to increase woodland visits, promote physical activities and foster healthier lifestyles. The Cannock Chase 'Route to Health' project promotes woodlands as a venue for health and well being, using artworks with a health theme created by the local community to engage with people and promote woodland walks. In contrast, the Forest of Dean Life Cycle project encourages people to use Forestry Commission trails, and focuses in particular on engaging under-represented Black and Minority Ethnic groups (cited in O'Brien, 2005a). All of these woodland activities also offer opportunities for friends and families to meet and socialise together, as well as making new friends and joining new social networks, and this is often a critical factor in people using and benefiting from woodlands.

Bedgebury Forest in Kent, which includes the National Pinetum, is a major regional outdoor activity centre offering 'adventure' in a world of trees. The Forestry Commission gained funding from Sport England in 2005 for a project to improve the on-site infrastructure and target specific groups such as women, those over 45 years of age and the under 16s, encouraging them to become more active through organised health walks and cycle rides. Through the project, new cycle routes, both for families and more serious top-speed single-track mountain bikers, walking trails and an adventure playground have been created. More recently in 2007 a high wire forest adventure course in the tree-tops was installed. Both walking and cycle hire facilities cater for disabled people, and schools regularly use the facilities and education centre.

Psychological well-being

Health and well-being is not just about physical fitness, but also has a major psychological dimension, which includes happiness, optimism, self-esteem, satisfaction with one's life and other positive states of mind. The World Health Organisation (WHO) Mental Health Declaration for Europe (2005) states: "Mental health and mental well-being are fundamental to the quality of life and productivity of individuals, families, communities and nations, enabling people to experience life as meaningful and to be creative and active citizens". WHO estimates that depression and related illnesses will become the greatest source of ill-health by 2020 (Bird, 2007b). Even now, it is estimated that close to 10% of adults in Britain will suffer anxiety and/or depression at some time in their lives. If this level increases, the cost to the National Health Service (NHS) could be enormous. One way of helping to alleviate this problem is physical activity, which can improve mood and self-esteem, both of which contribute to psychological well-being (O'Brien, 2005a).

Contact with nature is becoming rare in our increasingly urbanised society, and hence a valuable commodity. Woodlands offer an opportunity to escape from stress and can enhance people's enjoyment of physical activity, especially if they find some empathy with nature (e.g. Laitakari *et al.*, 1996; Pretty *et al.*, 2005). Periods spent in woodland can be both relaxing and therapeutic; leaving some of the worries about one's aches and pains at home. Research confirms that woodlands and nature spaces are restorative, allowing people to recover from the stress of focusing for long periods of time on work (Kaplan, 1995). Even the sight of trees from hospital wards may help people in their recovery from illness (Woodland Trust, 2004a). In the most urban areas, street trees which have not been too heavily pruned provide a green, leafy environment which most people find welcoming. Furthermore, the benefits of trees may be reflected in house prices, which tend to be more expensive near woodland and greenspace (Garrod and Willis, 1992).

Studies have emphasised that people's sense of their own identity is related and has often been developed through experiences in woodland and nature as children, which influence their visits as adults (O'Brien, 2005b), which may have deep personal significance, and be shared with their own children. Woods can trigger memories of childhood play amongst trees, and positive feelings may return in adulthood when visiting woodland in times of stress (Henwood, 2001, cited in Tabbush and O'Brien, 2003).

3.1.3 Children and woodland

Woodland and countryside experiences can make a particularly important contribution to the health, well-being, and social well-being of our children, particularly through education, extra-curricular activities and play. However, children spend less time in the countryside now than in the past, often experiencing nature second-hand through television and computer screens. This can be due to changing values in society, but also to parental concerns about children's safety outdoors. Many children have become disconnected from nature and are unaware of threats to habitats and species. They also miss out on adventure and fun. Whilst most children cannot realistically experience the delights of camping on wooded islands in the Lake District, battling with pirates (cf. Arthur Ransome's *Swallows and Amazons*), local woodland still offers unique

BELOW LEFT **A purpose-built woodland playground surrounded by chestnut coppice and conifer plantations.**

BELOW RIGHT **Children using brash in a sweet chestnut coppice to construct a den.**

ABOVE LEFT **Children (and adults) can learn about plant hunters and the collection of rare trees from a Forestry Commission information board.**

ABOVE RIGHT **Teachers use imaginative games to teach children about seed dispersal.**

elements for creative play and opportunities to build confidence. Building dens in woodland is a case in point, which was taken up by the Eden Project in its 'Let's get Den building' project, designed to encourage children's imagination and development and "enable children to experience, understand and celebrate their sense of place and purpose in the natural world and human community" (Eden Project, 2008). The Forestry Commission has held National Den Building Days to encourage young people and parents into the woods. It is clear that the more such opportunities the child has, the greater will be the chances that they will regard woodlands as enjoyable, creative and relaxing places as young adults (Ward Thompson, 2007). Forest School, in which children take classes in a woodland setting, where they learn not only about the environment but also maths and English, is becoming increasingly widespread in Britain (Murray, 2003). Sessions are run by Forest School leaders and teachers can be trained to do this as well. The key aspect is the woodland setting and the regular long-term engagement with the setting: which can last from 2–12 months.

This is not to say that television does not have a part to play. For example, the very popular BBC *Springwatch* and *Autumnwatch* shows are watched by millions of adults and older children. *Breathing Places*, which grew from *Springwatch*, encourages young and old to go out into the countryside to enjoy nature, and to take part in practical events such as survey work or conservation work parties. Younger children are catered for through the junior versions of *Springwatch* and *Autumnwatch* on the BBC young children's channel *CBeebies*, which encourages children to become 'nature detectives', and to explore their local patch; while the *Autumnwatch Spotter's Club* encourages children to explore local woodland and other habitats.

A fallen tree provides a natural woodland playground.

Studies in America have suggested that children will play much longer in areas with trees and green space, and that their play will be more creative, fostering collaborative and language skills, which are very important aspects of child development (Faber Taylor *et al.*, 2001). Woodland and other natural areas can be particularly beneficial to children with special needs. For example, Attention Deficit Hyperactivity Disorder (ADHD) can be devastating for young children, who are often overactive and find it difficult to concentrate and maintain attention. ADHD affects 5–10% of school children in the UK (Bird, 2007a). Faber Taylor and her colleagues carried out extensive studies on ADHD in urban America, and found that when children play in greener spaces they exhibit less severe symptoms than during similar play sessions in hard landscapes. Even a 20-minute walk in a park results in greater attention from children with ADHD than a similar time walking in a built up environment (Faber Taylor and Kuo, 2009).

Other initiatives which benefit children include the many local community woodlands created by local authorities and other bodies, and 12 'Community Forests, established in England in 1989 by the Countryside Commission (now Natural England) and the Forestry Commission, which aimed to create woodland for urban social and economic regeneration close to half of the population. One of the key objectives was to provide opportunities for children in urban schools. Children also benefit from the *Forest Education Initiative*, which teaches young people in particular about the environmental, social and economic potential of trees and woodlands, and shows how trees supply raw materials for environmentally sustainable building materials and many other products which we take for granted.

3.1.4 Involving people in woodland creation and management

Every year, an army of volunteers work on environmental projects across Britain for national organisations such as the Forestry Commission, British Trust for Conservation Volunteers (BTCV), National Trust, the Woodland Trust and the Royal Society for the Protection of Birds; others work with local organisations such as the Wildlife Trusts and in community woodland projects. Work is undertaken across a wide range of habitats from ancient woodland to the seashore. The experiences of woodland gained from practical 'hands on' management activities are very different from those gained from recreational activities such as walking or cycling (Weldon *et al.*, 2007).

People from all walks of life become volunteers, such as those with differing ethnic backgrounds, professions and social status. Some may have suffered social exclusion, for example through unemployment, poverty or poor health. Colleges and schools provide volunteers, and many community projects have been set up to encourage their members to volunteer, as for example in the Woodland Trust's Community Woodland Network. This network comprises more than 200 groups in England, all sharing responsibility for local woodland and offering opportunities for communities to share information and resources. Attending a single tree planting event as part of a woodland creation scheme may stimulate some people to undertake other conservation work, or to join or even initiate new community woodland groups.

Maintaining woodland and other habitats for wildlife includes habitat management, restoration and creation. Volunteers play a crucial role in helping conservation organisations to achieve

Children learn how to plant trees at an event organised for schools by the Woodland Trust.

Children may be encouraged to write and illustrate their experience of tree planting.

their often ambitious management targets. In a detailed study of environmental volunteering O'Brien *et al.*, (2008) found that a desire to improve landscapes and to live in a more sustainable manner were important motivators for many volunteers. Many other reasons were given, forming a continuum from altruism to learning useful skills to help in finding employment.

Some people undertake practical conservation because of growing community concerns over climate change and other pressures on the environment. This is reflected in lifestyle choices, such as the increasing interest in recycling and saving energy. Volunteers gain satisfaction from the tasks they undertake and the opportunity to socialise and make new friends. Some will learn new skills, whilst improving their health and well-being. The 'Green Gym' run by BTCV makes explicit the links between practical conservation and mental and physical health.

In the field, volunteers may be involved in habitat management, habitat creation or wildlife monitoring. Habitat management is likely to involve routine maintenance following an established site management plan, or possibly habitat restoration. The tasks are diverse, from ride mowing and removal of scrub through to fencing. Woodland creation involves similar tasks, particularly land preparation and tree planting and accounts for smaller numbers of volunteers. Wildlife monitoring is also extremely important, but often undertaken by amateur naturalists with a particular expertise or interest in a one group, such as birds or plants. Some organisations such as the British Trust for Ornithology (BTO) and Butterfly Conservation rely heavily on volunteers to support various schemes such as the BTO's ongoing *Breeding Bird Survey*, Butterfly Conservation's *South East Woods Project* and their *Wider Countryside Butterfly Survey* which started in 2009. Volunteers also get involved in other types of activity such as campaigning, education and administration.

In addition to fieldwork, communities and individuals are becoming increasingly involved in environmental planning and decision making. This is now included in the Forestry Commission's policy framework, particularly in relation to the woodlands being created and managed in and around urban areas (Tabbush, 2005). The *Strategy for England's Trees, Woods and Forests* (Defra, 2007a) points out that early involvement of stakeholders in woodland creation programmes will improve plans and enhance the chances that woodland will make a longer-term contribution to sustainable development. This is reflected in the activities of organisations such as the Woodland Trust, the National Forest and Forest Enterprise.

3.2 Ecosystem services

The Millennium Ecosystem Assessment (2005) defined ecosystem services simply as *the benefit that people obtain from ecosystems*. In addition to the obvious benefits of woodland ecosystems for biodiversity, woodlands also provide services directly to people and communities. These goods and services can be divided into four categories of ecosystem function: regulation, habitat, production and information (De Groot *et al*., 2002). Regulation functions refer to the capacity of an ecosystem to regulate ecological processes and life support systems, such as the climate and water. Habitat functions describe the provision of habitat for wildlife and conserving genetic diversity. Dependent on these two functions are production functions, which include biomass, food and energy resources; and information and cultural functions such as recreation, which also contribute to human well-being. For many people living in the urban environment it is the non-material services obtained from woodland that are most important, gained through spiritual enrichment, cognitive development, recreation, and aesthetic experiences of nature.

The UK Government's Low Carbon Transition Plan (HM Government, 2009) states that "woodland creation can make a significant contribution to tackling climate change" with an ambitious target announced in 2009 for planting 10,000 ha of new native woodland per year over a period of 15 years. If this new planting is carried out, it is estimated that by 2050, it will have locked away 50 million tonnes of carbon. Adaptation to climate change will also require resilient ecosystems which will ensure adequate and clean water, provide timber, wood fuel and other forest commodities, provide shade in urban areas, improve air quality and offer some resilience against flooding.

Food security is another issue which will be significantly affected by climate change. Food production in the UK will need to cope with a rising global population and diminishing natural resources, but it is unlikely to be solved by increasing national food self sufficiency alone (Defra, 2006). Energy security and climate change will also have a major impact on food security. Expanding woodland cover is compatible with, and indeed will support successful and sustainable agricultural production in the UK. Natural ecosystems will need to provide key services to support production, including a stable and thriving ecosystem, unpolluted soils, clean and reliable water supplies, habitat for pollinating insects and predators of crop pests, and opportunities to diversify farm income and energy supplies (Woodland Trust, 2009b).

3.2.1 Regulating services

Apart from their wider role in regulating climate change, trees benefit people in a number of ways. One important function is maintaining air quality, especially in cities, by absorbing, extracting and intercepting pollutants and particulates. Pollutants such as carbon dioxide, nitrogen monoxide, sulphur dioxide and ozone are known to cause respiratory problems. Trees absorb these compounds, thus improving air and water quality. They also filter particulate matter and soot from the atmosphere, which exacerbate some chronic lung diseases. Small woods and street trees play an important role in noise absorption in some settlements. Street trees can also offer some protection to buildings through shading in the summer and as windbreaks at other times of the year. Such a role could reduce the use of energy in buildings for heating and cooling. Shade provided by trees in the summer months also has direct health benefits for people; apart from the pleasure and comfort of finding cool shade on a hot summer's day, shade is known to offer some protection against harmful UV radiation – which is an increasing cause for concern over the rise in cases of skin cancer – and can reduce stress induced by heat.

Woodland cover is also important to prevent soil erosion, and in water regulation by controlling the timing and magnitude of runoff and flooding in river catchments. In the latter case, riparian woodland offers a number of possibilities. Riparian woodlands are recognised as being potentially some of the richest and most diverse of semi-natural habitats, mainly due to the mosaics and multiple ecotones between aquatic, open land and woodland components. They form natural edges and linking networks through landscapes often dominated by agriculture, providing continuous corridors for wildlife to disperse and forage. Wet woodlands and floodplain forests are specific targets of the UK Biodiversity Action Plan, involving both restoration and creation of new habitat.

There are few substantial floodplain forests now left in Britain, apart from good examples such as along the Beaulieu River in the New Forest and the lower reaches of the Spey in Scotland (Peterken and Hughes, 1995). Remnants, consisting of willow and alder carr, are often secondary in origin, forming patches along many streams and small rivers in the lowlands. In their pure form, floodplain forests are dynamic ecosystems, responding to disturbances as the channel shifts and braids in flood, leaving scoured areas and alluvial flats to colonise with pioneer alder, black-poplar and willow. Over time these disturbances create a succession of even-aged stands, with some areas consolidating into mixed woodland, and a river topography consisting of meanders, pools, riffles, backwater channels, old river terraces and wetlands.

Where a river remains constrained within an engineered channel, restoring floodplain forests will not achieve the degree of habitat complexity created by unmanaged river systems, but planting native woodland will improve water quality by regulating flows and buffering runoff from farmland, benefiting fish and invertebrate populations as well as a range of other species. If, on the other hand, engineering constraints can be removed and the river is allowed to meander and flood naturally, the 'hydraulic roughness' of a restored or re-created floodplain forest may assist by holding back and regulating flood water threatening downstream settlements (Forestry Commission, 2003b). While the area occupied by the trees themselves should have little influence on the flood storage capacity, there would be a need to remove coarse woody debris that could accumulate and block bridges and dams.

3.2.2 Provisioning services

Perhaps the most obvious of these services in this particular context is the provisioning of wood and timber products for society. Wood production in the UK is steadily rising after the huge investment in afforesting open land made in the latter half of the 20th century. Current utilisation is around 9–10 million green tonnes per year (roughly the same amount in cubic metres), of which the vast majority, 95%, is from conifer plantations, almost equally supplied by the Forestry Commission and all other ownerships respectively; while most production from broadleaved forests originates from non-Forestry Commission woods. However, compared with the general picture of self-sufficiency in wood products, averaged across the 27 EU countries, Britain supplies less than a fifth of its own needs.

Annual consumption of wood in the UK is currently around 50 million m^3 (WRME[1]), of which more than two-thirds is for paper and paper products, with the remainder, in descending order: sawn wood, wood-based panels and other materials including roundwood, woodchips, charcoal and residues. Very little is currently used as woodfuel: only about 1 million oven-dry tonnes (over 2 million m^3) of wood chips, logs, wood pellets and other forms of wood fuel were supplied in the UK in 2008. Some of this, about 0.6 million m^3, is harvested directly from forests for fuelwood, with the rest made up of forest harvesting residues, arboricultural arisings from urban trees and along transport routes, sawmill products and other processed residues (Forestry Commission, 2009b).

A great deal more could be made of woodfuel as a renewable energy source, which at present contributes less than 1% of total UK energy needs. A Forestry Commission (2007) study found that only 40% of the annual increment of English woodlands was currently being harvested to market, but there was potential to harvest a further 2 million green tonnes per year, the equivalent of heating 250,000 homes, and an annual saving of 0.4 million tonnes of carbon. This could be supported by increased utilisation of arboricultural arisings, sawmill co-products and recovered wood from businesses and households. A staggering 6 million tonnes is lost each year to landfill.

Woodland creation clearly has a role in extending carbon storage and potential energy use in the future. Although they cannot compete with the savings of greenhouse gas emissions made by faster-growing, short-rotation forestry systems and conventional conifer plantations, new native woodlands grown on long rotations will retain higher carbon stocks in their living biomass.

---

1 Wood Raw Material Equivalent, underbark

4 WOODLAND CREATION IN A CHANGING CLIMATE

4.1 Britain – a changing climate

The concentration of CO_2 in the earth's atmosphere is increasing rapidly because of human activities, particularly the burning of fossil fuels, and also the continued destruction of rainforests. It is projected that the levels of greenhouse gases will continue to increase during the 21st century (Intergovernmental Panel on Climate Change, 2007), causing the global mean surface temperature to rise. Everyone in Britain must be aware of climate change, and many will have seen media coverage of changes which are already happening, such as melting glaciers and the thinning of the polar ice sheets. Future changes to our climate have been widely publicised, but the full implications are not yet being taken sufficiently seriously by the public or their elected representatives, although climate change is now high on the political agenda.

The UK Climate Projections (UKCP09) published in 2009 (Murphy *et al.*, 2009) provides climate information for the UK to the end of this century, updating earlier projections published in 2002. Scientists have shown that some degree of climate change is inevitable as a result of past emissions of greenhouse gasses, but beyond this, climate change will be determined by the actions of governments and society over the next few years. Under the medium emissions scenario for example, changes in mean summer temperatures are projected to be greatest in southern England (up to 4.2°C) and least in Scotland (just over 2.5°C). Over the coming decades, Britain's summers are expected to get warmer and its winters milder. Summers may be drier in many parts of the country, such as Wales, eastern Scotland and the South East, with the risk of droughts. In contrast, winters will be wetter, with more high-intensity rainfall leading to flooding. Overall, little change is expected in the annual rainfall. Frost days in many areas may be fewer. Climate change will alter the length and duration of the seasons, affect wind speeds and increase the frequency of extreme weather events. Sea levels are also expected to rise.

For woodland practitioners interested in overall projected climate change and possible implications for habitat management and creation, UKCP09 includes various pre-prepared maps and graphs, in addition to the user interface. Maps are available at a national and regional level for a range of climatic variables, such as rainfall and temperature. Maps are presented for the 2020s, 2050s and 2080s; for low, medium and high emissions scenarios (see examples in Figures 4.1 and 4.2). These maps demonstrate a plausible range of projected changes for different times in the future, on a regional and national level. The UKCP09 maps are still only projections, not future climate forecasts. Consequently they only provide broad and uncertain signposts when thinking about different options for adaptation to climate change, and different degrees of risk. Nevertheless, the precautionary principle demands that we think seriously about how to accommodate present woodland conservation plans and new woodland creation projects in the light of this information.

4.2 How climate change might affect woodland communities

Although some species in Britain are likely to expand their range in response to climate, it will pose serious threats for a great many others. Forests are highly sensitive to climate change (IPCC, 2007) and there is evidence that British woodland is already being affected. Climate warming is advancing some spring and summer events whilst shortening the winter season. Woodland ecosystems are complex, and changes in synchrony and competitive advantage between species could have profound consequences for the community as a whole, especially as different organisms are responding to climate change at different rates. Data from the UK Phenology Network, managed by the Woodland Trust in association with the Centre for Ecology and Hydrology, has shown how responsive nature's calendar is to changes in temperature in response to climate change (Collinson and Sparks, 2008). A study on pedunculate oak in Surrey has shown a dramatic trend towards earlier leafing, which by the late 1990s was 21–28 days earlier than in the 1950s (Cannell *et al.*, 1999). In the 1980s and 1990s alone, leafing of Surrey oaks advanced by 10 days; ash by six days, hawthorn by 10 days and lime by 11 days (Dudley, 2001). Oak is reported to gain a four-day advantage over ash for every 1°C rise in temperature (Collinson and Sparks, 2008). If oaks continue to advance faster than ash, this could shift the species balance in oak-ash woodland in favour of oak.

Figure 4.1 Changes in summer mean temperature for the 2080s under the UKCP09 medium emissions scenario (published on the UKCP09 website).

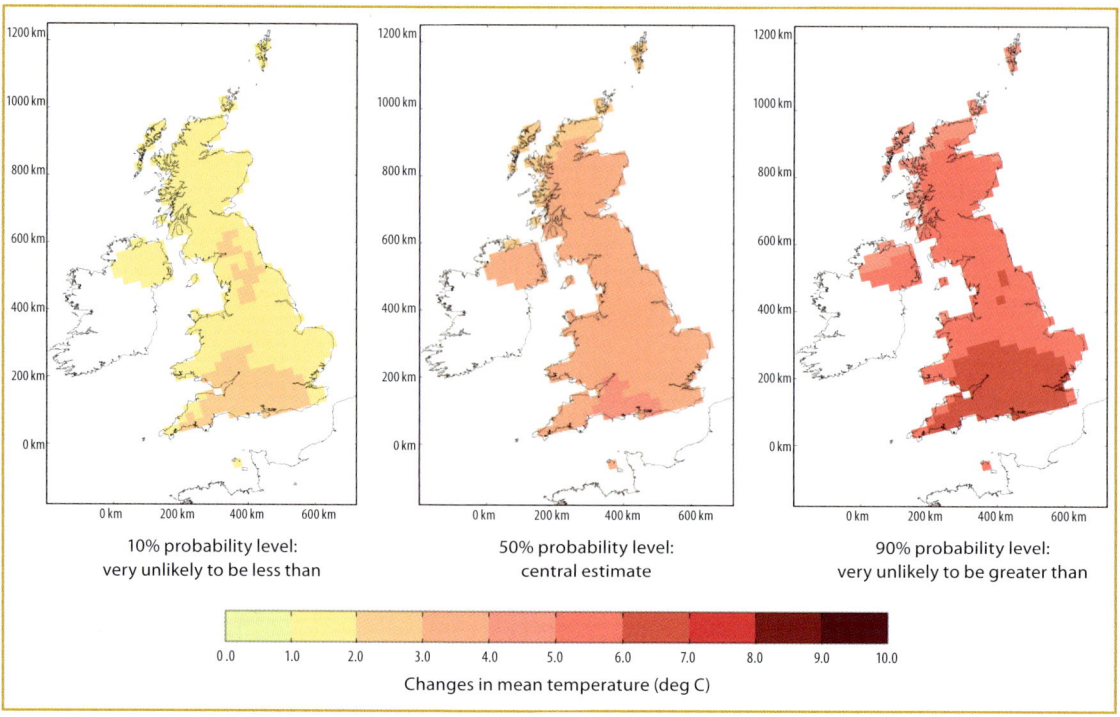

Figure 4.2 Changes in summer precipitation for Eastern Scotland for the 2080s under a medium emissions scenario (published on the UKCP09 website).

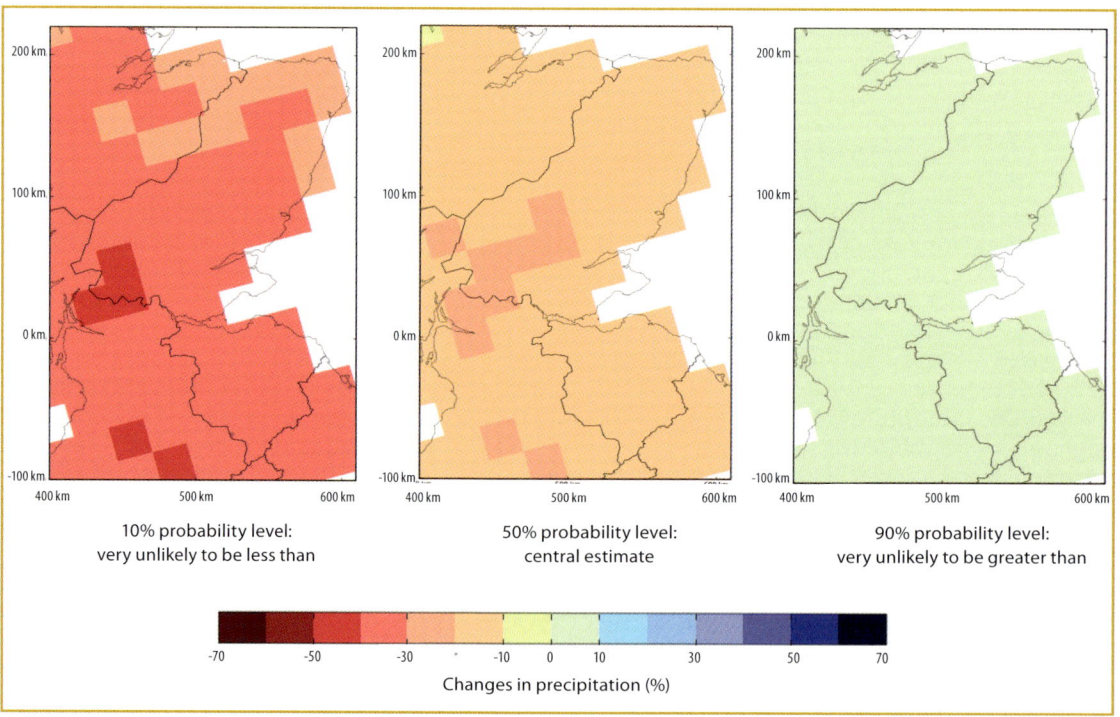

Earlier leafing trees would cast shade across the woodland floor, inhibiting the growth of plants which (currently) flush later. Species such as cow parsley and garlic mustard which come into leaf in late spring could be in direct competition with bluebells and wood anemones if they flush earlier in the year. Changes in flushing, flowering and fruiting of plants are particularly important because many insects, animals and birds rely on nectar, pollen and fruit resources. Migrant birds may arrive too late to capitalise on their main insect food source, which may have peaked sooner due to warmer temperatures and earlier flushing. Some plants rely on pollinators, as do species which feed on seed and fruit later in the year. Climate-induced changes in phenology which disrupt the synchrony of ecosystems could have serious implications for the survival of some members of our woodland communities and species assemblages will inevitably change.

Drought stress caused by reduced summer rainfall may have serious implications for the health of trees, making them more prone to plant pathogens. Increased winter rainfall may cause waterlogged soils and flooding in low-lying areas. Trees may be less susceptible to waterlogging during the dormant period, but if the period is shortened by climate change the flooding risks to roots could increase. Any damage to roots suffered in the winter may be compounded by the effects of subsequent summer droughts. Storms with heavy rainfall and strong winds are also projected to increase in frequency with climate change, but with less certainty. Whilst occasional storms have little impact on woodlands, more frequent storms could cause longer term damage and bring about changes in woodland ecosystems.

Insect pests are likely to increase in diversity and plant pathogens in severity with a warmer climate, and plants already under stress due to changes in the climate will be more susceptible. Insect pests of trees such as some bark beetles and moth larvae may benefit from a warmer climate. Exotic pests may colonise such as the oak processionary moth, the previously native gypsy moth and the Asian longhorn beetle which attacks healthy trees such as birch, ash and elm. Soil-borne pathogens such as *Phytophthora* fungi are already spreading, and would benefit from more frequently waterlogged soils and more susceptible trees. Increased summer drought stress in trees may increase the frequency of oak and beech decline, whilst sooty bark disease of sycamore may increase in severity.

Bluebells and ramsons in competition with earlier-leafing cow parsley.

4.2.1 Community composition and plant dispersal

Some years ago it was suggested that for every 1°C rise in temperature, some species may have to move as much as 150 km north, or 100 m uphill (Dudley, 2001). If such a projection were to prove correct, it would have profound consequences for those species which are unable to move, either because of an inherently poor capacity for dispersal, or habitat fragmentation. Many barriers in the landscape can prevent the dispersal of woodland organisms, such as large expanses of open land. In the longer term therefore, climate change may have significant effects on the composition of woodland communities across Britain, including trees, shrubs and ground flora.

For these reasons, scientists have devised approaches to simulate the impact of climate change on the distribution of selected species in Britain. Researchers at the Environmental Change Institute, University of Oxford have led the way with a computer simulation model known as

Hawthorn (right) and field maple (left) may flush earlier in the year as the climate changes.

Damage to young trees may increase if winter mortality of mammalian pests such as the grey squirrel is reduced.

SPECIES (Spatial Estimator of the Climate Impacts on the Envelope of Species) as part of a programme on Modelling Natural Resource Responses to Climate Change (MONARCH) (Walmsley et al., 2007). This allows future suitable climate space to be modelled for a variety of species under varying climate scenarios (Parallel Climate Model, the Hadley Centre Model, and projections of global carbon emissions produced by the IPCC). Whilst these models provide a useful insight into the potentially dramatic impacts of climate change on biodiversity, they cannot forecast with any precision the actual effects on communities, species or the competitive interaction between species. Each is subject to a range of caveats and assumptions, any of which could significantly change the projected outcomes (Smithers et al., 2007).

Phase 1 of the MONARCH programme assessed threats and opportunities for critical species, habitats and geological features on a national scale. Woodland was represented by a study of beech woods, upland oak woods and native pinewoods. Beech is projected to make a northward and westward shift (Harrison et al., 2001; Berry et al., 2002), depending on the severity of climate change. Although its continued presence in the south should not be threatened, it could become unsuitable as a productive timber tree in Kent and Sussex under the medium high scenario, and across much of central England and East Anglia under a high emissions scenarios (Broadmeadow and Ray, 2005; Broadmeadow et al., 2005). A significant decline in the number of beech trees, or a change in their contribution to the canopy could have major implications for the ground flora and shrub layer. In contrast, in upland oak woods, the oaks themselves may persist, but again the understorey and ground flora could change. Ash is another example of a species which could suffer in the South East, but become more widespread in Scotland. Under the 'medium high' climate change scenario, the MONARCH models project that ash would decline in much of the South East and parts of central England – certainly as a timber species – and possibly from much of central Europe by the 2080s.

Colonising heather may alter the composition of montane communities and lowland acid communities with a greater frequency of warmer, drier summers, depending on grazing pressure.

Western gorse (left) may colonise higher altitudes and have a major impact on upland heath and grassland communities (right).

It is also important for conservation practitioners to be aware of areas in Britain considered to be particularly sensitive to climate change, and the populations, distribution and dispersal of species within these regions. Phase 2 of MONARCH focussed on such areas, including Snowdonia, which is projected to be particularly sensitive to climate change by the 2050s, and the Central Highlands of Scotland (Berry *et al.*, 2005). In the upland oak woods, sessile oak may become less prominent in drier regions, and spread further into the Scottish pinewood zone at lower latitudes and north along the west coast of Scotland. Ancient woodland plants in these sensitive communities show limited opportunities for dispersal, and might be threatened. Bracken and western gorse may colonise higher altitudes and have a significant impact on the composition of upland heath, while colonising heather may similarly impinge on montane communities. In the Central Highlands, the projected climate of the 2050s will favour upland rather than montane communities across much of the region, resulting in a dramatic decline in suitable climate space for montane habitat and dwarf shrub cover. However, Scots pine is projected to remain the dominant species of Caledonian pine forests over the next 50 years. The MONARCH programme indicates that the trees and shrubs in the communities studied will still be present in 50 years time, partly due to their longevity and partly to the fact that most species are not on the edge of their range. However, the models do not project changes in species abundance, which are almost certain to occur and are likely to cause significant change in the composition of local communities.

4.2.2 Climate space for individual species

Species which are better able to disperse such as birds, butterflies and moths are already responding to climate change by altering their ranges, as well as their phenology and ecology. Butterflies are particularly interesting because many British species reach the climate-induced limits of their ranges in the UK. Eleven out of 46 southern species have already demonstrated northerly range extensions in response to the warming climate (Hill *et al.*, 2002). These tend to be the more mobile, wider countryside species such as the peacock and comma. The red admiral and clouded yellow which are migrants to Britain, breeding in the summer months, are now able to overwinter, and may soon become residents. Climate change has also had some benefits for habitat specialists, for example the silver-spotted skipper is now able to exploit chalk grassland on previously cooler aspects. However, most habitat specialists have declined because the loss of breeding habitat prevents range expansions. Three northern species – northern brown argus, Scotch argus and mountain ringlet – have exhibited range contractions to more northerly latitudes and higher altitudes (Franco *et al.*, 2006).

The Environmental Change Institute used the SPECIES model to examine future climate space across Europe for 389 species as part of an EU-funded project called BRANCH. The potential for change in the ranges of 120 species selected for nature conservation action in the UK BAP has also been modelled under Phase 3 of the MONARCH programme, commissioned by various conservation

The mountain ringlet is a high altitude species at risk from climate change (reproduced with the kind permission of Peter Eeles and Butterfly Conservation).

The range of the small skipper is steadily expanding.

agencies in the UK and Ireland. These studies suggest that there are likely to be both winners and losers as a result of climate change. They begin to quantify the effects of climate change on wildlife, and inform nature conservation policy and wildlife issues in adaptation planning across the British Isles. However, there is still a great deal of uncertainty surrounding the effects of climate change on species distribution, and there is no guarantee that if climate space for a species or community moves, that the species concerned will be able to move with it.

In spite of extensive modelling and experimentation, it is difficult to predict how exactly plant communities will change in response to different warming scenarios. This is because plant responses resulting from changing weather variables are confounded by those mediated by altered competitive relationships between species within the vegetation community. Positive feedback between the species benefited by climate change and increasingly warmer or droughty conditions may have the effect of magnifying and accelerating community change. On the other hand, species that retain projected climate space in future warming scenarios may still suffer because the equilibrium established with other species in the community may have altered.

4.2.3 The future for Britain's woodland including UK BAP priority habitats

The effects of climate change on native trees and woodland habitats in Britain have been considered by many authors (e.g. Berry *et al.*, 2002; Broadmeadow and Ray, 2005; Broadmeadow *et al.*, 2005; Wesche *et al.*, 2006; Ray, 2008a, 2008b). The Forestry Commission have employed a decision support system, the Ecological Site Classification (ESC) (Section 6.6) to make projections about the future distribution of native woodland communities (e.g. Figure 4.3). These studies indicate that climate change will affect species assemblages and succession, alter the frequency and severity of natural disturbances and lead to gradual, possibly subtle, but widespread changes in woodland communities. Species pools of vegetation associated with woodland between widely separated regions may already be quite similar, as Wesche *et al.*, (2006) have shown for beech woodland in Cumbria and Derbyshire compared with southern England; so it may take decades before marked changes become detectable. While in some cases it may be possible to mitigate the effects of change by woodland creation to allow species

The frequency of broadleaves may increase in native pinewoods with a warming climate.

PART ONE GENERAL PRINCIPLES – **WOODLAND CREATION IN A CHANGING CLIMATE**

to disperse across fragmented landscapes, it might be more realistic for conservation managers to recognise that classifications of habitats based on the status quo are likely to become increasingly untenable (Hossell *et al.*, 2003). Changes are unlikely to result in transitions from one National Vegetation Classification (NVC) community to another, but result in new associations that may no longer fit current NVC definitions. The following scenarios for UK BAP priority woodland types give some impression of what might happen as the climate changes:

Lowland beech and yew woodland: although restricted to southern England and South Wales, this woodland type could potentially spread north and west (Figure 4.4); where the resulting woodland community may differ from that in the south, as different species respond differently to the new environmental conditions (Wesche *et al.*, 2006). The effects of climate change on the flora and fauna of beech woodland may be independent of its effects on the tree itself. The sensitivity of beech in particular to drought and seasonally fluctuating water tables suggests that climate change may result in increased colonisation by species such as oak, and a shift towards W10-type communities.

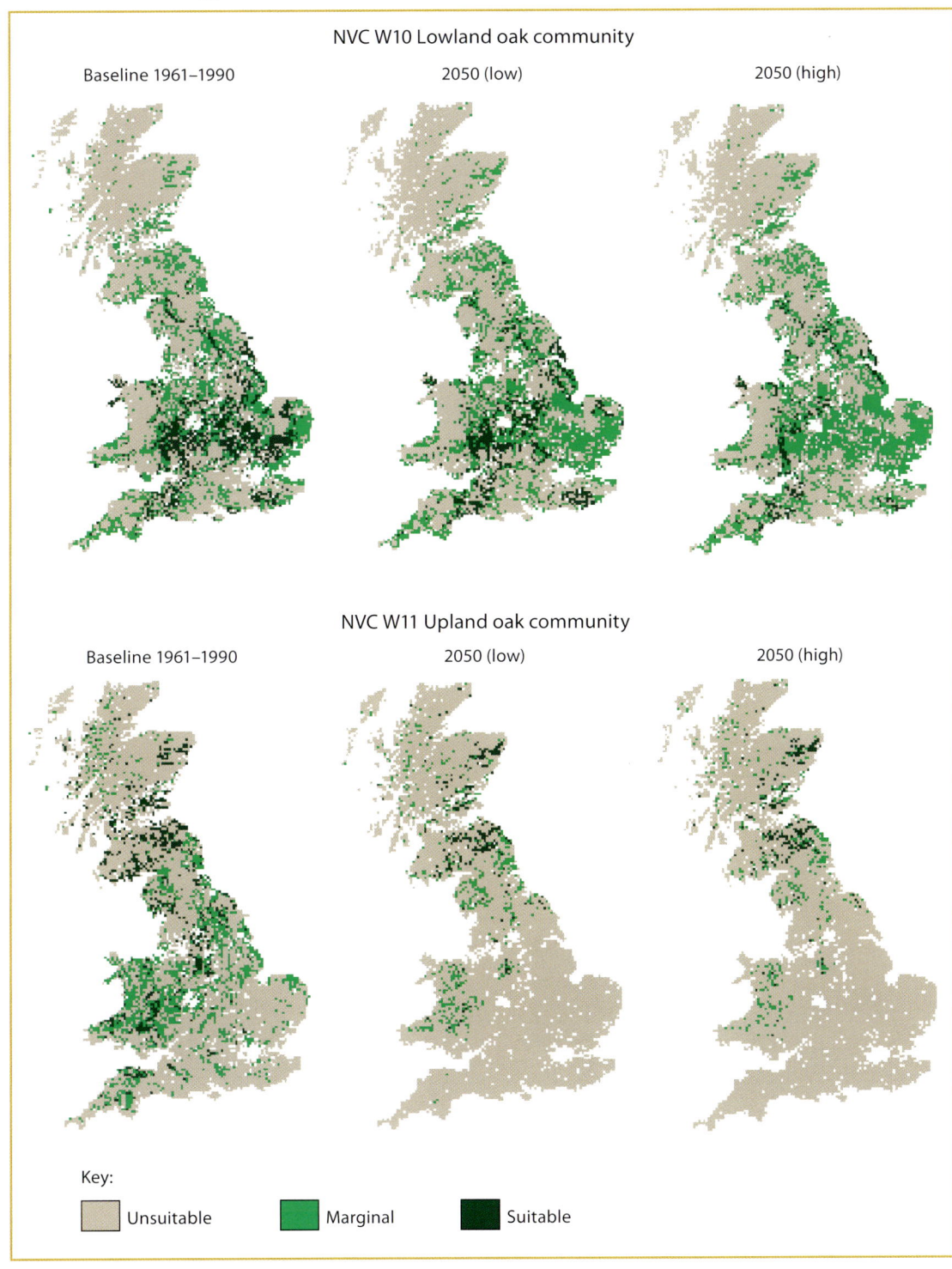

Figure 4.3 Projections of the effects of two climate change scenarios on the suitability of sites for lowland and upland oak communities by the year 2050 (NVC W10 and W11) using the Forestry Commission's Ecological Site Classification. (Source Broadmeadow and Ray, 2005; © Crown copyright, reproduced with the kind permission of the Forestry Commission). © Crown copyright and/or database right. All rights reserved. Licence number 100049759.

Lowland mixed deciduous woodland (ash-elm woods and oak-ash woods): winter storm damage and summer drought may increase scrubby areas; fire damage could become a concern in woods visited by the public; colonisation by beech and sycamore may increase in Wales and northern England/Scotland; and age structure may change as old trees become susceptible to wind damage. Simulation models indicate that the extent of sites suitable for lowland oak wood communities (W10) in England should change little by 2050, with possible extensions into parts of Wales and Scotland. However, under the high emissions scenario some areas within the current W10 range, such as central and Eastern England, may become more marginal, presaging change in the community structure (Broadmeadow and Ray, 2005).

Wet woodlands: winter flooding may be more frequent throughout Britain, favouring wet woodland, with possible expansion on to wetland such as bogs and wet meadows in some areas; wet woodland may be used as a natural defence against flooding. Ash may colonise riparian woods in areas with drier summers.

Upland mixed ash woods: in Wales and Scotland, natural disturbances may bring down trees and branches, opening woodland to colonisation by a greater range of herbs; tree species composition may change more slowly than in oak woods. On these relatively fertile soils the W9-type communities may gradually lose ground to southerly, W8-types.

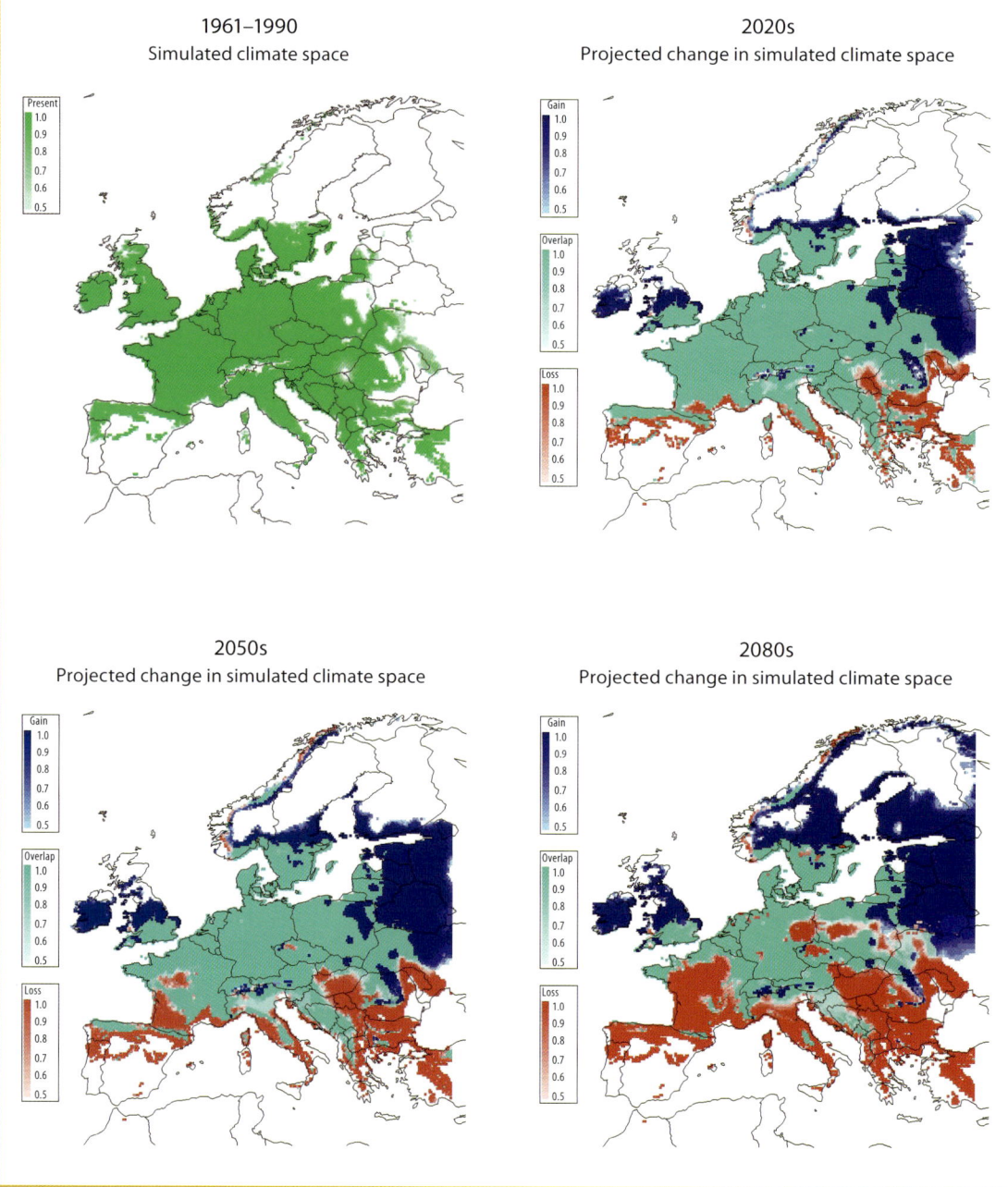

Figure 4.4 Climate space projections for beech under the 'medium high' scenario for the 2020s, 2050s and 2080s, using a single modelling method to fit species distributions for specific climate change scenarios (HadCM3). Green indicates the simulated current climate space (1961–1990). In the projection maps, red indicates areas where climate space for the species could be lost; turquoise indicates where climate could continue to be suitable (overlap) and deep blue indicates areas of potential gain (assuming effective dispersal and colonisation). (Source: BRANCH project, reproduced with the kind permission of the Environmental Change Institute, University of Oxford). © Crown copyright and/or database right. All rights reserved. Licence number 100049759.

Upland oak woods, including 'Atlantic oak woods': these communities account for large areas of semi-natural woodland in Wales and on the western seaboard of Scotland. Simulations of site suitability indicate that the range of W11 upland oak woods could contract significantly, although the woods would not disappear, but their community structure would change (Figure 4.3) (Broadmeadow and Ray, 2005). Milder winters, warmer and drier summers, and more severe gales (in Scotland) may adversely affect epiphytes; increased winds and gales may also cause disruption, possibly leading to more scrubby woodland. Milder conditions in winter, spring and autumn may also result in broadleaved colonisation, e.g. beech and sycamore in the Atlantic oak woods of Wales and Scotland. The higher temperatures should make conditions more suitable for a greater diversity of species, making possible a transition from W11 towards W10-type communities. The fire hazard in woods adjacent to moorland or woodland used for recreation could increase.

Upland birch woods, including 'Atlantic oak woods': in parts of the Highlands and eastern Scotland, recently planted upland birch woods may need to be enriched with oak or hazel to increase their resilience to climate change (Ray, 2008b). The oak-birch W17 communities at the edge of their range may become more favourable for W11 woodland community species.

Native pinewoods: summer drought may favour drier sub-communities in parts of the Highlands; warmer summers may encourage colonisation by broadleaves (oak, birch, and rowan); scrub may extend above the current treeline; and the risk of fire in pinewoods adjacent to moors frequented by visitors will increase (Ray, 2008b).

4.3 Specifying sources of seeds of trees and shrubs

Specifications for sources of trees and shrubs in Britain usually assume that 'local seed is best'. But this paradigm raises a number of issues at a time when climate change is of such concern: what is meant by the term 'local'; why do practitioners believe that it is best to plant locally sourced seed; and should this ethos be reviewed in light of the challenges of climate change?

4.3.1 Origin and provenance

First of all it is necessary to consider the terms 'origin' and 'provenance'. The origin is the natural range from which a species was originally derived. Plant provenance refers to the location from which seed or an individual was collected but says nothing about its true geographic or ecological origin. Local provenance is yet another confusing term that has been widely misinterpreted. A useful definition is: *"any individual of a population comprised of genetically similar individuals related by common descent and occupying a particular biogeographic area to which it is likely to have become adapted, and that has not been introduced by humans"* (Forest Service of Northern Ireland, 2008). This implies that individuals of local provenance should be naturally indigenous to a particular biogeographic or 'local' area, but there is still no guarantee that they were not brought in by humans in the distant past. Some organisations refer to material collected from the nearest available indigenous woodland area adjacent to the selected planting site as 'local provenance' whereas others adopt much wider regional criteria, such as the Forestry Commission's local seed zones (Section 4.3.3).

Most forest agencies, conservation bodies and environmental groups traditionally recommend planting native trees and shrubs indigenous to an area or region. This follows the precautionary principle that, through natural selection, such plants should already be well adapted to local conditions and will therefore survive and perform better than the same species imported from elsewhere. There is, for example, already good evidence that native British nursery stock is better adapted to growing conditions in this country compared with material from parts of continental Europe, which can be susceptible to late spring frosts. Furthermore, there are strong biodiversity arguments: trees grown from imported seed that depart significantly from the normal times of leafing out, flowering or fruiting may upset the fine balance between locally native trees and the wildlife they support. The use of local plants also reduces the potential for hybridisation with imported, improved or domesticated stock, so that the risks of outbreeding depression should be limited. These principles are also widely applied by encouraging the practice of natural regeneration in ancient, semi-natural woods. However, there is no guarantee that in future local populations will possess sufficient adaptive genetic diversity and resilience to cope with the challenges of climate change and other environmental pressures. Including some non-local seed may increase genetic diversity and hence the potential for improved future adaptation, although it may not cope any better with climate change. This notion is explored in more detail in the following section.

4.3.2 Gene flow and genetic diversity

Genetic variation is responsible for the ability of an individual to survive, reproduce and respond to 'change'. Consequently populations with a broad range of adaptive genetic variation will have the best chance of coping with climate change. Individual trees of the same species might possess different versions (alleles) of a gene. If, for example, one of these versions functions better in warmer climates, those individuals might survive better if the temperature rises due to climate change and so would be more likely to pass on their version of the gene to subsequent generations.

Genes introduced into a population by pollen or seed from another population of trees – so called 'gene flow' – may increase the diversity of that population, which could help it cope with changing environmental pressures such as climate-induced stress or attack from new pathogens. This occurs over much larger distances than might be expected, often tens and sometimes hundreds of kilometres (Broadhurst, 2007). For example, in remnant native broadleaved populations of rowan and ash surviving in denuded areas of the Southern Uplands of Scotland, significant amounts gene flow from outside the study area have been detected (Bacles *et al.*, 2004, 2006). In wind-pollinated ash, 25–35% of seeds resulted from pollination by 'foreign' trees, while 50–75% germinated from seeds dispersed from trees outside the area, probably assisted by strong winds. Meanwhile, rowan, an insect-pollinated species, also maintained high genetic diversity, primarily through effective seed dispersal by birds. Despite this evidence of gene flow, trees which are currently 'adapted' to a particular site or set of environmental conditions will not necessarily have sufficient adaptive variation to cope with new challenges resulting from climate change. It is for this reason that sourcing seed from areas which are not 'local' is now being seriously considered.

Most native trees are outcrossing (i.e. cross-pollinated), which has helped to maintain a high level of genetic adaptability within their populations (Hubert and Cottrell, 2007). However, conservationists, foresters and geneticists alike must consider whether the local gene pools of woodland plants have sufficient adaptive genetic diversity and resilience to meet the challenges of climate change, and to respond quickly enough. Climate projections suggest that many species of plants and animals will suffer significant range changes, a loss of adaptive genetic diversity and, in some cases, local extirpation, particularly in temperate and arctic forests (e.g. Peters, 1990).

These issues raise serious concerns for the long term future of woodland in Britain, but there is also the more immediate issue of phenotypic responses to climate change, and the tolerance of individuals. Within a population of trees, or a number of populations through which genes flow, there may be enough inherent adaptive genetic diversity for that species to eventually adapt to climate change, although there is no guarantee that large numbers of individuals would survive. Many might not have the ability to adapt their physiological processes – such as growth and transpiration rates and phenotypic traits such as budburst – to cope with climate change. The effects on other members of the woodland community, particularly those which rely on services provided by trees could be profound.

4.3.3 Regions of provenance and seed zones in Britain

The Voluntary Scheme for the Certification of Native Trees and Shrubs is a Forestry Commission initiative that aims to match native seed sources to planting sites (Figure 4.5), particularly for semi-natural and new native woodlands (Herbert *et al.*, 1999). This scheme, with 24 zones across Britain supersedes the much broader Regions of Provenance (for native species only) that were defined by the Forest Reproductive Material Regulations of 1977 for timber-producing forest trees. The local seed zones are based on major climatic, geological and landform divisions in Britain, each divided into two altitude bands, above or below 300 m. The natural distributions of 26 trees and 27 small trees and shrubs within these zones have been taken into consideration. There is also a special set of designated collection zones for indigenous Scots pine in Scotland (Figure 4.5).

In the absence of sufficient knowledge about genetic variation and adaptation in native trees and shrubs (with the exception of Scots pine), the British seed zones are relatively uniform in area and do not relate to particular species: hence they are likely to be rather conservatively drawn. This relatively fine-scale zonation has been questioned, suggesting that it could be overly restrictive in the face of projected climate change (Hubert and Cottrell, 2007). Alternative approaches have yet to be adopted in general forestry policy or recognised in planting grant schemes, but are currently under review.

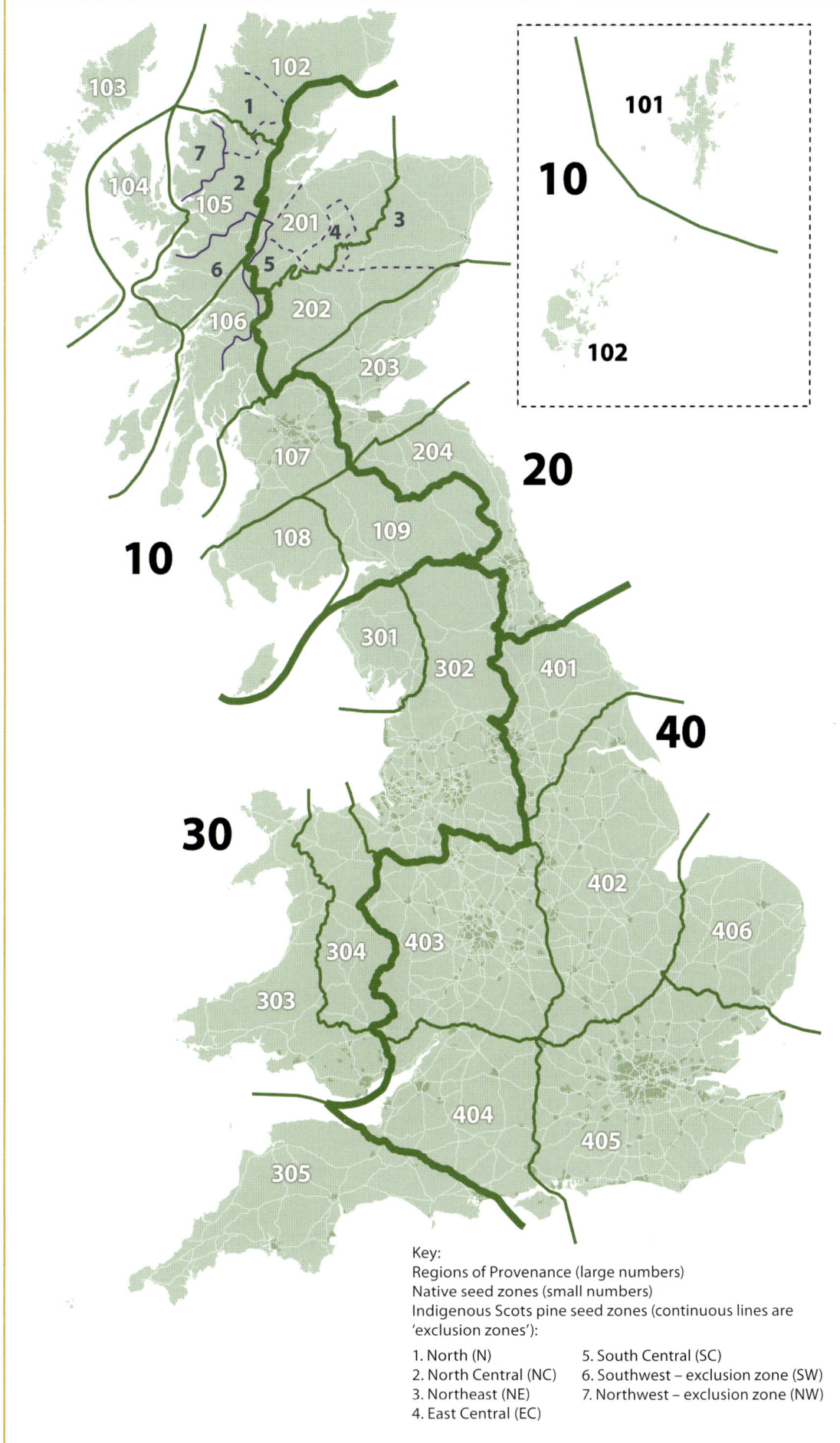

Figure 4.5 Forestry Reproductive Material (FRM) regional provenance map showing native seed zones. (Source: Forestry Commission Scotland, 2006; Crown copyright, reproduced with the kind permission of the Forestry Commission.) © Crown copyright and/or database right. All rights reserved. Licence number 100049759.

Under present day conditions, provenance trials and reciprocal transplant experiments, particularly those comparing British and continental populations, have consistently shown that local tree seed is best 'adapted' to local environmental conditions. Local trees are less likely to fail through poor adaptation to the local environment; they often grow better than 'imported material'; are phenotypically adjusted to local conditions (trees flush and flower in synchrony with local ecosystems); and do not dilute the local adaptive gene pool. However, across much of the British Isles, woodland is highly fragmented, and in some areas almost certainly contains planted native trees of non-local origin. As trees live for long periods of time, there is no guarantee that any population will be best adapted to a particular site. Prior to human intervention, a geographical continuum of tree populations across Britain would have allowed more effective gene flow containing potentially well-adapted genotypes, but also wider variation in adaptation to soil type, aspect, altitude and competition.

4.3.4 Consideration of seed sources in a changing climate

Recommendations for where and how to use locally-sourced trees and shrubs tend to be influenced by forestry and nature conservation policies and the availability of grant–aid schemes. Typical guidance tends to be a blend of the precautionary and pragmatic, with locally–sourced, indigenous material recommended for restoring or extending ancient woods, while a much wider range of origins and provenances may be suggested for forestry and landscaping purposes. Many organisations, for example the Joint Council for Landscape Industries (2002); the Forestry Commission (Forestry Commission Scotland 2003, 2006; Hubert and Cundall, 2006) and the Woodland Trust have their own best practices for sourcing plant material appropriate to one or more of a range of different planting situations. Such situations include:

- extending or restoring ancient woodland
- creating new native woodland for biodiversity
- planting mainly for timber production
- urban landscaping and planting to restore post–industrial, derelict land.

This list also represents a hierarchy for selection, in which the strictest interpretation of local provenance is usually applied to situations such as ancient woods and the least rigorous to landscape plantings in urban situations. Perhaps the most clearly defined category is that of indigenous, self–regenerating woods identified on the Ancient Woodland or Caledonian Pinewood Inventories. Some authorities suggest that using natural regeneration should be the first recourse when seeking to restore or expand such woodland. Although sound in principle, there may be cases where there are too few individuals of the previous canopy present to provide either an adequate seed rain or sufficient genetic variation, following Gould's (1997) principle that natural selection can only work on the material available (see below).

The local seed zones pre–date recent advances in molecular genetics which have improved our understanding of gene flow and the effects of habitat fragmentation. They represent a current 'best estimate' in terms of capturing local adaptive genetic variation, both in terms of the area of collection, identification of suitable populations and selection of parent trees. However, with projected changes in local environments, sourcing from the local seed zones alone may become increasingly untenable. If planting stock were to be selected from several sources, including non–local provenance, this would:

- enable new gene combinations which may help the population to respond to future environmental changes
- increase the chances that some planted trees would be well adapted to the future climate
- avoid the risk of inbreeding depression.

If woodland creation were to rely solely on the 'precautionary principle' of 'local is best' – through planting or natural regeneration – the resulting populations may lack sufficient adaptive genetic diversity to cope with progressive climate change, thus compromising restoration efforts. Plant material taken across the oceanic and continental range represented by north west and south east Britain, respectively, may already contain useful adaptive genetic variation that can be exploited in the warmer conditions projected to occur. Plant material may be moved from the south to the north of Britain; in addition, the maritime climates of France and other parts of Western and Southern Europe may yield genotypes that closely match future climatic scenarios in Britain. Importing material from these regions is less likely to lead to outbreeding depression in resident populations than material imported from continental, Northern and

Eastern Europe. A new, less restrictive precautionary principle, that of maintaining high levels of genetic diversity, may be the key to ensuring adaptability in the face of global change.

This is not to say that local tree seed should not be planted, or even that it should not constitute the bulk of the planting. Given the current gaps in our knowledge of tree genetics, new native woodland planting could be based on seed from native trees of local origin (sourced from Forestry Commission native seed zones) combined with seed sourced from other areas, provided these have similar environmental and climatic conditions to the planting site. Composite provenancing (Broadhurst *et al.*, 2008) and the similar 'portfolio approach' of mixing provenances (Hubert and Cottrell, 2007) both suggest such a strategy, although the methods differ in the amount of foreign material introduced. The implementation of such strategies is considered in Section 7.3.

4.4 Coping strategies for climate change

4.4.1 Ecological networks

To cope with the changing climate, natural ecosystems will need to respond and adapt quickly, and in many cases some intervention will be required, particularly where semi-natural habitats are fragmented, degraded or threatened by development. In the past two decades there has been a paradigm shift in conservation theory, particularly in heavily industrialised countries, where the traditional approach of protecting and tending usually small, strictly designated nature reserves has given way to a wider mission of managing dynamic, patchy landscapes in order to maintain metapopulations of significant species. It has been realised that limited reserves cannot guarantee long–term protection of the biodiversity that they contain, and that the wider countryside also plays an important role in maintaining their viability. The conservation problem then becomes one of a) understanding the ecological permeability of the landscape and the dispersal capabilities of the species in question, b) deciding how best to manipulate the landscape to improve functional integrity and c) designating wider landscape regions for conservation protection where the return on investment is likely to be greatest for Habitat and Species Action Plans.

Planners and practitioners will need to apply a broad approach which includes the creation of ecological networks – through habitat creation and restoration – in addition to conserving existing biodiversity by maintaining and expanding protected areas. These actions are widely viewed as two of the most important mechanisms for minimising the effects of climate change on semi-natural habitats and wildlife in Britain (e.g. Hopkins, 2007; The Wildlife Trusts, 2007). In addition, the UK Biodiversity Partnership's guiding principles to help practitioners take account of climate change also highlight the development of ecologically resilient and varied landscapes; and the reduction of threats not linked to the climate, such as the intensification of farming practices and the abandonment of traditional management (Hopkins *et al.,* 2007).

In the case of woodland, this seems to be justified ecologically by historical evidence suggesting the existence of a well-connected mosaic of forest cover prior to human disturbance, whether as open 'savanna', as postulated by Vera (2000) or more-or-less continuous forest tracts punctuated by gap-dynamic processes. From this perspective the restoration of habitat connectivity is not an artificial change to the landscape: to prevent species loss, it is important not only to preserve or develop areas that are large enough for the persistence of populations, but also to maintain possibilities for genetic exchange between patches.

An ecological network may be defined by its interactions, which can be at any scale, provided the parts function as a whole, so a cluster of small sites would need to function similarly to a single, extensive site. Such a network will improve functional connectivity between 'good' habitat patches, allowing wildlife to disperse more freely, and increasing the chances that species and habitats will survive the changing climate. Irrespective of size, most ecological networks will include core areas, buffer zones and dispersal routes; each having a different ecological value within the network.

Core areas

In any planned ecological network, the first step is to conserve all areas of high quality habitat which have some conservation value, whatever the current level of protection afforded to these sites. These areas will be important for resident species and for migrants displaced by climate change. They must also be regularly monitored and management plans should be in place to ensure that they are being managed to provide the best outcome for wildlife. In some cases this may require management plans to be revised to increase the chances of survival of the species and habitat which they protect. For example, coppicing and grazing regimes may be altered to suit all threatened species on a site, not just the more charismatic species.

Buffer zones

In our highly fragmented landscapes, many protected areas and sites of high conservation value are vulnerable to damaging activities in the immediate vicinity such as agricultural sprays, the impacts of nearby development or invasion by non-native species (Corney *et al.*, 2008). Enlarging these sites through the designation of buffer zones could help to protect them in the longer term. Planting new woodland may be one option for buffering existing ancient woodland (see also Section 5.2).

Dispersal routes

Functional landscapes of high quality habitat should provide the best chance for plants and animals to disperse and colonise new areas. For some groups, such as the generalist woodland birds (Section 2.3) this may already be possible, but for many others, landscapes are still hostile to movement. Dispersal might be achieved through physical corridors between sites; islands of habitat known as 'stepping stones' located at intervals between core areas; or permeable landscapes with some characteristics of semi-natural habitat, maintained for example in farmland through lower intensity land use (see Section 5.2).

Networks comprising specific habitat types such as woodland will be important, but wildlife will benefit most from landscapes with as wide a range of habitats as possible, so spatial planning will be critical. Functioning ecological networks will be particularly important in intensively farmed areas. Diverse landscapes will also provide opportunities for wildlife to find new habitat niches as the climate changes. In many instances, habitat creation and restoration will be necessary to fulfil these aims.

Although the theories of ecological networks have been extensively developed, few studies have yet been carried out to provide the evidence base to prove their success (Eycott *et al.*, 2008). Whilst some insects are already extending their range northwards, there is concern amongst many conservationists that even in the best-developed and managed ecological networks, many plants and animals will remain relatively immobile, unable to move, even if their own habitat becomes unsuitable. This is the case for some ancient woodland vascular plants and flightless saproxylic insects. Nevertheless, ecological networks are thought to provide the best chance of supporting a diverse flora and fauna in the British countryside, and without them, the outcome for wildlife could be much worse.

Scale

Ecological networks are being proposed and designed on varying scales, from the linkage of specific habitats at a very local level through to regional and national projects which encompass a wide range of habitats in their respective areas. On the Continent, international networks spanning many countries are also being developed. Irrespective of the scale, creating habitat such as new native woodland will play an increasingly important role.

Ecological networks are already being developed at the county level, e.g. Cheshire County Council's Ecological Network for People and Wildlife; Norfolk Wildlife Trust's Ecological Network Mapping Project for Norfolk. 'Living Landscapes' – a concept launched by the Wildlife Trusts – also aims to implement nature conservation at a landscape scale (Wildlife Trusts, 2007), and implementation is taking place locally across the UK, where 100 Living Landscape schemes now cover one million hectares. For example, the West Weald of West Sussex and south Surrey is one of the South East Living Landscapes identified as a proposed regional ecological network. Within this, the West Weald Landscape project aims to enhance identified ecological pathways, using the barbastelle bat as a focal species to guide efforts to increase landscape connectivity. This includes planting small areas of floodplain woodland, riparian woodland and planting or reinstating hedgerows.

The actions necessary to develop ecological networks on a regional basis are challenging and complex, even after the case has been made (Hopkins *et al.*, 2007). The Wildlife Trusts, however, envisage that their local networks will link together to form regional networks, such as that planned for the South East (Wildlife Trusts in the South East, 2006), which will integrate with other regional and national programmes to enlarge and reconnect areas of wildlife habitat, providing large interconnected areas through which animals and plants can move.

There are a number of good examples of ecological connectivity plans in Europe, including the Dutch National Ecological Network (EHS), which is an ambitious project to sustainably preserve, restore and develop important national and international ecosystems, through a network of existing protected areas and habitat creation/restoration sites, which are scheduled to be ready by 2018 (Ministry of Agriculture, Nature and Food Quality (Netherlands), 2004).

Spatial planning

Spatial planning for existing and future land use must support the adaptation of biodiversity to climate change through its policies and planning, consequently new mechanisms need to be developed to design and implement successful ecological networks. A major source of information on this topic is the BRANCH project (Section 4.2.3), which reviewed spatial planning mechanisms designed to help wildlife adaptation to climate change across North West Europe. BRANCH projects modelled how wildlife might respond to climate change; demonstrated good adaptation practice in spatial planning and protected area management; and presented case studies to develop planning options and tools to help wildlife in the South East adapt to climate change. For example, Hampshire Biodiversity Records Centre developed a GIS model to identify land suitable for habitat restoration or creation of chalk grassland and lowland heathland. This model examined habitat quality; geology and soil type; land use; topography; indicator flora and fauna records; habitat clusters; and used this information to produce maps indicating where suitable habitat might be created. These models also considered the impact of climate change on existing habitat and the implications for habitat restoration and creation opportunities.

Agricultural landscapes are hostile to the movement of many woodland species.

In this woodland, trees were cut to create a corridor to allow Duke of Burgundy butterflies to move between two isolated colonies.

4.4.2 Woodland habitat networks

Woodland habitat networks are patches of woodland that are projected to be functionally connected, with species able to move, to some extent, through intervening habitats. Woodland habitat network maps have been produced for many parts of Britain, based on the Forestry Commission's GIS approach to modelling and analysing habitat fragmentation and connectivity called BEETLE (Biological and Environmental Evaluation Tools for Landscape Ecology) (Watts *et al.*, 2005a, 2005b, 2007; Eycott *et al.*, 2007). BEETLE uses various evaluation tools including 'focal species' which are usually 'generic' species representing habitat and dispersal preferences of particular groups of 'real' woodland species (e.g. poorly dispersing woodland plants or butterflies using open habitats within woodland) for which we have little spatial data or ecological knowledge. This methodology was originally developed to evaluate the effects of management within existing forests and to project benefits of habitat restoration and creation in the wider landscape, but it is now also being used by the Forestry Commission to target woodland grants in some areas.

A key feature of such GIS models is the measurement of not just distance *per se* between habitats, but the ecological permeability of the landscape to the species concerned, recognising 'least cost' pathways of negotiable habitat and barriers to dispersal. GIS models can then be constructed using land cover data, core habitat presence and dispersal permeability to recognise potential habitat networks. BEETLE should help to target conservation actions, including the creation of habitat linkages through woodland planting. One of the first examples of its use was to target native woodland expansion in a Locational Premium scheme linked to the former Scottish Forestry Grant Scheme (Watts *et al.*, 2007).

The development of woodland or forest habitat network maps, their availability to conservation organisations and landowners, and their implementation through grant schemes for woodland creation differs across Britain, both within and between countries. For this reason, the three countries are considered individually.

Wales

Using the BEETLE model, the Countryside Council for Wales (CCW), in collaboration with Forestry Commission Wales and Forest Research produced maps of functional woodland habitat networks (Figure 4.6) for the whole of Wales (Watts *et al.*, 2005b; Latham *et al.*, 2008). The model used a focal species module, and land cover data from the CCW Phase 1 habitat survey; the Centre for Ecology and Hydrology Land Cover Map 2000; and datasets on ancient woodland (held by CCW) and topography (Ordnance Survey). Core networks are designed for generic focal species with poor dispersal ability (1 km) and a large habitat requirement (minimum 10 ha). focal networks represent species with greater dispersal ability (5 km) and a small minimum patch requirement (2 ha). In both cases, these have been mapped for broadleaf woodland and ancient woodland. Core networks can also be nested within the larger focal networks to aid the implementation of the strategy at local levels.

Habitat network maps are already being widely used by CCW and its partners, including the Forestry Commission, Wildlife Trusts and local authorities, as a practical tool to help guide landscape management decisions such as improving woodland connectivity. For example, CCW's Tir Gofal agri-environment scheme made a major contribution to ecological connectivity by using habitat network maps to meet its objectives of protecting and enhancing habitats of importance to wildlife. However, it is very important that before any decisions are made based on habitat network maps, ground truthing must be undertaken to confirm habitat quality, and identify landscape features not included in the maps, because of the limitations of the original Phase 1 survey data.

Scotland

Scottish Natural Heritage, in collaboration with Forestry Commission Scotland and Forest Research also produced maps of functional woodland habitat networks for the whole of Scotland using BEETLE (Moseley *et al.*, 2008). A wide range of data sources were used, including Phase 1 habitat survey, the Caledonian Pinewood Inventory, the National Inventory of Woods and Trees, the Riparian and Wet Woodland Indicator dataset, designated conservation areas and many more. The resulting Forest Habitat Networks (FHN) aimed to improve existing woodland and target new woodland creation sites in order to reverse the effects of fragmentation on woodland biodiversity; thus expanding the areas of continuous woodland cover in Scotland. One of the core objectives of the expansion of the woodland network was to protect woodland ecosystems

PART ONE GENERAL PRINCIPLES – **WOODLAND CREATION IN A CHANGING CLIMATE**

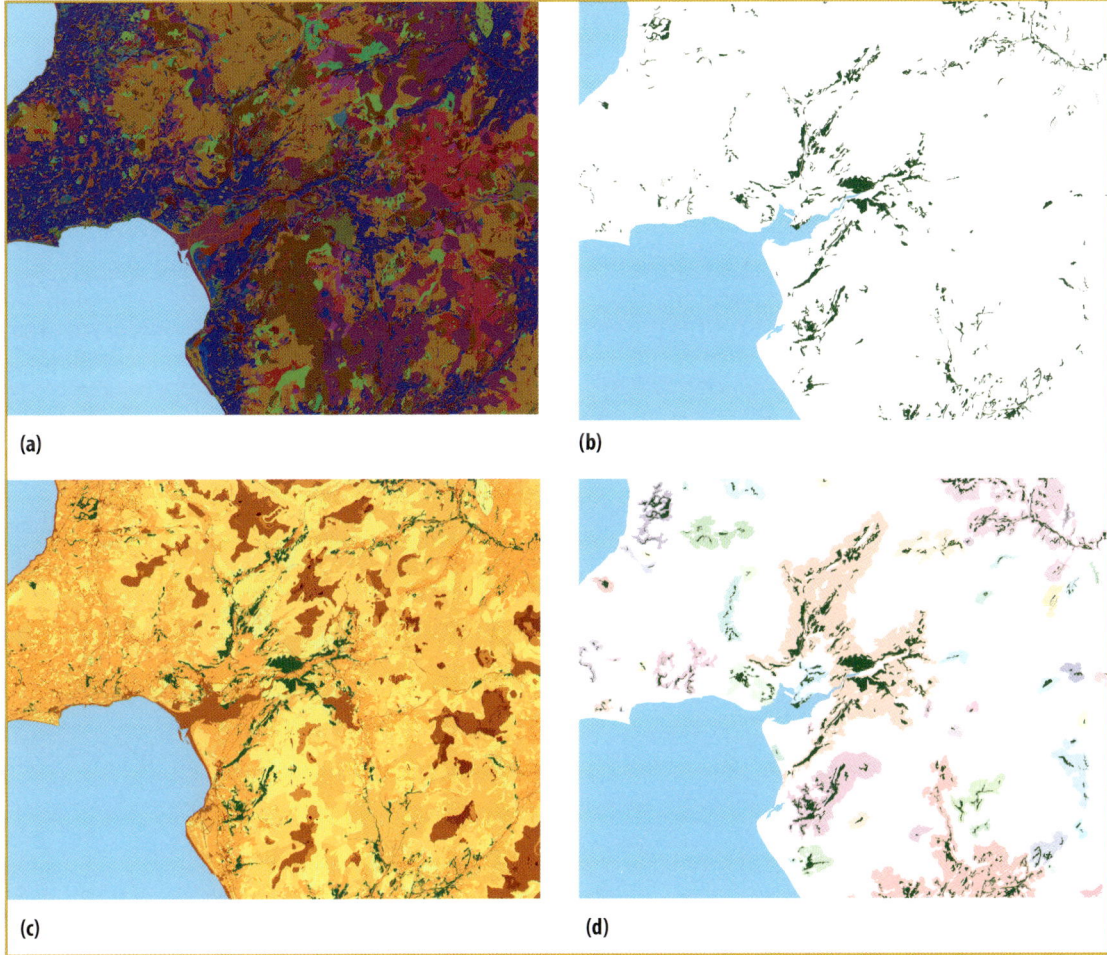

Figure 4.6 These maps illustrate the BEETLE modelling approach applied to a wooded landscape in North West Wales: (a) data from the land cover module; (b) the focal species model defines habitat areas, in this case deciduous woodland; (c) the connectivity model assesses landscape permeability – which ranges from high (yellow) to low (reddish brown); these models allow the identification of potential habitat networks which can be studied within the network analysis model (d). (Map reproduced from Watts *et al*., 2005b and kindly supplied by Forest Research.) © Crown copyright and/or database right. All rights reserved. Licence number 100049759.

against the changing climate, to sequester more carbon and expand future timber and wood fuel resources. Overall, the forest habitat network project aims to support the strategic development and integration of FHNs and open habitat networks in Scotland.

The FHN maps and reports support the strategic decisions of forestry policy makers and facilitate practical operational planning at national, regional and local scales. Some of these plans were agreed with local stakeholders as a basis for prioritising further native woodland creation to develop networks. Forestry Commission Scotland also developed guidance and a consistent set of GIS maps for use across Scotland to help with targeting native woodland creation and developing networks around 'high nature value' woodlands. At all scales, the FHNs are being used to prioritise habitat network improvement, in conjunction with local authority indicative forestry strategies, and other decision support systems such as the Forestry Commission's Ecological Site Classification (Section 6.6.1). They may also support habitat action plan (HAP) targets for expansion and restoration of woodland. Decision support systems are also used to identify areas where it would be inappropriate to create new woodland, such as heathland. At a local scale, woodland practitioners, biodiversity officers, planners and others should be able to study woodland networks to identify areas where woodland creation could be used to expand high quality core woodland patches and/or strengthen connectivity. Interpretation of the Scottish maps requires as much care as the Welsh maps, due to limitations in the quality of the data defining mapped habitats.

England

Each Forestry Commission Region publishes its own Regional Forestry Framework, which collectively contribute to national strategies such as "England's Trees, Woods and Forests" for fostering an ecosystem approach to the integration of trees, woods and forests into wider land management (Forestry Commission and Natural England, 2008). The South West of England region was the first to utilise woodland habitat networks derived from BEETLE with a view to establishing resilient, landscape-scale ecological networks as part of the regional response to the earlier UK Government's *Keepers of Time* policy (Defra and Forestry Commission, 2005) for protecting and enhancing England's ancient woodland. A woodland habitat network map was produced for the South West by Forest Research identifying high concentrations of ancient woodland. Working in partnership with organisations such as the Woodland Trust, Natural England and the Exmoor and Dartmoor National Parks Authority, the Forestry Commission initially identified 'Ancient Woodland Priority Areas' – Exmoor, Dartmoor and the Tamar Valley, the Forest of Dean and the Cotswolds. Within these areas grant aid was targeted towards woodland creation and other activities which would improve habitat networks at the landscape scale. Woodland creation outside these areas was also considered for grant aid if some element of linkage with other ancient woodland or semi-natural habitat could be demonstrated.

Other regions did not initially utilise BEETLE, but continued to follow local landscape guidelines, although with some geographical targeting for woodland creation. The East of England region, for example, began to target the restoration and extension of ancient woodland within particular clusters identified using a less complex GIS mapping system, developed in collaboration with local Wildlife Trusts, but still requiring extensive ground truthing. All regions used a variety of other research and documentary evidence to determine whether a woodland creation proposal should be supported at a particular location, using a points system in their evaluation. For example, points were allocated in the East of England for planting within 30–100 m of established semi-natural woodland, and for meeting the objectives of local authority Local Character Areas. In the West Midlands, woodland creation in key locations such as the Forest of Feckenham was identified as a priority, to create climate-adaptable core habitat areas. In the South East, woodland creation schemes scored additional points in districts with low woodland cover, together with urban growth areas and areas targeted for community access and involvement.

5 LANDSCAPE PLANNING FOR WOODLAND CREATION

5.1 Landscape Character Assessment in Britain

Landscape character has been defined as the distinct and recognisable pattern of elements that occurs consistently in a particular type of landscape, and how these are perceived by people (Swanwick, 2002). It reflects particular combinations of geology, landform, soils, vegetation, land use and human settlement, which together create a particular 'sense of place'. Scale is important in landscape character assessment, and there is a spatial hierarchy between various levels, including national, regional, county or district level, and the local landscape. When a woodland creation scheme is at the planning stage, the potential impact on the character of the local landscape should be considered, and an assessment undertaken to assist the site selection. Here we present an overview of landscape character assessment in England, Wales and Scotland.

Landscape character assessment is an important tool which should be considered whenever actions are likely to influence the landscape, including changes in land cover through new woodland planting. It confirms what makes the landscape distinctive and helps to inform planning and landscape management decisions, ensuring that landscape change occurs in a considered way, respectful of the character of an area. In the case of new woodland, a landscape character assessment will review the ability of the landscape to absorb new planting without significantly altering its character.

Much of the necessary information required for a woodland creation project can be derived from existing landscape character assessments, but in most cases some field work will still be necessary, particularly for ecological aspects.

5.1.1 Landscape character in England

National Character Areas

England has a Landscape Character Assessment mapped at 1:250,000, which is administered by Natural England. The Character of England map was produced in 1996, and combines the former Countryside Commission's Character Areas and English Nature's Natural Areas into 159 National Character Areas (NCAs, formerly known as Joint Character Areas) with similar landscape character (Figure 5.1). These are available on the Natural England website. The NCAs constitute a national spatial framework, which can be used for a wide range of applications.

NCAs provide an introduction to the landscape character of an area, including information on its key characteristics; physical influences; historical and cultural influences; land cover; and how the countryside is changing. Linked to the NCAs are Defra's Environmental Stewardship Targeting Statements, which list priority targets for stewardship schemes in areas where environmental outcomes are likely to

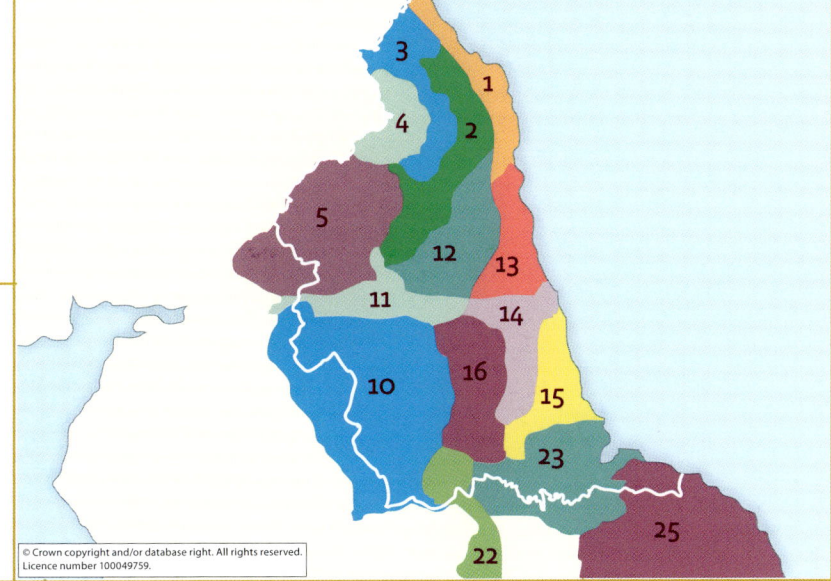

Figure 5.1 Natural England's North East National Character Areas map; the features defining the landscape of each area are recorded in individual descriptions. © Natural England (2010) material is reproduced with the permission of Natural England from its website. http://www.naturalengland.org.uk/copyright

Key
1. North Northumberland Coastal Plain
2. Northumberland Sandstone Hills
3. Cheviot Fringe
4. Cheviots
5. Border Moors and Forests
10. North Pennines
11. Tyne Gap and Hadrian's Wall
12. Mid Northumberland
13. South East Northumberland Coastal Plain
14. Tyne and Wear Lowlands
15. Durham Magnesian Limestone Plateau
16. Durham Coalfield Pennine fringe
22. Pennine Dales Fringe
23. Tees Lowlands
25. North Yorkshire Moors and Cleveland Hills

View from Box Hill on the North Downs across the well-wooded Low Weald, where woodland creation may be appropriate in certain locations.

The open landscape character of the South Downs where extensive woodland creation would be inappropriate.

be greatest, in support of the NCA. All NCAs are due to be refreshed and updated by spring 2011, still providing a contextual and strategic description of character, whilst more consistently representing the natural and cultural components that influence or contribute to the character of the areas.

Together, the NCA and Higher Level Stewardship documents give an impression of how appropriate it might be to plant new native woodland in the area in question. For example, NCA 122 *High Weald* draws attention to the loss of characteristic features such as hedgerows and wooded ghylls and the desirability of creating new native broadleaved woodland. The *High Weald* Target Area Statement (SE03) also highlights restoration and creation of woodland as a target. In contrast, NCA 116 *Berkshire and Marlborough Downs* emphasises the large-scale rolling chalk downland with its sparse woodland cover, where woodland creation would be detrimental to the open nature of the higher areas of downland.

Natural Areas

In addition to the NCAs, Natural England previously defined a comprehensive series of 120 Natural Areas, each with its own set of conservation priorities. Natural Area Profiles summarise wildlife and natural features, and their interaction with land use, geology and human history. They describe important habitats, species and physical features, providing a useful background for woodland creation schemes. Natural Areas are geographic rather than political, so they do not always match NCA boundaries. They offer a more effective framework than NCAs for conservation objectives such as the creation of new native woodland and other semi-natural habitat.

PART ONE GENERAL PRINCIPLES – **LANDSCAPE PLANNING FOR WOODLAND CREATION**

Local Landscape Character Assessments

In England, the national schemes are supported by an excellent coverage of local landscape character assessments, mapped at 1:25,000 or 1:50,000. These have been produced by a range of organisations, including local authorities, Areas of Outstanding Natural Beauty (AONBs), National Park Authorities etc. These assessments may have more detail than the NCAs, and focus on very much smaller areas. Many are available on the internet, and are also listed on the web-based Database of Landscape Character Assessments in England.

5.1.2 Landscape character in Wales

The landscape character assessments for Wales differ in approach to England, but essentially achieve the same landscape management objectives, underpinned by the Planning Policy Wales and the European Landscape Convention. Landscape character assessments in Wales include the National Landscape Character Map for Wales; the Seascape Assessment; LANDMAP; and Historic Landscapes.

National Landscape Character Map for Wales

The National Landscape Character Assessment of Wales, undertaken by the Countryside Council for Wales (CCW) provides a landscape context to spatial planning in Wales through the Welsh Assembly's Environmental Strategy. Forty-eight regional landscape character areas have their own distinctive character and 'sense of place' (Figure 5.2), and can be viewed on the CCW website. Each has its own narrative description of land form, land cover, land use and landscape qualities, broadly similar to English NCAs. Although there are some methodological differences, where comparisons can be made in the border areas, there are good agreements between the Welsh and the English NCAs (Briggs, 2008).

Whilst the Welsh landscape character areas provide important regional background information on landscapes, local areas might have their own distinct landscapes, particularly in areas where the landscape changes quickly from lowland to upland. Consequently, in many cases, local landscape character assessments are also useful.

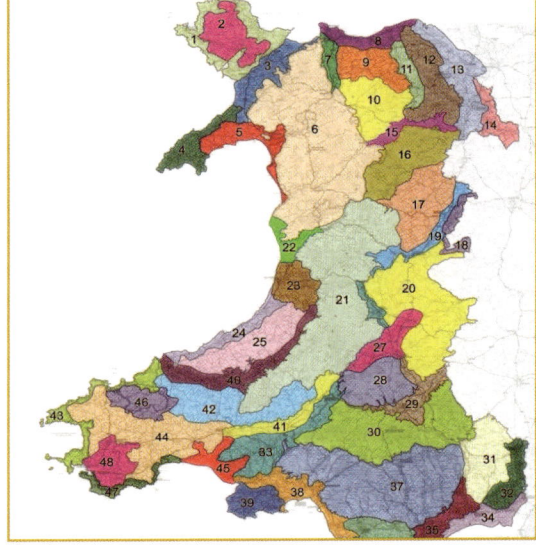

Figure 5.2 The Landscape Character Map for Wales divides the country into 48 regional landscape character areas.
(Reproduced with the kind permission of the Countryside Council for Wales). © Crown copyright and/or database right. All rights reserved. Licence number 100049759.

Conifer plantations in Beddgelert Forest march up the slopes of Mynydd Mawr, North Wales.

Upland oakwoods and conifer plantations in Coederyr on the shores of Llyn Gwynant in Nantgwynant, North Wales.

Local landscape character assessments

LANDMAP is the equivalent of the English local or county scale landscape character assessments. The assessments were carried out by CCW on behalf of the National Assembly for Wales, in partnership with local authorities and National Park authorities. LANDMAP has five layers: geological landscapes, landscape habitats, visual and sensory landscapes, historical landscapes and cultural landscapes. All five layers may be used to inform decisions on landscape management, given that each aspect may have some relevance to the same landscape location. LANDMAP is being used for informing landscape management plans and to provide information for forestry and woodland strategies, for example in forest design strategies for Welsh Assembly-owned forests in support of the Blaen Rhondda Forest design project, which was reviewed and updated to include the guiding principles laid out in the 'Woodlands for Wales' Forest Strategy.

Seascape assessment

This is a coastal landscape characterisation which includes a defined visual setting zone for each coastal section. The Welsh coastline divides into 50 seascape units on a headland to headland basis. Coastal character is distinct and often different to the prevailing inland character, and provides a means of relating developments offshore, such as wind farms, to coastal landscapes. As much of the description relates to the coastal landscape, up to 10 km inland, there may be relevant information to consult if habitat creation is being considered in these areas. Seascape descriptions are available on CCW's website.

Historic landscapes

Wales has a large number of historical features which help to create a 'sense of place', and add a feeling of time and depth to the landscape. A joint project between CCW and the 'Welsh Historic Monuments and the International Council for Monuments and Sites' has identified the best surviving examples as 'historical landscapes', aimed at protecting these landscapes from inappropriate development and change. This Register of Landscapes of Outstanding Historic Interest in Wales contains 58 landscapes in two volumes. Although many historic sites will be found within these registered landscapes, others may be located outside. The registers are informal designations, but they do constitute a 'material planning consideration' when considering potential developments in the wider landscape. All landscapes included in the registers have been characterised and can be viewed on the relevant Welsh Archaeological Trust website.

5.1.3 Landscape character in Scotland

Scottish Natural Heritage's (SNH) National Programme of Landscape Character Assessment consists of a series of 30 assessments that were carried out for each local authority and a small

Scots pine with birch, including some veteran trees on the upper slopes, Glen Affric in the Scottish Highlands.

number of National Park Authorities, covering the whole of Scotland (Martin and Swanwick, 2003). The studies identified 3,967 distinct landscape character areas, grouped into 366 landscape character types. For practitioners involved in woodland creation, each of the 30 Landscape Character Assessments provides useful information, including geology, vegetation, climate and soils at a local level. The study reports can be purchased from SNH, or freely downloaded from the internet. In addition, the mapped landscape types have also been digitised.

Landscape character types also informed the development of the Natural Heritage Futures programme (NH Futures, formerly the Natural Heritage Zones) which describes the distinctive identities of 21 natural heritage areas covering the whole of Scotland (Scottish Natural Heritage, 2002). The programme details national priorities and objectives for different settings, including 'Forests and Woodlands'. Each NH Futures area is presented in an individual plan (the equivalent of Natural England's NCAs, although more detailed in the Scottish version). The plans are used by SNH to inform its input into plans and strategies for various sectors such as Indicative Forestry Strategies, Development Plans and local and national Biodiversity Action Plans. Each plan includes the following sections: description of the main features of the area, including geology and agricultural land; key influences on the landscape, such as agriculture, forestry and development; vision – based on better stewardship of natural resources; objectives – future priorities and action required, which is particularly pertinent to woodland creation schemes.

SNH also has a database of 'Areas of Wildland', which are described as "uninhabited and often relatively inaccessible countryside where the influence of human activity on the character and quality of the environment has been minimal" in National Policy Planning Guidelines. SNH's policy objectives for these areas are to: safeguard their wildness and wildland; enhance nature; ensure responsible recreational use; recover past damage; and promote awareness.

5.2 Siting new woods: the landscape context

5.2.1 Planting strategies

Whilst woodland habitat network maps are excellent tools for identifying areas which would benefit from woodland creation, decisions still have to be made about where to plant new woodland in specific locations. Plans to increase woodland biodiversity at a local landscape scale will need to consider a range of different approaches, such as a) maintaining and enhancing the condition of existing ancient/native woods; b) restoring plantations on ancient sites; and c) creating new native woodland. Such priorities are addressed in Biodiversity Action Plans, a number of landscape planning strategies produced by county authorities and wildlife NGOs, and in future climate change scenarios. In all cases the planting of new woodland can assist significantly in producing more resilient habitats, but there is rather limited guidance on whether areas for woodland creation should be used to buffer existing sites, expand the available habitat or improve the connectivity between sites.

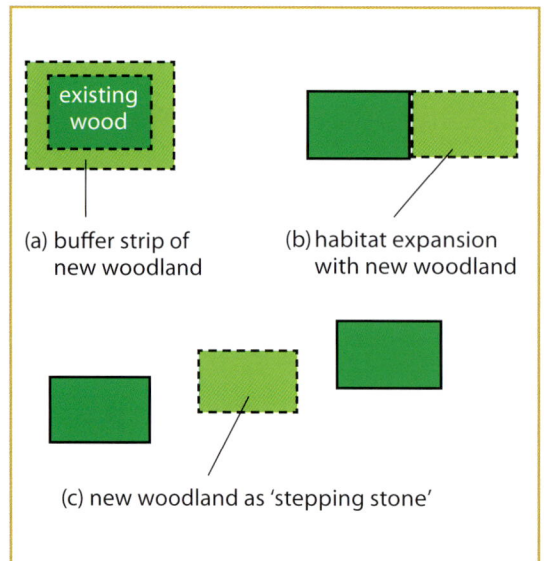

Figure 5.3 Parent strategies for increasing woodland habitat, based on the occurrence of existing woodland, by (a) buffering; (b) expanding; and (c) increasing connectivity between sites.

Examples of three parent strategies are shown in Figure 5.3. In Figure 5.3a, an isolated wood has a new woodland strip created around it to act as a buffer against spray drift. The buffering benefit is effective almost immediately, although initially the strip largely benefits only non-woodland species. As it matures other species move in, but its value for woodland specialists may still be somewhat limited. It is also likely to have little effect in improving connectivity between woods. In Figure 5.3b the same area of woodland is concentrated along one edge so its buffer value is much lower, but ultimately, when it matures (in 75 yrs+) its value for woodland specialists will increase, as will also be the case for the existing wood buffered in Figure 5.3a. Again, there may be little connectivity gain. In Figure 5.3c there is no buffering benefit and no additional habitat gain for woodland specialists in the short term, but on the other hand there is a benefit to connectivity through the creation of a 'stepping stone' patch. Each of these functions is further explored below.

5.2.2 Buffering existing woods

Edges of woodland often have distinct species assemblages and may be the richest parts of the wood. However where the edge abuts arable, improved grassland, or is close to roads or urban areas, there can be negative effects that may be offset by creation of a woodland buffer strip between the wood and the impact. The depth of 'edge impact' will vary according to conditions and type of impact: agricultural sprays, fertilisers, drainage, urban pollution, noise, etc. (Gove et al. 2007; Corney et al., 2008). The width of buffer needed should probably be, in most cases, equivalent to the depth of the edge effect; but in practice, depending on the nature of the impact and the type of buffer it might be wider or narrower. To avoid shading out the existing edge, it is an advantage if a gap can be left between the buffer planting and the wood perimeter.

In terms of where the technique should be applied, buffering will tend to have the greatest benefits in small to medium-sized patches, protecting the woodland core from edge effects in landscapes where the surrounding land use is intensive, as in arable or on the urban fringe. Relatively less extra benefit comes from buffering large patches because most of their area is (depending on woodland shape) already sufficiently distant from the edge. The relative benefit from the edge area released is greater with small woods, because the edge area released comprises a greater proportion of the whole. Therefore an approach would be to target ancient woods of c.2–10 ha in intensively farmed regions, with a lower priority given to larger woods and to landscapes with a high level of semi-natural cover, where other techniques such as habitat extension and linking networks can be explored.

5.2.3 Habitat extension – adding to existing woods

In general, species richness increases with increasing woodland size and with it the potential size of species populations present, making them less likely to go extinct. For some species or species assemblages there may be a minimum threshold size at which they are first likely to occur, or at which there is sufficient habitat to maintain their long-term viability. If the wood is too small to supply the requirements of a particular species of conservation concern there is no benefit (in the short term) from adding area to sites which still fall short of the critical threshold, but on the other hand there is a gain to be had from bringing other sites from below to above the threshold. Thus habitat expansion is most usefully targeted towards patches at the smaller end of the spectrum, or where it will move sites across critical size thresholds (Box 5.1).

As a wood increases in size, habitat complexity usually increases with the wider range of topography, hydrology, soil types and natural disturbances covered. Open space and structural complexity is also likely to be better represented in larger woods where there is a greater chance of continuing management, through the presence of rides, coppicing, felling and windblown areas

Box 5.1 Modelling farmland bird populations

In 1990–1992, repeat surveys of farmland bird populations were carried out by the Institute of Terrestrial Ecology (now the Centre for Ecology and Hydrology) in Cambridgeshire and Lincolnshire in order to establish relationships between the presence of resident, breeding bird populations and a number of landscape measurements. The latter included 24 variables, such as woodland size, perimeter, distance to the nearest wood, surrounding land use, etc.; allowing the probability of a species being present in a given woodland situation to be calculated. The methodology was then applied to an intensive arable area of 60 km^2 on the western edge of the Cambridgeshire Fens containing a majority of small, relatively isolated woods with virtually no connecting habitat of any description (Swetnam et al., 1998). This showed, for an 'interior' forest bird such as the treecreeper, that the probability of finding it was greatest in the largest woodlands (Figure 5.4a): there also appeared to be a source-sink effect where birds present in the large (source) woods were able to disperse to nearby, smaller woods (sinks).

The effect of landscape change was then modelled in various ways. In one scenario of aggressive agricultural expansion, the removal of small, isolated woodland fragments had little effect on the treecreeper population. However, reducing the size of small (<20 ha) woods of by removing 40 m of perimeter from each, effectively discouraged any breeding populations. Conversely, expanding the woodland perimeter of the same small woodlands by adding a theoretical 60 m of new edge, dramatically increased the probability of treecreepers colonising all but the smallest and most isolated woods (Figure 5.4b). This scenario also benefited other species limited by woodland size and density in the landscape, such as great spotted woodpecker and long-tailed tit.

This theoretical exercise illustrates how different planting strategies (or the converse, fragmentation) can have a dramatic effect on the numbers of bird species using woods within a region. Generally, increasing existing woodland size through buffering or expansion in predominantly open landscapes will tend to benefit most species, including those that can breed in small woodland parcels as well as the specialists requiring larger woods. However, at some point, as with most species groups, ever-increasing forest cover will begin to disadvantage 'edge' species such as whitethroat and yellowhammer. Providing that enough is known about the habitat requirements of species of conservation concern, modelling their responses to alternative landscape configurations can be an effective way of evaluating a different planting strategies.

Treecreeper.

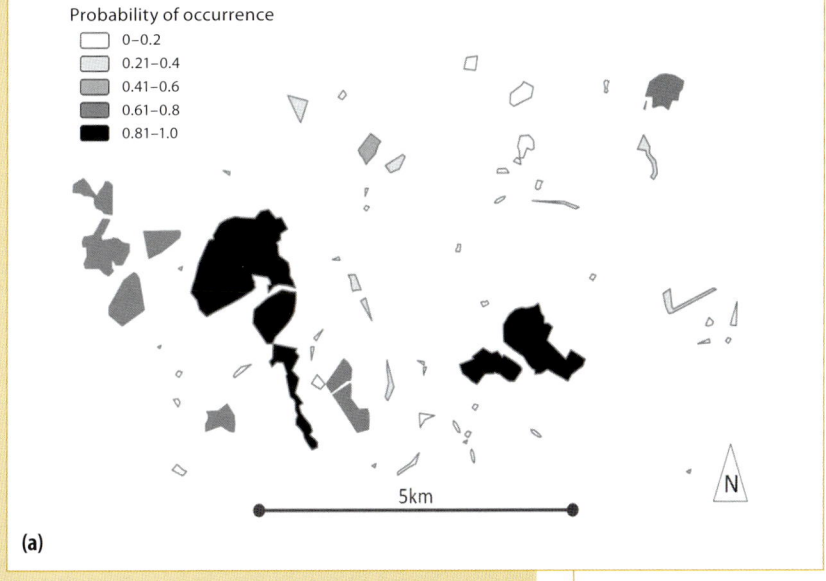

(a)

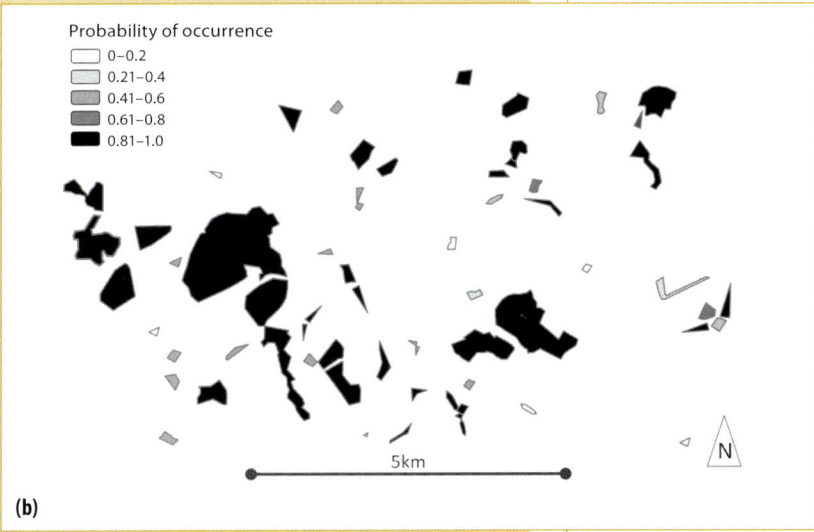

(b)

Figure 5.4 Modelled effects of woodland expansion in a farmed Cambridgeshire landscape on the probability of treecreeper occurrence, showing (a) the status quo; and (b) the effect of buffering the perimeters of all small woods (<20 ha) with 60 m of new perimeter. (Source: Swetnam et al., 1998; reproduced with the kind permission of Elsevier Ltd.)

(Peterken and Francis, 1999). Most species are associated with a particular age or growth stage in a wood, so that the threshold for maintaining a viable species population in unmanaged woods is likely to be higher than for actively managed woodland because in the latter case the age structure can be controlled such that all age classes are always present. This is most obvious if gap-phase species are considered, but it applies also to other growth stages in the cycle.

It can be argued that greater habitat expansion benefits can be derived from adding woodland in sparsely wooded regions than in densely wooded ones, because the *relative* increase in habitat area is greater (Figure 5.5). In both cases, the additional new woodlands attached to patches A and B may increase the chance that a species will be able to survive in the enhanced patch and not go extinct. (It is assumed that any impact on the extinction risk in the other patches is minimal.) However the benefit of that reduced extinction risk is greater in the poorly-wooded area (B), because in the densely wooded areas there is a greater chance that some species will be able to re-colonise patch A from surrounding sources, whereas in the sparsely wooded region extinction may be final.

5.2.4 Increasing connectivity between woods

Much work on developing connectivity models and woodland habitat networks has already been referred to (Section 4.4.2), based either on simple distances between sites or modifying the effective distance by incorporating elements of matrix quality. These can suggest which areas of a landscape may be considered part of the same core or focal 'network' for a given class of species (real, generic or focal) sharing common dispersal characteristics. While these techniques are highly effective in presenting the broad framework of planting opportunities, less work has been done on where to dispose new woodland parcels within the given framework, given that the process of infilling may inevitably be piecemeal, long drawn out and incomplete in practice.

Improving connectivity may be achieved using linear corridors, belts or 'stepping stone' patterns of tree planting. An obvious advantage is that some species, especially more mobile mammals, birds and insects, may be able to use these connections as transit stations to more favourable habitat, facilitating the formation of a viable metapopulation. At the same time the presence of several adjacent patches may collectively satisfy the minimum size requirements of some species. With the increased connectivity spread over a wider range of environmental variation than previously, several new small woods also have the potential to contain more species than the original configuration of existing woods.

Exactly where to site new woodlands within a network of existing woods is an issue that also has to be resolved. If a new patch is added at position X there is a very high chance that it will be colonised by a species present in the surrounding patches (Figure 5.6), given a relatively permeable matrix. However, if the species population within the network is already robust, with regular immigration and emigration between patches, then the value of new woodland at X is limited – it is like adding a small amount to an already large, single wood. If the wood is added at position Y it may be less likely to be colonised, but should eventually be (assuming no

Figure 5.5 The relative benefits of adding new woods to (a) clustered or (b) isolated woods.

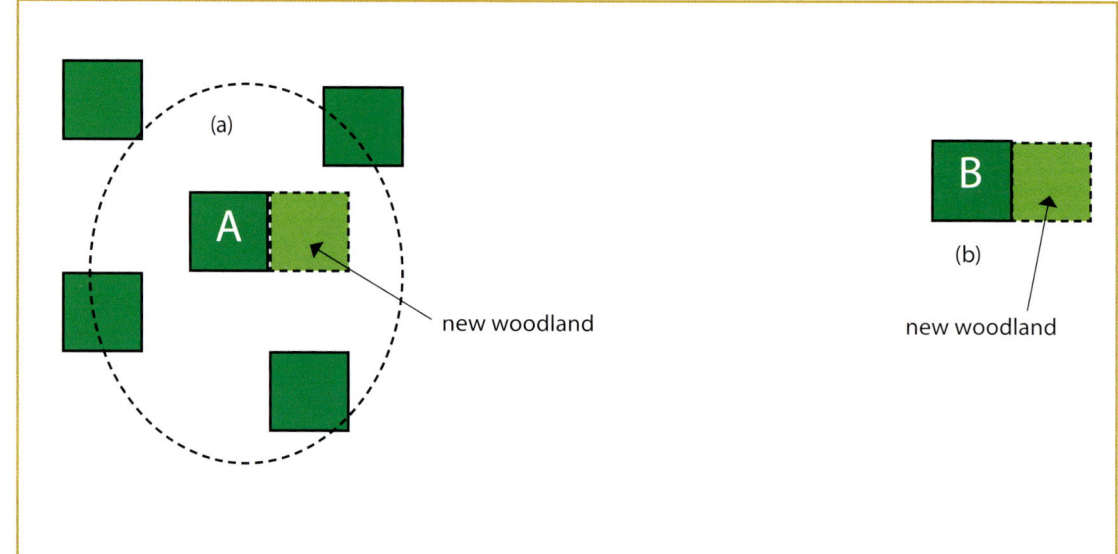

PART ONE GENERAL PRINCIPLES – **LANDSCAPE PLANNING FOR WOODLAND CREATION**

ecological barriers) as it is within the network envelope. However in addition a new wood in this location extends the 'network area' both in itself and by potentially bringing in a wood currently outside the network. Similarly, in Figure 5.7, adding the wood at Z potentially provides a link between two large 'networks' but if these networks are both large and relatively robust it may be less useful than adding the wood at V which helps to link a relatively small, less robust network to a larger one. More work is needed on the relative merits of linking networks of different sizes and integrity, with actual monitoring of individual species in case studies.

More work is also needed on the best ways of using a given amount of new woodland to improve the connectivity between woodland areas. In Figure 5.8, for example, is it better to place one large 'stepping stone' of new planting between the two blocks of woodland (or two networks) or to divide up the new woodland into small patches, so reducing inter-patch distances? This latter arrangement may be a more efficient use of resources in some landscapes and for some species. In effect it becomes an argument for developing mosaic habitats such as wood-pasture or networks of trees along boundaries such as hedgerows – a layout that might be expected to aid the dispersal of mobile species, such as bats, small mammals, butterflies and birds that can move along boundaries (Kirby, 2009). On the other hand, neither configuration is likely to work for poorly-dispersing species that require large areas of woodland habitat.

5.2.5 Which strategy?

A number of conclusions emerge from this very brief review of landscape planting strategies. Across the country as a whole buffering tends to provide the most immediate and certain returns, as it builds intimately on the ecological capital already present in existing woods and helps to protect them from the impacts of adjacent land use. As diminishing returns apply to buffering larger and larger existing woodlands, the greatest relative conservation gains are only likely to occur at smaller patch sizes. However, this advantage may well be offset by the consideration that very small woodlands are likely to contain only a limited suite of species in the first place.

The same diminishing returns operate with habitat expansion, where the new woods are planted adjacent to existing ones. Other things being equal, the greatest relative benefit per unit of new woodland is most likely when adding to small, rather than to large woods, again bearing in mind that smaller woods tend to support fewer species. Any species of conservation concern will add a further dimension to this judgement, as expanding the wood above a certain size could now reach the critical threshold area able to support, say, a less mobile species requiring 'interior' woodland conditions. The tendency in this case would be to make the woods bigger if that species already occurs in low numbers, or is present in similar habitat nearby. Conversely, in the case of slowly moving woodland plants, there may be no benefit in expanding the new

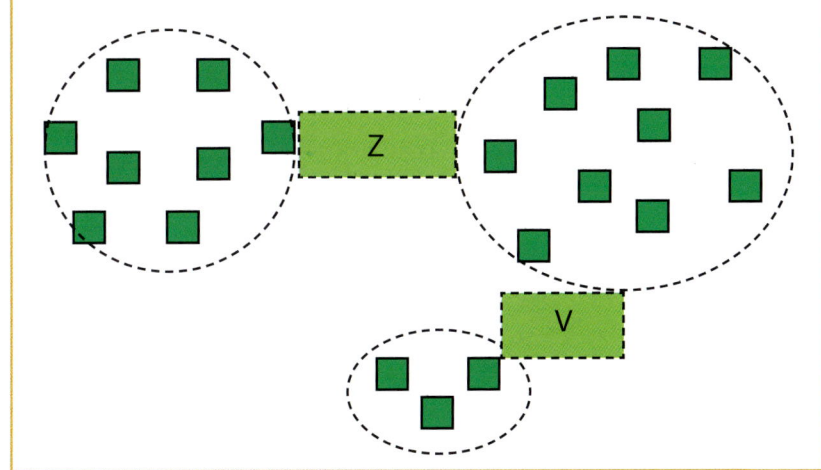

Figure 5.6 Adding new woodland to networks – in the middle or on the edge.

BELOW **Figure 5.7** Linking networks – large to large, or large to small.

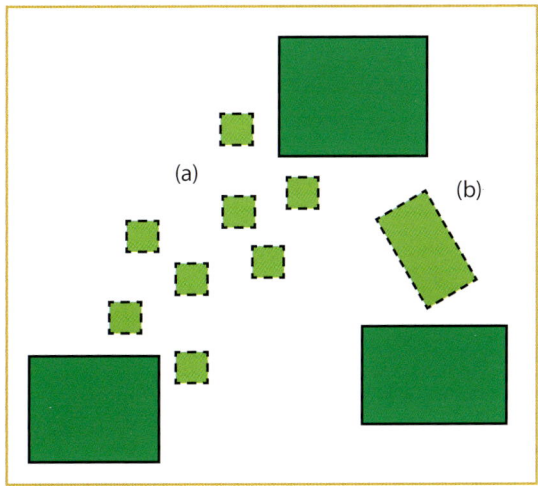

Figure 5.8 The connectivity between woods is likely to be greater with the subdivision of the new woodland patches (a) compared to the same area as a single block (b). The large blocks can either represent existing large woodlands, or networks of woodlands.

New woodland to the left of the path has been planted too close to the south-facing shrubby edge of an ancient wood, which will suffer from the resulting shading.

area beyond that likely to become colonised in the medium to long term. In general, however, habitat extension will tend to have relatively more impact in landscapes with little woodland cover or with predominantly small woods – beyond this it may be worth considering the role of new woodland for connectivity gain.

New woodland to improve connectivity is of least value in very poorly wooded landscapes (where there is nothing to link up, and when the patches are extremely isolated), but also in very heavily wooded landscapes where connectivity is already likely to be relatively high. Its value thus lies in intermediately wooded landscapes where the patches are very isolated. In these cases, linking outlying patches to larger ones may be most effective, applied as small blocks in areas where the opportunities arise.

5.2.6 General conclusions

The balance of new planting for wildlife will depend heavily on conservation priorities and the ecological capital held within a particular landscape. Arguably, maintaining and enhancing the existing woods is a first priority (Hopkins *et al.*, 2007) because they are currently the richest in wildlife and will be the source of species to spread through the rest of the landscape, even if their long-term survival is uncertain because of climate change. By the same token, restoration of plantations on ancient woodland sites is a most cost-effective way of using resources and is the only way of increasing the area of ancient woodland with semi-natural characteristics in the short term because of the legacy of species and features they contain. Both of these options may involve some new planting or natural regeneration within or around the sites concerned.

Creating new woodland is essential for the longer-term survival of many species and habitats, but in the short term is more limited in its effectiveness because it will take time to provide suitable habitat space for any species under threat. Which of the immediate strategies of buffering or expansion is more effective will depend on the size and species-richness of the existing woodland to be enhanced, whether it contains important specialist species, and the density, type and configuration of the surrounding woodland habitat. Improving general landscape connectivity by linking networks will be important in the longer term. In practice, the strategy adopted will depend on what funding sources are available and the willingness of the landowner to undertake woodland creation. Buffering and linking existing woods (the latter through expanding boundaries and corridors such as hedgerows, and less intensive use of intervening land) may be more suited to agri-environment schemes and small ownerships; whereas using large blocks of new woodland to expand habitats and to reinforce networks may be more feasible for large landowners and conservation trusts, aided by Forestry Commission grant schemes.

PART TWO
WOODLAND CREATION PRACTICE

6 PLANNING A WOODLAND CREATION PROJECT

Introduction

This chapter provides guidance on landscape and ecological issues which affect the planning of new native woodland creation schemes. Planning requires some understanding of the likely impact that new woodland will have on the character of the local landscape (see Section 5.1) and the wildlife already present on the site. The steps necessary to achieve this are outlined in Sections 6.1 and 6.2 of this chapter. Decisions must then be made on the type of woodland most suited to the site, guided to some extent by the soil type and by the composition of semi-natural woodland communities in the local landscape, which can provide useful 'reference sites' (Sections 6.3 and 6.4). Information on the ecology of the site can then be reviewed and the assessment completed (Section 6.5). If the new woodland is likely to have a significant impact on the environment, consent may be required from the Forestry Commission, under the Environmental Impact Assessment (Forestry) Regulations (Section 6.6).

The level of detail in an assessment of landscape character will depend to some extent on the scale of the project. Large scale woodland creation projects, such as the Woodland Trust's Victory Wood in Kent, may require a new landscape character assessment (LCA). In such cases, Natural England's *Landscape Character Assessment Guidance for England and Scotland* (Swanwick, 2002) may be helpful, and is available on the internet. A similar assessment may be required for small scale planting, if the exact site has yet to be determined.

If a relatively small area of woodland is to be created on a predetermined site, a detailed assessment of landscape character may be unnecessary, although the historic environment and landscape should still be considered. In this case the planning process could effectively start with an assessment of biodiversity on the proposed woodland creation site and its environs (Section 6.2).

Whatever the extent of survey work undertaken, individuals should be responsible for their own health and safety, and should adhere to risk assessments completed prior to the commencement of any field work.

6.1 Assessing landscape character

6.1.1 Published information on local landscape character

National sources of information

An overview of the key characteristics and character of the wider landscape is a good place to start. In England, this information is included in Natural England's National Character Area (NCA) assessments (Section 5.1.1). NCAs also describe how the area is changing and how future changes might be managed. A further useful source of information is Natural England's Environmental Stewardship, an agri-environment scheme providing funding to land managers who deliver effective environmental management on their land. The Higher Level Stewardship (HLS) Target Area Statements and Theme Statements describe priorities for HLS schemes. Target Area Statements cover high priority areas across England, and indicate the land management activities viewed as a priority in that particular area. The relevant Natural England 'Natural Area Profile' (NAP) should also be consulted, as NAPs focus more on the wildlife and natural features of the area, and identify objectives for these; useful information for woodland creation schemes. They can be found by following the conservation and biodiversity links on Natural England's website. Additional information can be found in NAPs on geology and woodland communities present, although these are not mapped and therefore do not preclude the need for field surveys.

In Wales, the National Landscape Character Map for Wales, together with the appropriate regional LCA (Section 5.1.2), includes similar information to the English NCAs. These can be found on the Countryside Council for Wales (CCW) website. Scotland also has a series of 30 comprehensive LCA reports which provide invaluable information for the purposes of woodland creation, available on the Scottish Natural Heritage (SNH) website. More up to date LCAs can be

An assessment of the character of Pevensey Levels indicates that woodland planting would be detrimental.

accessed from SNH in the form of 21 Natural Heritage Futures, although these provide less detail than the original Scottish LCAs. The SNH database of 'Areas of search for Wildland' (Section 5.1.3) should also be consulted to check whether the proposed locality for woodland creation falls within one of these areas.

Local sources of information

Natural England's 'Database of Landscape Character Assessments' in England provides local LCA information designed for use in planning, biodiversity action, targeting of agri-environment schemes and so on. The database is updated regularly by the LCA community and can be found on the associated Landscape Character Network website. It should be consulted at the outset, although not all local LCAs are listed and further web searches may be necessary. However, for some areas the search may reveal more published local LCAs than the researcher can realistically cope with. Nevertheless, these local LCAs address similar topics to the NCAs and NAPs, but are usually more relevant as they focus at a local scale. In Wales, some local authorities have prepared their own LCAs, so web searches for these should be undertaken in the local area.

Maps

A good map of the area – preferably an Ordnance Survey (OS) 1:10,000 – is essential, both for planning visits and surveying. Portions of OS 1:25,000 maps can be viewed on the OS website. In England, 1:10,000 scale maps can be viewed on the Government's web-based interactive map 'Multi-Agency Geographic Information for the Countryside' (MAGIC). Aerial photographs show how landscape cover fits with topography, land use and settlement; the patterns made by trees, fields, hedges and woods; and how these patterns change across an area. This evidence will support decisions on integrating new woodland into existing patterns of fields, hedgerows and other features. Aerial photographs may be viewed on a number of websites, of which Google Earth is one of the most up to date.

Historic landscape and archaeological assessment

New native woodland should not be planted without some reference to the historic environment and landscape. This should ensure that the historic character of the landscape is protected, and not adversely affected by any tree planting. It is important that both above and below ground archaeological sites are protected, many of which are unrecorded. Features which might be present on a site include:

- above-ground features such as earthworks, prehistoric humps or hollows, historic field systems identified by historic extant boundaries and earthworks, settlements of all periods
- industrial sites of all periods; wetland sites which preserve palaeo-archaeological remains such as pollen, invertebrate macrofossils, etc.
- below-ground features such as archaeological sites identified by soil and crop marks on aerial photographs; settlements of all periods; industrial features of all periods; prehistoric field systems

- historic routeways such as sunken lanes and relict boundaries with remnant features such as trees, earthbanks or collapsed stone walls
- historic buildings of varying uses
- parkland and designed landscapes.

In Scotland, environmental assessment and consultation processes ensure that woodland creation respects archaeological features and historic and designed landscapes. If planning permission is required for woodland creation in England, applications would be viewed by a county archaeologist and checked against the county Historic Environment Record; in Wales, one of the four regional Historic Environment Records would be consulted. For larger woodland creation schemes, accredited experts may be engaged to undertake the necessary desk study and field survey. A surveyor should follow methodology in English Heritage's *Understanding the archaeology of landscapes – a guide to good recording practice* (English Heritage, 2007).

Old hollow way lined with ancient hornbeam coppice on the High Weald near Hempsted Forest.

Wood bank and ditch on the edge of Park Wood, near Robertsbridge in the Sussex High Weald.

English Heritage guidelines include different levels of survey which depend on the nature of the site and the resources and time available. In many cases involving woodland creation, a non-intensive survey would be appropriate, combining a desk-based assessment of known records together with field visits, equivalent to level 2 of the English Heritage guidelines.

Initially, a desk study may be undertaken, utilising sources of information such as:

- Historic Environment Record (formerly the Sites and Monuments Record)
- county Historic Landscape Characterisation map and documents
- historical maps; pre-OS, such as tithe maps, estate maps and enclosure awards
- aerial photographs; sources include the National Monuments Record and the Unit for Landscape Modelling, and county councils
- County Records Offices
- archive material to trace past land use, such as manorial records, terriers and deeds.

The resulting report should present an historical perspective of the landscape; an outline of the historic or archaeological character of the site, including a summary of previous studies in the area; a site inventory and maps of the area; and a comprehensive list of features. It should also include management recommendations for the conservation of any archaeological features found, which can be combined with information from the landscape evaluation to determine the likely overall impact of tree planting on the site (Section 6.5). Finally, it is important when considering potential sites for woodland creation to understand where woodland has been lost in the past and what form it took, and if possible, how it was managed.

Woodland habitat network maps

Woodland habitat network maps based on the Forestry Commission's BEETLE model have been produced for Wales, Scotland and parts of England (see Section 4.4.2). One of their uses is to improve woodland connectivity through the identification of target areas for woodland creation, although all require some degree of ground truthing. If these have been produced for the area in question, they should certainly be consulted at an early stage, not only to inform decisions on woodland location, but also with respect to planting grants for new native woodland (see Section 6.7). In Wales, these can be obtained from CCW and its partners, including the Forestry Commission, who use the maps as one criterion for their Welsh grant schemes. In Scotland the forest habitat network maps can be accessed from Scottish Natural Heritage and the Forestry Commission. In South West England, woodland habitat network maps are available for key areas from the Forestry Commission Regional Office. Other Forestry Commission Regions in England follow local landscape guidelines to varying extents, and some have targeted areas for

Woodland creation is not always the best option – having been cleared of conifers, this site is being restored to heathland.

woodland creation based on simpler mapping systems. The local Regional Office should be consulted to see what resources are currently available for that area.

6.1.2 Undertaking a landscape evaluation

Whatever the scale of woodland creation, it will be necessary to undertake some fieldwork to examine the ecological characteristics of the wider landscape, and the proposed woodland creation site itself. For larger areas of woodland creation, of the order of 50 ha or more, a local Landscape Character Assessment (LCA) may be required to guide the location and design of the planting. The information collected can be reviewed alongside published landscape character assessments to assess the overall impact of the proposed woodland creation scheme (Table 6.1). The creation of relatively small patches of new woodland may also benefit from a LCA, if the planting site has yet to be chosen. If existing woodland habitat network maps are being consulted, some ground truthing will be needed to reassess woodland characteristics and also the presence of other semi-natural habitat and features not included, such as ancient hedgerows.

Preparing the local landscape description – Lamberhurst Farm, a worked example

The ground where woodland creation is proposed should be walked beforehand to analyse the landscape, using a field survey sheet, similar to that illustrated in *'Landscape Character Assessment Guidance for England and Scotland'* (Swanwick, 2002). A series of photographs and/or sketch maps, some made from a distance, will provide an invaluable aid to identifying the key landscape characteristics of the area (Figure 6.1a).

For larger scale woodland creation schemes, we illustrate the process with a series of sketches of Lamberhurst Farm in Kent, the site for Victory Wood, an area of new native woodland created by the Woodland Trust. The site comprised 140 ha of arable land underlain by London Clay, and bordered on two sides by ancient woodland; to the east by Ellenden Wood, and along the south western boundary by Blean Wood. Consultation of *The Landscape Assessment of Kent* (Kent County Council, 2004) showed that Lamberhurst Farm straddles the border of two local character areas, the Blean and the Eastern Fruit Belt. The Blean is characterised by a domed landscape of densely wooded, rounded hill tops, with perimeter areas cleared for agriculture. In contrast, the Eastern Fruit Belt represents undulating farmland, characterised by woodland blocks, orchards, shelterbelts and large pockets of arable land, pasture and horticulture. Consequently it was necessary to check and refine any conclusions drawn from these contrasting published descriptions.

Table 6.1 Assessing the impact of new native woodland on local landscape character

	High potential	**Issues of concern**
Landscape character assessment	• Woodland creation identified as a priority in local LCA(s) • Wooded or historically wooded landscape • Landscape strengthened by planting • Ancient woodland close by • Woodland with access will benefit local communities	• Woodland creation not a priority in local LCAs • Woodland not a feature of the local landscape • Adjoining designated areas will not benefit from, or will be harmed by woodland creation • Area better suited to creation of other habitats, such as heathland
Historic Landscape Character	• Historic landscape character not adversely affected by woodland creation • No historic or archaeological features would be adversely affected by woodland creation	• Adverse effects on historic landscape character, including parkland and designed landscapes • Archaeological features within the site or beyond the boundaries adversely affected, e.g. through changes in water tables following planting
Contribution to habitat networks	• New woodland contributes to an ecological network • New woodland buffers ancient woodland and/or woodland SSSI • New woodland open space contributes to grassland habitat network	• New woodland makes no contribution to an ecological network, or interrupts existing network • Site too isolated to significantly benefit wildlife in the local landscape • Woodland planting would disrupt species dispersal from other habitats
Potential woodland creation site	• Area for planting >5 ha • Opportunity for extensive ride network and creation of open area habitat	• Site might be better used to create other habitat such as grassland • Compaction, waterlogging or drainage problems (excluding wet woodland)

Beyond the settlements, the hillside (Lamberhurst Farm) in the far distance will be entirely wooded, linking the two blocks of ancient woodland to left and right (see also Figure 6.1).

The sketches and photographs taken in the field confirmed these features and allowed a boundary to be drawn between the wooded landscape typical of the Blean, and the more agricultural landscape of the Eastern Fruit Belt (Figure 6.1a). The large arable fields which lie within the boundaries of Lamberhurst Farm, separated mainly by fence lines and thin strips of tall herb vegetation, contrast markedly with these landscape profiles.

Historic maps of the area dating back to the late 18th century show a much stronger, less fragmented landscape, with an area of woodland known as North Blean Wood linking Ellenden Wood and Blean Wood. North Blean Wood extended from the southern boundary of Lamberhurst Farm, over the ridge and on to the low lying area to the north (Figure 6.1b). These maps also show that the large arable field in the northern part of the site was formerly divided into much smaller fields.

Based on the historical evidence and landscape profiles for the area, it is possible to suggest new areas of woodland creation and other habitat restoration to strengthen the local landscape character (Figure 6.1c and 6.2). When reviewed alongside published landscape character assessments for the area, it is clear that woodland creation will have a very positive impact on the landscape (Table 6.2).

Table 6.2 Summary of the main landscape character criteria for Lamberhurst Farm in Kent, which support the planting of Victory Wood.

	Positive aspects	Issues of concern
Landscape character assessment	• Woodland creation identified as a priority in local LCA(s) • Heavily wooded landscape • Open access will benefit local communities	• No major issues of concern
Historic Landscape Character	• Prehistoric communities likely to have used the area • Little of the medieval landscape survives • Opportunity to restore historical woodland cover and system of small fields/hedges • Historical evolution of the site should be presented to visitors through interpretation displays	• Archaeological and cultural aspects of the area should not be subsumed by the landscape character and ecological aspects of the site
Contribution to habitat networks	• New woodland contributes to a habitat network by restoring a link between Blean Wood and Ellenden Wood • New woodland provides buffer and habitat for colonisation from adjacent woods • Ample open space provides an opportunity for species-rich grassland creation	• No unimproved grassland in the area to support natural colonisation
Potential woodland creation site	• Large area for creating woodland with an extensive network of rides and glades • Large area for creating species-rich grassland	• Heavy clay soils may cause problems with tree establishment in places

Figure 6.1 Sketch maps drawn to identify key characteristics of Lamberhurst Farm and the wider landscape, viewed from the north west.

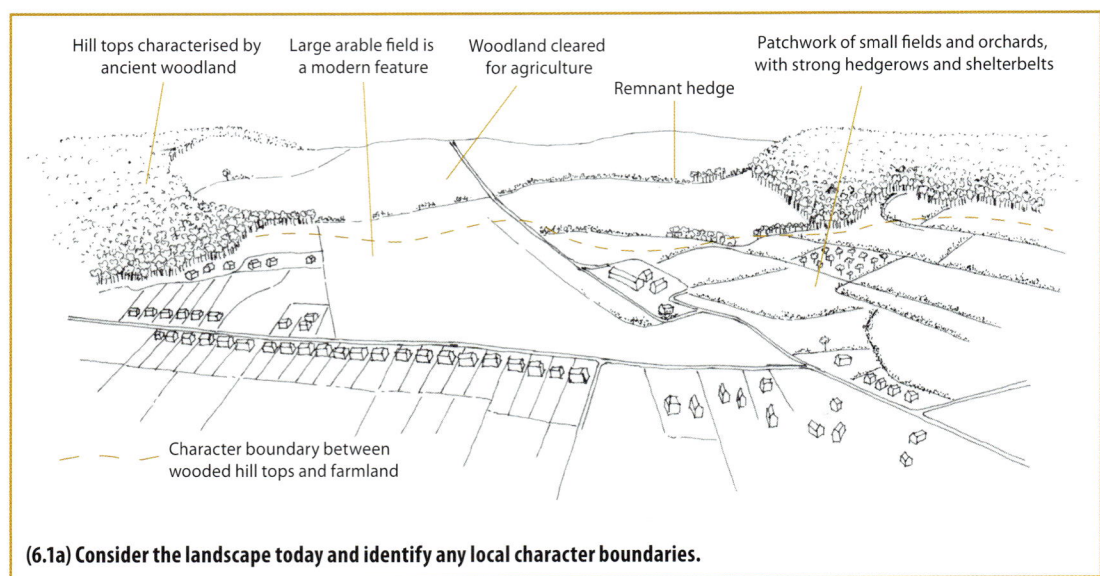

(6.1a) Consider the landscape today and identify any local character boundaries.

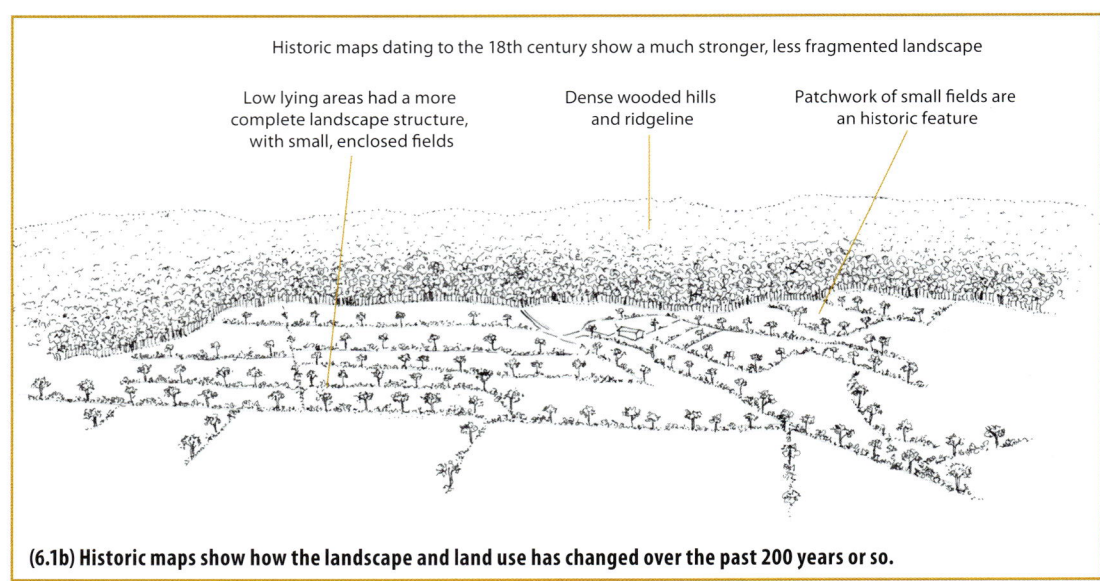

(6.1b) Historic maps show how the landscape and land use has changed over the past 200 years or so.

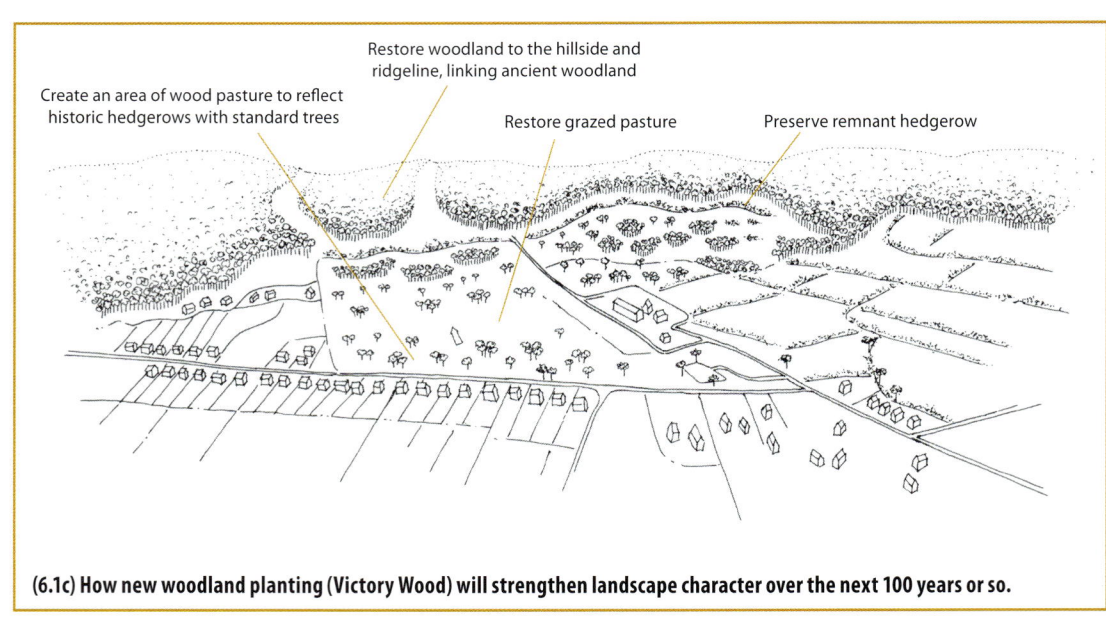

(6.1c) How new woodland planting (Victory Wood) will strengthen landscape character over the next 100 years or so.

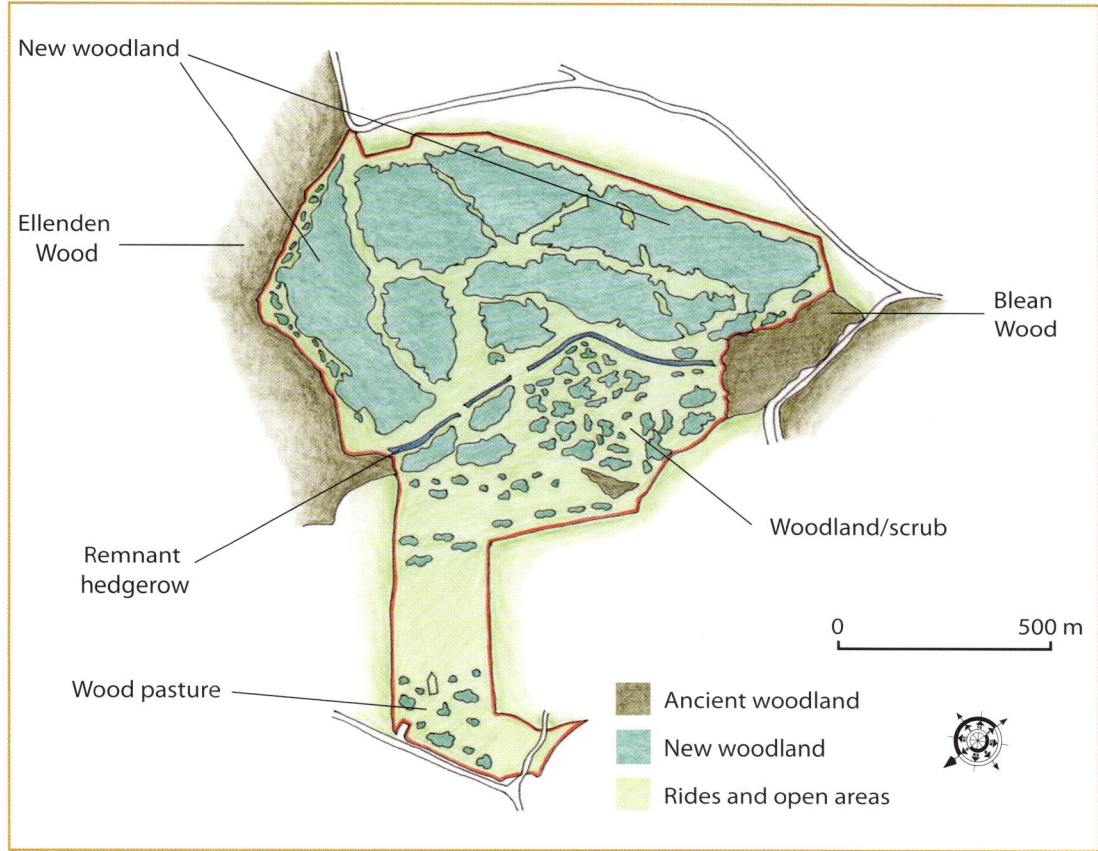

Figure 6.2 Sketch map of Lamberhurst Farm, the site of Victory Wood; showing the location of new woodland, scrub, rides and open areas.
© Crown copyright and/or database right. All rights reserved. Licence number 100049759.

6.2 Biodiversity of the proposed woodland creation site and its environs

It is essential that any woodland creation scheme does not disturb wildlife of conservation concern, either on the proposed site or in the immediate vicinity. It is also important to establish that woodland is the most appropriate habitat for the site. For example, agricultural sites which have not been improved, or which are immediately adjacent to unimproved grassland or heathland might be better restored to this habitat, rather than woodland.

6.2.1 European Protected Species

It is important to establish at an early stage whether there are any European Protected Species in the proximity of the proposed woodland creation site(s). These are species protected under Annex IV of the EC Directive on the Conservation of Natural Habitats and Wild Fauna and Flora (92/43/EEC). In Britain, this directive is implemented through the Habitat Regulations 1994 (as amended in 2007, 2008/9), and all listed species have full protection under the Wildlife and Countryside Act 1981 (as amended). Species include: all British bats; wild cat; dormouse; otter; great crested newt; natterjack toad; sand lizard; smooth snake; large blue butterfly; and a number of very rare plants including early gentian; marsh saxifrage; and Killarney fern. In Britain, any development that adversely affects any European Protected Species will require a special Development Licence, issued by Defra. 'Development' in this context is a broad term, including any project which 'carries out operations on, over or under land', or involves the 'material change in use of land'. If European Protected Species are present at or near the planting site a thorough evaluation will need to be made of any disturbance likely to be caused.

The local Biodiversity Records Centre may be able to help with this, or it may be necessary to employ an ecological consultant who would be also responsible for any licence applications. More details and an up to date list of European Protected Species can be obtained from the Defra or Natural England websites. The critical question to ask is whether the development – in this case the management operations required for woodland creation – is likely to have any impact on European Protected Species. Examples include disturbance to: areas of scrub inhabited by dormouse; trees with cavities or splits, especially older trees and ash, beech, oak, sycamore and Scots pine used by bats; or land within a few hundred metres of a great crested newt breeding pond, particularly during hibernation time when newts can be found in refugia in dense undergrowth, under turf or

The presence of any European Protected Species such as the dormouse in the proposed woodland creation site must be established.

rocks, and in mammal burrows. If any disturbance is possible, further details on European Protected Species licences can be obtained from the Forestry Commission website.

6.2.2 Undertaking a Phase 1 habitat survey

A number of general habitat survey methods have been published, but the most widely used technique is the rapid Phase 1 habitat survey (Joint Nature Conservation Committee, 2007b). Some more sophisticated methods, such as the Integrated Habitat System originally developed by the Somerset Environmental Records Centre, integrate Phase 1 with existing classifications in use in the UK, including Biodiversity Broad Habitat Types and the European CORINE and EUNIS classifications (Section 1.2).

Based principally on vegetation structure, with topographic and substrate features, Phase 1 gives a broad picture of areas that might be of conservation importance, which can be followed up in more detailed surveys. The output is a coloured, digital map that can be easily interrogated and interpreted. Surveys are supported by a comprehensive field manual (Joint Nature Conservation Committee, 2007b). Another very useful source of information is the *Farm Environment Plan Features Manual* (Natural England, 2008) which was designed to help farmers and land managers appraise the environmental value of land for Defra's agri-environment schemes. The Phase 1 habitat survey may constitute a new survey or it may be used to ground truth woodland habitat network maps where available.

Fieldwork

The Phase 1 habitat classification and its associated field survey is a relatively simple, standardised technique which maps semi-natural communities and other wildlife habitat. Additional habitat codes have been created for the *Phase 1 Habitat Survey of Wales*. Even if Phase 1 survey data is available for a site, it may be out of date and will not contain the target notes of an Extended Phase 1 habitat survey (see below) or highlight the value of different habitats for different communities.

Site topography and elevation are recorded, together with the 10 structural habitat categories, which include woodland and scrub, grassland and marsh, and heathland. Further qualitative descriptions may be made, for example relating to substrate type (acid, neutral or basic) or wetness (wet, dry) and to management status (improved, unimproved). Within these broad categories are a further 155 more specific habitat types, each with its own name and alpha-numeric code. These are still fairly general and do not distinguish vegetation at the community level, for example recognising only broadleaved, coniferous and mixed woodland types, but vegetation structure such as high forest, coppice, linear woodland and grassland is included. The final output is usually a habitat map identifying habitats and areas of importance for flora and fauna.

Target notes are recorded for each semi-natural area, including detail such as the management type, the dominant species, damage to the site, etc. Target notes are also used to record information on sites too small to map. The aim is to make a preliminary assessment of the nature conservation value of the site, providing enough background for more detailed surveys, defining the vegetation more precisely in terms of the plant communities present (e.g. as defined by the National Vegetation Classification). The choice of which areas to target-note is subjective and depends on the time available, but the larger *interesting* areas with wildlife potential are usually detailed. It is also important to target-note habitats that are damaged or are known to have been destroyed.

When the area has been mapped, the information is transferred by hand or digitally to a base map and a coloured fair copy produced. These in turn can be overlain on to geological, soil or topographic maps for interpretation and planning purposes. At the same time accurate area measurements of all habitats within the region are provided for future reference. There are 'grey areas' in the methodology and inconsistencies when comparing practices by different surveyors and counties. Grassland is a particularly difficult area, for example distinguishing between semi-improved neutral grassland (pastures subject to fertilisation, herbicide treatments, intensive grazing or drainage), improved grassland (lacking in broadleaved herbs) and amenity grassland.

Extended Phase 1 habitat survey

Phase 1 surveys identify the main structural habitat types, and highlight areas which might be affected by any proposed change of land-use such as a woodland creation scheme. The Extended Phase 1 habitat survey methodology was a modification made by the Institute of Environmental Assessment (IEA; now the Institute of Environmental Management and Assessment) (1995) to provide a record of habitats which are ecologically important. This is necessary because Phase 1 botanical surveys do not highlight habitats of value, or potential value to other wildlife which may otherwise be overlooked, for example:

- veteran trees
- holes and loose bark for bats in mature trees
- bare ground
- sunny banks
- deadwood
- fungi
- habitat boundaries
- ponds, streams and seepages
- habitats of low botanical interest which support species-rich invertebrate communities.

This agricultural landscape at Theydon Bois in Essex was surveyed before a new native woodland creation scheme was planned.

Stream bordering the site of a new native woodland creation scheme in Essex, which was described in an Extended Phase 1 habitat survey.

It is important to ensure that such habitats are protected and provided with a sufficient buffer area to avoid damage. The survey may include targeted searches for signs of protected species.

6.2.3 Wildlife surveys

Relatively simple baseline surveys of the main groups of flora and fauna may be all that is necessary to establish the wildlife value of a site and its immediate surroundings and to inform future management. For larger sites, where there is interest in monitoring the changing status of the flora and fauna over a number of years, more sophisticated methods may be needed, and advice should be sought from professional ecologists or conservation organisations such as the British Trust for Ornithology (BTO) or Butterfly Conservation.

LEFT **Veteran beech tree highlighted in an Extended Phase 1 habitat survey.**

RIGHT **Ancient hornbeam pollards would feature in an Extended Phase 1 habitat survey.**

Before undertaking field surveys of wildlife, local naturalists, county Biodiversity Records Centres and conservation organisations (e.g. the Botanical Society of the British Isles, the Bat Conservation Trust, and Butterfly Conservation) should be consulted for records of species of conservation concern. These include UK BAP priority species, Red Data species, Nationally Notable species or any species protected under Schedule 5 of the Wildlife and Countryside Act (1981). The National Biodiversity Network Gateway contains a vast amount of biological data from a wide range of sources and provides national and regional species distribution maps, and allows searches for all species recorded in SSSIs and 10-km squares; a useful starting point when considering the conservation value of an area.

Vegetation of potential woodland creation sites

The existing vegetation on any prospective woodland creation site and its environs must be considered. For arable land, sophisticated survey techniques may not always be necessary, unless rare or endangered plants such as cornfield annuals are present; or remnants of unimproved grassland remain along field margins. In other areas, for example in the uplands, more extensive semi-natural grassland, heathland or marshy communities might be present. If this is the case, a National Vegetation Classification (NVC) survey is suggested, which is widely accepted as a robust classification of semi-natural vegetation in the British Isles. For the purposes of this exercise, we suggest a minimalist approach to data collection such as the following:

1. First identify an homogeneous area within the site for survey.
2. Set up the first of three 2 x 2 m quadrats and record the species present and their percentage cover. The abundance of each species can be recorded using percentage cover or the Domin scale; note any other species present in the environs.
3. Repeat for the remaining quadrats spread evenly around the area.
4. If in other homogeneous areas different community types are present, repeat the process for each.

Domin scale	Vegetation cover
10	91–100 % cover
9	76–90 % cover
8	51–75 % cover
7	34–50 % cover
6	26–33 % cover
5	11–25 % cover
4	4–10 % cover
3	<4% cover with many individuals
2	<4% cover with several individuals
1	<4% cover with few individuals
+	1 individual, with no measurable cover

Use the data collected to determine the most appropriate NVC community classification, referring to the keys given in Rodwell (1991 *et seq*). Computer programs are also available to calculate the 'goodness of fit' of data collected from quadrats to the expected species composition of semi-natural woodland communities and sub-communities recognised by the NVC. One such program, 'Tablefit' (Hill, 1996), is freely available from the Centre for Ecology and Hydrology.

Hedgerows

Hedgerows might be included if they are likely to be affected by woodland creation, for example by shading. A hedgerow is defined as any boundary line of trees and shrubs over 20 m long and less than 5 m wide at the base, provided that at one time the cover was more or less continuous (Defra, 2007b). An ancient or species-rich hedgerow is classified as one where a minimum of five woody species (four in northern and eastern England, Scotland and upland areas of Wales) are present in a 30 m length; these may include both native and species naturalised prior to 1500 AD.

For the purposes of informing woodland creation schemes, survey a 30 m length of hedgerow, starting 30 m in from one end of the hedge. If this section is particularly gappy, a more continuous section should be selected. All woody species present in the hedgerow should then be identified, and the percentage cover recorded by visual assessment. Where woodland herbs still survive, 2 x 2 m or 2 x 1 m quadrats may be located under the hedgerow canopy 10 and 20 m along the transect, and the abundance of ground cover species recorded using the Domin scale above. Alternatively, a list of woodland species could be compiled along the length of the hedgerow.

Hedgerows may be surveyed for a range of other purposes, including: identification of hedgerows of conservation value for wildlife; assessing condition attributes for hedgerow BAP targets; and cultural or historical importance. In these cases, a large amount of additional information would be required, and comprehensive guidelines on hedgerow surveys are included in Defra's *Hedgerow Survey Handbook* (Defra, 2007b).

Bird surveys

Bird surveys should be undertaken if there is any prospect that the proposed woodland creation site might support rare or uncommon birds. Birds can also be used as biodiversity indicators both at the local and landscape scale. The abundance of insectivorous birds e.g. warblers is directly related to the abundance of invertebrate prey and the vegetation structure. However, in most cases, surveys may only assess whether the habitat supports scarce breeding birds such as:

- declining farmland birds, including skylark, corn bunting, tree sparrow and grey partridge
- wet meadows and any lowland or upland habitat which might support breeding waders such as lapwing and redshank.

Other vulnerable habitat includes heathland and montane areas over 600 m. In exceptional cases, desk studies might indicate that species on Schedule 1 of the Wildlife and Countryside Act (1981) or Annex 1 of the EC Birds Directive are breeding, or that the woodland creation site is in close proximity to known populations of these species. A winter bird survey can also be considered if the area might include important feeding or roosting habitat for waterfowl or raptors, etc.

Before undertaking a bird survey, the surveyor should be familiar with UK legislation protecting Britain's flora and fauna, which protects all wild birds, their nests and eggs by law, with limited exceptions. Nesting is considered to have started as soon as the first twig is positioned. Some rare species are given special protection; in Britain it is a criminal offence to disturb, at or near the nest, a species on Schedule 1 of the Act. In Scotland it is also an offence to disturb capercaillie and ruff at their leks. For more detailed information it is advisable to consult the Act itself.

Various survey methods might be considered (Hill *et al.*, 2005), although in many cases, surveys based on the British Trust for Ornithology's (BTO) Breeding Bird Survey may be most appropriate. This is a national project aimed at monitoring changes in breeding populations of widespread bird species across the UK. Typically, two visits are made to the site; the first between early April and mid-May, to coincide with the main period of breeding activity of resident birds, although this may be later in the north. The second visit should be made between mid-May and late June, during the main breeding period for migrant birds, which again will vary depending on the location. Surveys are carried out early in the morning, avoiding poor weather conditions (heavy rain or strong winds), when notes are made of all species heard and seen along a predetermined transect. Further details and other survey methods such as the Common Bird Census can be obtained from the BTO website. Additional information on rare and declining farmland birds can be found on the RSPB 'Birds on your farm' web pages. Other survey methods are summarised in the Joint Nature Conservation Committee's (JNCC) *Common Standards Monitoring Guidance for Birds* (2004) which can be downloaded from the JNCC website.

Grey partridge – a declining farmland bird which may be found during the survey of a prospective woodland creation site on agricultural land.

Invertebrate surveys

Broad-ranging invertebrate surveys are likely to be very costly and time-consuming, consequently in most cases it is more practical to identify habitat of high invertebrate biodiversity value. Natural England's Features Assessments (Natural England, 2008) provide useful guidance: if four or more of the following features are present, the site is likely to have a high potential for invertebrates:

- some species-rich semi-natural vegetation
- abundant seed or flower production throughout the year
- good structural variation within the vegetation
- patches of scrub; ancient trees; natural springs and flushes; or other water bodies
- variable topography or near vertical areas of exposed soil
- free-draining soils
- frequent patches of bare ground
- anthills
- fibrous dung attractive to beetles
- dry stone walls.

In addition, selected groups such as butterflies or hoverflies may be chosen as 'indicators' of the diversity of other species in the community, and of habitat health, providing they are expertly surveyed using recognised transect methods. Butterflies are the easiest invertebrates to survey: they are highly visible and most are relatively easy to identify. The requirement of adults for sunny rides and abundant flowers for nectaring can be indicative of both the structural quality of open areas, and potential feeding sources for a range of other invertebrates. The diversity of species and the presence of colonies will also give some indication about the quality of existing vegetation in surrounding open areas.

For sites with little suitable habitat for butterflies, such as arable land lacking conservation field margins; or improved, reseeded pasture, it may be sufficient to visit the site on four occasions during the flight season and note the species present. Provisionally, plan to visit in early to mid May; the first two weeks of June; mid to late July; and mid August, but if necessary, modify the schedule to encompass the flight periods of all possible butterflies and second broods.

If there is any promising semi-natural habitat on the site, consider monitoring butterflies using a more formalised site transect method, again based on four, evenly-spaced visits during the flight season (see above) noting species and numbers. A route or transect should be identified which includes the most promising habitat. Transect walks are usually carried out between 11.00 and 16.00 hrs in suitable weather conditions for butterfly activity: dry and sunny (at least 60% sunshine); no more than a moderate breeze (wind speed less than Beaufort Scale 5); at least 13°C in sunny conditions or 17°C if overcast. Strictly, only butterflies occurring within a 5 m line transect are recorded, up to 5 m ahead of the recorder. This will allow data to be compared with other years, but for assessing the conservation value of a site, butterflies identified outside the transect should also be recorded. Monitoring which is to be repeated year-on-year will benefit from more frequent visits; every two weeks, particularly during the period of peak activity from late June to mid August.

Mammal surveys

If species of conservation concern are known to be present on or adjacent to the site, then surveys should be undertaken. These include UK BAP priority species such as dormouse, harvest mouse, pine marten and wild cat; species protected under Schedule 5 and/or 6 of the Wildlife and Countryside Act (1981); the EC Directive and the Bern Convention. If protected species are suspected, then advice from the statutory conservation agency must be sought prior to undertaking surveys appropriate to the species concerned (for a summary, see Institute of Environmental Assessment, 1995). The services of a professional ecologist will almost certainly be required if surveys are necessary.

Amphibian and reptile surveys

Six reptiles and seven amphibians are native to Britain and all are protected to varying degrees. Four species have European Protected Species status, and are also UK BAP priority species. Of these, the natterjack toad, sand lizard and smooth snake are rare; the species most likely to be encountered in woodland creation schemes is the great crested newt. The other British reptiles (viviparous lizard, slow-worm, grass snake and adder), together with the common toad, have

The common toad (left) and adder (right) are both UK BAP priority species which may be present on prospective woodland creation sites.

undergone declines in status in recent years and are now UK BAP priority species. Consequently, these species should also be considered in any change of land use.

Great crested newts are widely distributed in England, and are also found in parts of Scotland and Wales. The NBN gateway is a useful starting point to gather information on local populations, although absence of records does not mean that the species is not present in the area. The Local Biodiversity Records Centre can be contacted, or the local amphibian and reptile group. If there are breeding ponds within 250 m of the site, newts will use the surrounding area for foraging, dispersal, resting and hibernation, and a survey may need to be commissioned. If nearby ponds are accessible, a herpetologist may survey them to assess their suitability for great crested newts.

Widespread reptiles are found in a range of habitats, from heaths and rough grassland to brownfield sites and woodland edge, although they are less abundant in intensively farmed landscapes and upland areas. Activities which could harm reptiles include: land clearance; cutting vegetation to a low height; and removal of wood piles or other debris. Where their presence is suspected, and they are likely to suffer from operations involved with site preparation or tree planting, surveys based on current best practice should be undertaken by professional ecologists, with a view to implementing a reptile mitigation programme if necessary. Reptile activity is highly seasonal; animals hibernate between October and March, and their activity during the summer months is dependent on the weather. Reptiles may even go into partial hibernation in prolonged periods of hot weather. Consequently reptile surveys should be considered well in advance of any land development. For further information, the *Herpetofauna Workers Manual* (Gent and Gibson, 2003) provides comprehensive guidance to all aspects of reptile and amphibian conservation and management, including site assessment, species translocation and the law. Natural England's *Reptiles: guidelines for developers* (English Nature, 2004) should also be consulted.

6.3 Geology and soils of the proposed woodland creation site

6.3.1 Published information on local geology and soils

The next step is to locate information on geology and soil types in the local landscape. This is particularly important to guide the eventual design and choice of species for the new woodland. Geological maps are valuable for predicting soil types, but only if they show drift deposits as well as solid geology, as whichever is at the surface forms the soil parent material – indeed, geological maps form the basis of many soil maps and are available at scales of 1:63,360 or in greater detail for some parts of the country. Geological information, as maps or digital downloads, can be obtained from the British Geological Survey, held by the Natural Environment Research Council.

Soils information was originally produced by two separate agencies, the Soil Survey of England and Wales and the Soil Survey of Scotland. For England and Wales, the Land Information System, hosted by the National Soils Resources Institute at Cranfield University, is an environmental information system containing soil and soil-related information. It provides a range of services, including site-specific soils information with maps, soil descriptions and the relation between soils and the environment. A charge is made for the 1:250,000 scale digital National Soil Map and other services. The 1:250,000 maps show the boundaries of polygons of different soil Associations, listing the main soil type or group to which it belongs, as well as brief details of soil characteristics and typical land usage. For full descriptions of the characteristics and properties of each soil Association (there are 99 in South East England alone) it is necessary to access the accompanying regional Bulletins: although even here the smallest soil units, the soil Series, are not fully described.

The precision improves with more comprehensive soil surveys, based on detailed field profile descriptions that can show soil units at the Series level and the soil boundaries at an individual field scale. These maps are produced at a smaller scale, mainly 1:25,000 or even at 1:10,000, but are few and far between: only a handful of 10x10 km sheets are available for each county, and in some counties only one. In addition to the Soil Survey of England and Wales, there is a separate classification for Scotland, the information for which is held at the Macaulay Land Use Research Institute. The Forestry Commission has produced its own soil classification system which is particularly applicable to the uplands and forestry plantations (Pyatt, 1982; Kennedy, 2002).

In England, the Government's web-based interactive map (MAGIC) includes a 'Soilscapes' option at a scale of 1:250,000, but this is only indicative of generic soil types across a region and more detailed information will be required to aid woodland design.

6.3.2 Commissioning a soil survey

Soil surveys are used to determine whether sites are suitable for planting trees, and if so, to help select appropriate species mixes and to plan site preparation. The digital National Soils Map indicates general soil types and hydrological properties, but laboratory-based analyses are required to determine pH, phosphorus index and other measures of soil nutrients.

After taking account of existing geological or soil maps, a detailed soil survey involves traversing the area and sampling the nature of the soil at intervals using auger borings and digging occasional inspection pits. Depending on the complexity of the site, a density of five

Useful information on soils can be gained by digging a small soil pit (left) or examining the root plates of fallen trees (below).

samples per hectare is usually sufficient for a very detailed survey at a scale of 1:2,500 and for areas up to 20 ha, which might take an experienced surveyor 2–3 days to complete. For larger areas and where less detailed information is needed, this could be reduced to perhaps one sample per hectare. At each sample location a note is made of the colour, texture and stoniness of the soil, together with a record of the soil layers or horizons present, up to a depth of one metre. Rooting density and depth is also noted, as in some soils the roots are killed off by a lack of oxygen if the lower profile is waterlogged. Such soils have gleyed horizons, where the iron compounds in the soil are reduced (deoxygenated), turning them grey or greenish in colour. If there is seasonal waterlogging, the upper parts of the profile become oxygenated as they dry out during the growing season and the iron compounds change to red and orange colours, causing a characteristic grey/orange mottling at the transition zone.

The type of humus at the soil surface is also a good indicator of fertility: on very acid, infertile soils the litter layer breaks down very slowly, and often forms a thick (>5 cm) deposit in recognisable layers representing varying states of decay – known as mor humus. Mull humus, on the other hand, is much thinner and forms over more fertile, less acid soils when there is a rapid turnover of litter. Moder humus types are intermediate. Altogether, the descriptive methodology outlined above should enable the surveyor to classify and map soil units to a reference soil Series.

The soil can be further tested quantitatively by removing soil samples with a screw, Dutch or tubular auger, usually inserted to 15 cm depth if a topsoil sample is required, and returning them to the laboratory for analysis. Many authorities suggest walking a W-shaped path across the sampling area, taking 5–6 samples per limb. Ideally at each sample point 3–5 separate cores should be taken and bulked. A simple physical 'finger' test, which can be performed either in the field or the laboratory, can be used to assess the soil's textural composition of sand, silt and clay particles. The large particles comprising sandy soils tend to promote good drainage but hold less available water (to plant roots) per unit volume. In clay soils the small particle sizes (<0.002 mm) tend to impede drainage but can hold twice the available water of sands; in silts available water capacity is still higher, despite the somewhat larger particles. Balanced mixtures of these three particle sizes produce loamy soils, which tend to deliver both good aeration and moisture-holding properties. The finger test, based on the degree to which soils cohere when moistened and rolled into a ball, or into thin cylinders and finer threads, indicates their textural status: for example clay soils have a plasticine-like consistency and can be rolled into thin threads which can be formed into narrow rings without breaking apart. More accurate laboratory methods to determine the proportion of sand, silt and clay involve shaking a soil:water suspension together with a dispersing agent and measuring the rate of sedimentation using a hydrometer.

Simple chemical tests, measuring the level of soil acidity (the pH) or the soil nutrient status, can be carried out using kits available from specialised suppliers and garden centres. Indicator papers or water-testing kits can measure the whole, or part of the pH range (1–14), but for more accurate determinations a portable or laboratory pH meter with electrode is used to test a solution of soil, made up with distilled water. Other routine laboratory tests of soil fertility usually measure quantities of the major plant nutrients – available phosphate, potassium and magnesium levels, plus total nitrogen and sulphur. Widely used standard methods (MAFF, 1986) involve using solutions of sodium carbonate or anionic resins to extract phosphorus, or ammonium nitrate in the case of potassium and magnesium. Results are given both as a concentration, mg per litre of extractable nutrient and as an index, ranging from zero, indicating deficiency, to 9, an excessively high value. Nitrogen can also be measured both as nitrate or ammonium, indicating the amount available to plants (mineralised) at the time of sampling, but a more reliable and consistent measure is the total nitrogen content of the soil, representing the pool available for mineralisation. If total carbon is also estimated from the loss on ignition of organic matter, the carbon:nitrogen ratio gives a useful indication of the potential for mineralisation.

6.4 Semi-natural 'reference' habitats in the local landscape

A central aim in creating new woodlands for wildlife is to accelerate the development of semi-natural woodland types and their associated wildlife, based on the most likely communities that would have been present formerly. It is therefore necessary to identify the geology and soil type(s) present at the woodland creation site from the start. Visiting examples of semi-natural habitat in the wider landscape – so called 'reference sites' – will be helpful to establish what communities naturally occur and thus inform the selection of species for planting.

On ex-agricultural land it is likely that the soil structure and chemistry will have been significantly altered, and its fertility increased, through decades of intensive arable farming. High pH levels from liming and elevated soil phosphorus may persist for considerable periods, depending on the soil type and previous farming history. Conversely, industrial activity can leave soils relatively infertile, compacted and sometimes contaminated with toxic substances. However, historical and chronosequence studies of forests in Britain and Europe show that after farmland abandonment, soils tend to become progressively more acid with natural leaching of the profile and as organic matter builds up, while soil available phosphate becomes increasingly immobilised as aluminium and calcium phosphates. Under trees, such attenuation may eventually return the soil fertility to levels comparable with long-established woodlands, due to a combination of nutrient uptake by woody vegetation, leaching and immobilisation, but the process is likely to be long drawn out and will depend critically on soil type. Parallel studies examining the effects on soil nutrients of continuous arable cropping or grazing of former arable land without fertiliser inputs, indicate that reversion to lower, more 'natural' phosphorus and pH levels might occur within a single forest rotation of c.30–100 years.

If soil analysis has been carried out, the site's fertility status will be known. The practitioner must then decide whether to plant a woodland type suited either to the present conditions, or to some future date dictated by the naturally attenuating fertility levels. As the rate of change is difficult to predict and is likely to be different at each site, a compromise would be to plant elements of both 'present' and 'future' community types, or to begin with the present one, and gradually to modify its composition through management over time, supported by further soil analysis. Once a decision has been made, it should be possible to identify ancient woodlands in the wider landscape as reference sites, based on their underlying geology and soil types.

6.4.1 Published information on potential reference sites

In England, the Government's web-based interactive map (MAGIC) is an excellent starting point to identify key environmental schemes and designations (statutory and non-statutory). These include ancient woodland, Sites of Special Scientific Interest (SSSI), National and Local Nature Reserves, Woodland Trust properties and RSPB reserves, although some sites with non-statutory designations are excluded. The grassland inventory is also included, but this does not distinguish between different grassland types. Grassland, and other UK BAP priority Habitats such as lowland heathland and fens can be found on Natural England's web-based interactive 'Nature on the Map' which includes a comprehensive coverage of SSSIs, nature reserves and agri-environment schemes. Scottish SSSIs are documented on the Registers of Scotland website, and information on Welsh SSSIs can be found on the CCW website.

In Wales, CCW's web-based interactive LANDMAP is the main source of information for identifying key environmental schemes and designations, and is similar to MAGIC. LANDMAP includes many of the statutory and non-statutory designated sites described above, together with primary habitats and Phase 1 habitat survey. The CCW website also includes an interactive countryside access map showing the location of nature reserves and Woodland Trust properties, etc.

The Scottish Natural Heritage website provides information on sites with conservation designations such as National Nature Reserves (NNRs), Local Nature Reserves, SSSIs, and Special Protection Areas. Sites can either be found by searching specific regions, or in the case of NNRs, SSSIs, Special Areas of Conservation and Special Protection Areas, by using various maps on SNH's information service.

Non-statutory wildlife sites should also be identified in the local landscape. Because these have evolved separately in different counties, they are known by many names, including county wildlife sites, Sites of Nature Conservation Interest/Importance (SNCI), Sites of Interest/Importance for Nature Conservation (SINC) and District Wildlife Sites. Selection of these sites in England and Wales is often undertaken by local Wildlife Trusts on behalf of Local Authorities, and details can be obtained from these bodies. In Scotland, 'Local Sites' identified for their high wildlife value by the Scottish Wildlife Trust are also officially recognised by local authorities through a non-statutory designation. Information on these sites can be obtained from the Scottish Wildlife Trust. Roadside Nature Reserves are included in the Welsh SINCs, but are listed separately in many English counties, where details should be obtained from the local Wildlife Trust. There is no Scottish equivalent of Roadside Nature Reserves, although some local authorities do identify roadside areas which have some value to wildlife, and may 'mark' and manage them accordingly.

A small number of English counties also have interactive maps available on their websites. One of the most advanced of these is the Kent Landscape Information System (K-LIS) on the County

Ancient woodland reference sites should be visited to inform the selection of trees and shrubs for planting.

Council website, which offers detailed descriptions of habitats derived from aerial photographs and backed up by ground surveys. Online maps are readily accessible down to field boundary level, which can be overlaid with various habitat data, including elevation, landscape character, soils, a limited number of habitat types, and maps describing statutory designations across Kent. K-LIS maps also identify locations where there are opportunities to create habitats or restore landscapes. Cheshire County Council hosts a similar interactive map on it's website as part of its Ecological Networks Programme. Some counties such as Shropshire direct enquiries to MAGIC and 'Nature on the Map'. Other interactive maps are hosted by AONB offices such as the Gower, and local authorities such as Solihull Metropolitan Borough Council.

The National Biodiversity Network's Gateway (NBN) provides a single point of access to wildlife information held by a wide range of organisations and groups, and can be accessed from the NBN website. It also includes an interactive map which allows designated sites such as SSSIs and Local Nature Reserves to be located. In addition, it provides occurrence data for a species, or species data for a site or geographical area, at a minimum 10 km level of precision. The NBN also supports a network of 70 Local Biodiversity Records Centres across the UK, facilitating the collation, management and provision of local environmental data. Some of these are based in the local Wildlife Trust, others within county councils. The contact details and website addresses for all these centres can be obtained from the website of the National Federation for Biological Recording. The level of services and the way in which they provide data varies from one centre to another. Some Centres such as the Sussex Biodiversity Records Centre can prepare local maps showing different habitat types and sites with conservation designations, and biodiversity information for an area, although there is usually a charge for this service. In Wales, details of the four Local Biodiversity Records Centres can also be found on the Welsh Local Records Centre website.

Species-rich meadow reference sites should be visited, but in lowland Britain such places are now rare.

6.4.2   Visiting reference sites

If information on potential reference sites is not available or is not sufficiently detailed, a simple NVC survey can be undertaken, either by a

Table 6.3 Key to the main National Vegetation Classification Types of woodland, based on the key canopy species, ground flora component and broad soil types (after: Forestry Commission, 2008; © Crown copyright, reproduced with the kind permission of the Forestry Commission)

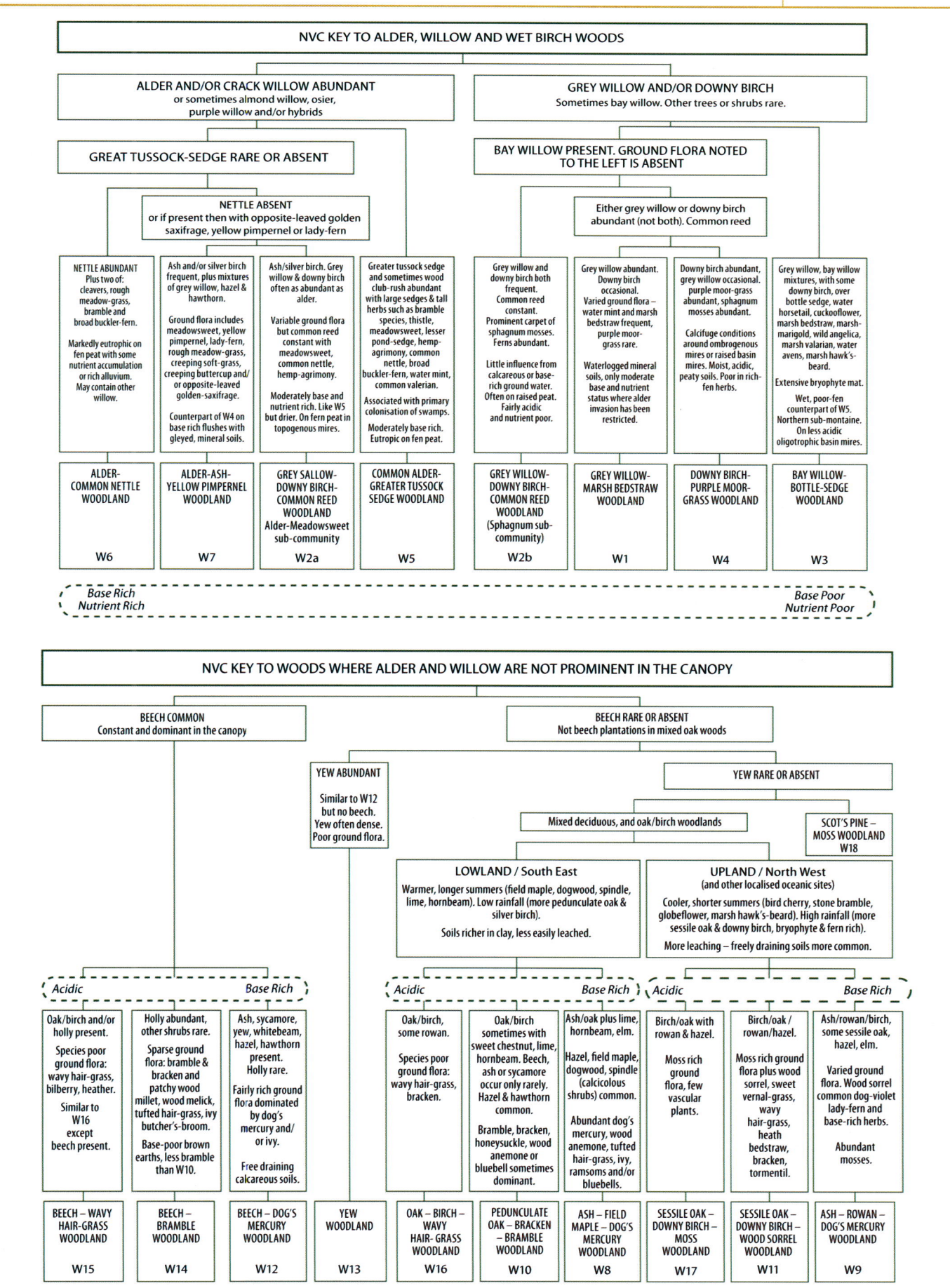

Vegetation surveys in ancient woodland reference sites can help to devise appropriate planting mixes.

Ancient hedgerows can help with species choice for new native woodland.

professional ecologist, or anyone confident in identifying woodland plants. A useful guide is the *National Vegetation Classification: Field Guide to Woodland* (Hall et al., 2004). If neighbouring woodland is at an early stage of succession, it may not be possible to accurately assess its NVC type. Old hedgerows or remnant patches of trees within, or close to the woodland creation site may also offer clues to the woodland type which formerly grew on the site.

Undertaking a woodland vegetation survey

Assuming permission to enter the woodland has been obtained, we suggest using the NVC (see Section 6.2.3) because it considers trees, shrubs and ground flora together. Ultimately, an NVC survey can guide the selection of trees and shrubs for planting and provide a framework that can accelerate natural colonisation and the development of a new woodland ecosystem. However it should always be remembered that every ancient wood is in some way unique, and that the objective should not be to copy a precise woodland type through planting.

In many cases, an experienced ecologist or forester will be able to provide a reasonably accurate assessment of woodland communities present simply by observing the vegetation types. Simplified guidelines based on key canopy species, prominent vascular plants and broad soil types for determining NVC types may help the practitioner to undertake a similar task (Table 6.3; descriptions of the main communities are given in Chapter 1). If more detail is needed, a series of sample quadrats can be recorded to compare with NVC summary tables (Rodwell, 1991) or the *Field guide to woodland* (Hall et al., 2004). For these purposes we suggest a method based on that described by Hall et al., (2004):

1. First, stratify the woodland into visually different types, and select homogeneous areas within each type for survey

2. Set up a 5 x 5 m quadrat and record species present in the field layer, and their percentage cover. If the data are unlikely to be used for comparative purposes, a 4 x 4 m or 10 x 10 m quadrat could be employed as in the NVC recording scheme

3. Record the canopy and understorey percentage cover of trees and shrubs in larger quadrats above (2): the NVC recording scheme uses 50 x 50 m quadrats, but smaller 20 x 20 m or 30 x 30 m quadrats may be sufficient.

   As an alternative to percentage cover, the abundance of each species can be recorded using the classification: dominant, abundant, frequent, occasional or rare (DAFOR), or the Domin scale.

4. Repeat this process five times, with quadrats spread evenly around the stand

5. If other community types are present, repeat the process for each.

Use the data collected to determine the most appropriate NVC community classification, referring to the keys given in Rodwell (1991) or Hall *et al.,* (2004), or the computer programs described in Section 6.2.3.

Hedgerows can also provide useful, but limited information for the design of planting mixes, particularly if they are ancient, and possibly remnants of ancient woodland present on the site in the past. For the purposes of informing woodland creation schemes, the method described in Section 6.2.3 should suffice.

Semi-natural open ground communities

In theory, semi-natural grassland and/or heathland communities in the wider landscape should help to identify species and species-mixes suitable for creating grassland or heathland communities in open spaces in new native woodland (see Section 7.5). The desk study will have identified the location of such habitat, and the underlying geology or soil types of these areas can be compared with the woodland creation site. For sites which match, records of the species present should be obtained if available. Otherwise, if permission is granted, the sites should be visited and a more systematic NVC survey undertaken (Rodwell, 1992). Once again, we recommend a minimalist approach to data collection as described in Section 6.2.3.

Use the data collected to determine the most appropriate NVC community classification, referring to the keys given in Rodwell (1992) or the computer programs described above. Species diversity and abundance data will be useful for designing the planting mixes.

However, in contrast to ancient woodland, high quality semi-natural grassland communities – particularly in the lowlands – are highly fragmented and rare. In many cases, it will simply not be possible to find good reference sites in the local landscape. Reference to historical records or typical NVC communities will then be the method of choice.

Vegetation surveys in grassland or heathland reference sites can help with decisions on sowing mixes for open spaces.

6.5 Reviewing ecological data

Survey work is needed to confirm that woodland creation will not impinge on semi-natural habitats and wildlife within the area, and to ensure that the site would not be more suitable for creating other habitats, such as grassland or heathland (Table 6.4). Phase 1 habitat and wildlife surveys will establish the conservation status of the proposed site and therefore whether it is suitable for establishing woodland. As a major objective of woodland creation is wildlife conservation, a good general knowledge of the flora and fauna of the wider landscape, together with an understanding of how species disperse and colonise is important; particularly for those species able to colonise new woodland and its associated habitats. With this knowledge, particular features can be incorporated to benefit priority species, such as hazel-rich woodland

Table 6.4. Checklist for determining the potential of new native woodland creation and its associated habitats for wildlife.

	High potential	Issues of concern
Soil survey		
	• pH similar to ancient woodland in the wider landscape • pH differs from reference sites by < 2 units • P index 0-1	• pH differs markedly from ancient woodland or unimproved grassland in the wider landscape • P index > 2.0 • Soil conditions on site suitable for recreation of other threatened habitat such as chalk grassland
Reference sites		
	• Reference sites close to the planting site, to guide species choice	• If no suitable reference sites, planting mixes can be based on geology, soil and site characteristics alone
Biodiversity of the woodland creation site and its environs		
Phase 1 habitat survey	• Vegetation indicates low fertility • Any ecologically important habitats not affected by woodland creation	• Weeds present indicate high fertility • Adjacent open habitats, such as semi-natural grassland or heathland would benefit from expansion • Woodland creation site contains habitat of conservation value
Vegetation	• No rare plants or communities	• Rare plants present • Species-rich grassland or other rare communities present which should be conserved
Birds	• No birds of conservation concern • Local priority bird populations will benefit from new woodland habitat	• Established population(s) of declining birds such as farmland or moorland species that would be adversely affected by proposal
Invertebrate habitat of high biodiversity value	• None present which would be adversely affected by woodland creation	• Valuable microhabitats present such as species-rich semi-natural vegetation
Butterflies	• Nearby populations of wider countryside might colonise new woodland open space	• Semi-natural habitat within the woodland creation site supporting habitat specialist butterflies
Mammals	• No protected species present • Protected species in the wider landscape benefit from habitat creation	• Woodland creation would cause disturbance to protected species
Amphibians and reptiles	• No protected species present • Protected species in the wider landscape benefit from habitat creation	• Woodland creation would cause disturbance to protected species such as great crested newts
European Protected Species	• Any species present that will benefit from woodland creation	• Disturbance requiring licences and mitigation
Future benefits for wildlife		
Wildlife in the wider landscape	• A range of woodland habitats designed and managed for wildlife • Wildlife in the wider landscape will benefit from woodland creation	• New woodland too small to include open space or edge habitat • Lack of source populations – species diversity in the new woodland will remain low for the foreseeable future
Rare species	• Target species of local BAPs such as dormouse will benefit directly from woodland creation • Young plantations will support species such as tree pipit and nightjar	• No obvious 'protected species' beneficiaries
Negative impacts on wildlife	• No obvious negative impact on habitat or wildlife of conservation concern	• Disturbance or loss of protected species • Damage or destruction of semi-natural habitats of conservation value such as ponds or grassland • Disturbance to adjacent habitats such as shading the edge of ancient woodland • New woodland forms a barrier between habitats which benefit from being linked, such as wetlands

edges for dormice or food plants for scarce butterfly species, or alternatively to enhance the value of the site for wildlife in the longer term. There may also be opportunities to create a mosaic of different, open habitats to add to the value of the project, and to create opportunities for a wider variety of species to colonise or disperse.

Finally, it is important to be realistic about how 'natural' the new woodland and other created vegetation communities can ever be. In the case of former agricultural sites, high fertility can strongly influence the species mix and the methods adopted for both woody species and the herbs and grasses of woodland rides and glades.

6.5.1 Ecological assessment of Lamberhurst Farm – a worked example

As described in earlier (Section 6.1.2), the landscape character assessment of Lamberhurst Farm in Kent suggested that it would be a prime site for woodland creation. The landscape assessment was augmented by specialist surveys of habitat, wildlife and soils. These ecological surveys confirmed the suitability of the site for woodland creation (Table 6.5) and the first phase of planting took place in 2005–2007 across much of the former area of North Blean Wood, which

Table 6.5 Summary of the main landscape character and ecological assessment criteria for Lamberhurst Farm in Kent, which support the planting of Victory Wood; including the creation of new native woodland, scrub and grassland

	Positive aspects	Issues of concern
Soil survey		
	• pH range 5.9–7.5 • P index 1.0–2.0 over much of site • Soils good for tree growth	• pH higher than neighbouring ancient woodland • Base-rich from liming • P index >2.0 over parts of site
Reference sites		
	• Adjacent ancient woodland primarily lowland sessile oakwood (W10a), with ash-maple woodland (W8a) along stream gully; small patches of rare acid sessile oak-beech (W15)	• Soil fertility levels should be considered when choosing species, but reference communities still appropriate • No unimproved grassland reference sites in the local landscape
Biodiversity of the woodland creation site and its environs		
Phase 1 habitat survey	• Ancient woodland and species-rich hedgerow are present within and bordering the site • Good sources of colonists in adjacent ancient woodland • Site protected from spray drift • Evidence of natural regeneration	• Weeds present indicate high fertility in places
Vegetation	• No rare arable plants or semi-natural grassland communities • Hedgerow linking adjacent ancient woods	
Birds	• Birds of woodland and scrub will benefit from new woodland habitat • Open areas could be managed for ground nesting species such as skylark and meadow pipit	• Significant proportion of red-listed skylark population will be lost • Red-listed corn bunting may be lost
Invertebrate habitat of high biodiversity value	• Little habitat present which would be adversely affected by woodland creation	• Trackway with areas of bare ground will be lost
Butterflies	• Healthy populations of wider countryside butterflies in field margins would thrive in managed woodland open space	
Mammals	• Dormouse present in boundary hedgerows should benefit from habitat creation	• Woodland creation activities must not cause disturbance to dormouse
Amphibians and reptiles	• Grass snake (UK BAP priority species) present – should benefit from habitat creation • Great crested newt (UK BAP priority species) present in ponds close to the site – should benefit from habitat creation	• Woodland creation activities must not cause disturbance to hibernating animals
European Protected Species	• Dormouse and great crested newt should benefit in the long term	• Any disturbance would require licences and mitigation
Future benefits for wildlife		
Wildlife in the wider landscape	• Woodland habitats and meadows designed and managed for wildlife • Wildlife likely to benefit from woodland creation includes birds, bats, invertebrates, plants, fungi and lichens	• No unimproved grassland in the area to support natural colonisation of open areas
Rare species	• Target species of local BAPs such as dormouse will benefit directly from woodland creation • Young plantations may attract tree pipit and nightjar	
Negative impacts on wildlife	• Few negative impacts	• Skylarks and corn bunting highlighted above

originally linked the ancient woods of Ellenden and Blean. Grassland with wildflower seed inoculation areas were created in the woodland rides and glades, and more extensively in the northern meadow. The preservation of open areas on the northern part of the site maintains the original gradation from woodland, through pasture onto the grazing marsh of Seasalter Level, and the coast beyond.

6.6 Other landscape evaluation methods

6.6.1 Ecological Site Classification

Powerful decision support systems are now being developed to help foresters and woodland owners choose appropriate species for their site, whether for production or nature conservation objectives. An example is the Ecological Site Classification, software available for purchase from the Forestry Commission (Pyatt *et al.*, 2001) but the manual, which is useful in itself for surveys, can be freely downloaded. Basically, the inputs consist of a climate module, based on the National Grid position of the site and its elevation above sea level, and the soil type which can either be read directly from soil maps or more accurately inferred from actual field surveys (Figure 6.3). Indicator plant species present on the site can also be input as an optional addition in order to strengthen the soil classification. Climate data is based on the last 30 years of meteorological data (supplied) and uses two main indicators: seasonal accumulated temperature and moisture deficit, plus windiness and continentality, the latter a measure of the length and intensity of the growing season. Soil quality in the field can be judged from two standpoints: a) soil fertility, based on pH measures and humus type, and b) soil wetness and aeration, based on textural type and evidence of waterlogging and rooting depth observed in soil pits.

The outputs are of three types: tree species suitability, based on a knowledge of how different species perform with respect to climatic and soil limitations; predicted timber yields, again based on compartment records and experience of growth rates on different sites; and finally 'woodland suitability', which attributes the most likely NVC community type as if the site were of semi-natural origin, listing possible semi-natural mixtures of trees and shrubs that could be used as a recipe for planning new native woodlands.

Levels of sophistication in such decision support systems are set to improve dramatically. In the future releases, ecological site classifications have the potential to assess not only the suitability of species at present, but also in the future, anticipating climate change. The new version is also likely to be available as a Geographic Information System (GIS), allowing forest managers to test spatially the suitability of forest plans, for example the best options for tree species, native woodlands and open space, linked to the requirements of key species and non-woodland communities listed in Biodiversity Action Plans.

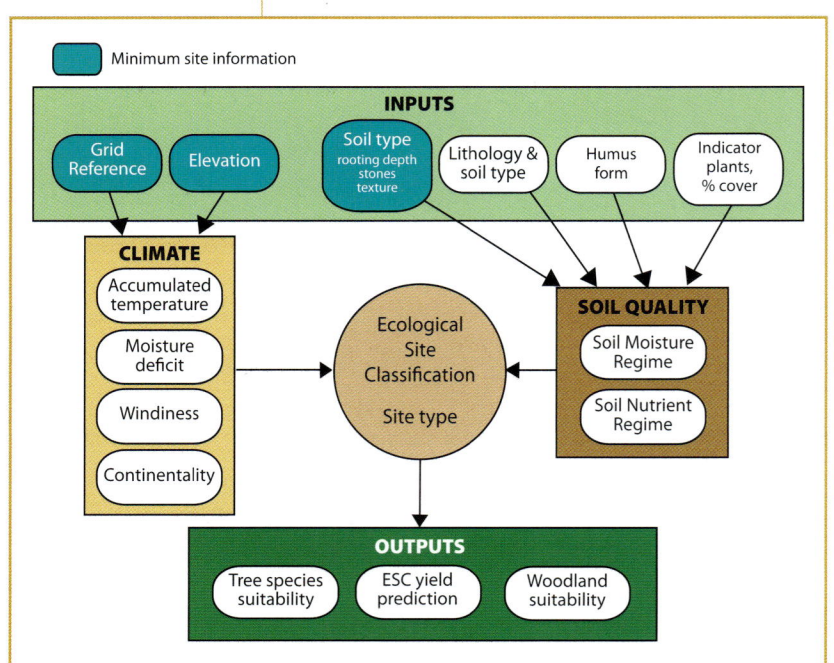

Figure 6.3 The Ecological Site Classification: inputs and outputs (after Forestry Commission, 2001).

6.6.2 Environmental Impact Assessment (Forestry)

The landscape and ecological assessments described in this chapter should enable the practitioner to identify the best opportunities for new woodland creation. At the time of writing, if the new woodland is likely to have a significant impact on the environment, consent is required from the Forestry Commission, under the Environmental Impact Assessment (Forestry) Regulations 1999 for England and Wales, or those for Scotland (1999), both amended in 2006. These regulations also apply to deforestation, forest roads and forestry quarries (Forestry Commission, 2009c).

Woodland creation (termed 'initial afforestation') includes tree planting on an area that has not had trees for many years, direct seeding, natural regeneration and short rotation coppice. Thresholds apply, above which the Forestry Commission is required to make a determination as to whether consent will be required. For sites within sensitive areas such as National Parks, AONBs and National Scenic Areas a threshold of 2 ha applies; in other sensitive areas such as an SSSI or National Nature Reserve, there is no set threshold. Outside of sensitive areas, the threshold is 5 ha.

A relatively simple Determination form is available on the Forestry Commission website which forms part of an initial screening exercise to determine whether the project is above one of the thresholds, and whether it is likely to have a significant impact on the environment. The information required includes a map of the area, a description of the proposed work and its possible 'significant' effects on the environment, and any other relevant information, such as the results of the survey work described in this chapter.

If, in the opinion of the Forestry Commission, the project will have a significant environmental impact, then consent must be applied for, and an Environmental Statement of work submitted, based on an Environmental Impact Assessment. Forestry Commission woodland officers work closely with applicants to help with the preparation of this documentation.

6.7 Finding out about planting grants for new native woodland

6.7.1 Forestry Commission grants

Most grant aid towards woodland creation and replanting in Britain is provided through the Forestry Commission, with different schemes operating in England, Scotland and Wales and also variations in prioritisation within different regions. Aid is given in return for certain public benefits, such as:

- woodland creation close to where people live, particularly within the urban fringe, giving access to countryside for recreation and sport, and improving air quality
- wildlife enhancement, particularly when buffering or linking important habitats and protecting ancient woodland
- enhancing the landscape
- restoring derelict and former industrial land
- increasing the timber resource and developing a sustained yield of wood products
- providing buffer strips along watercourses, preventing soil erosion or providing shelter
- increasing carbon sequestration to tackle climate change.

Woodland establishment grants are competitive and successful applications are typically judged on all of the above criteria, with priorities varying somewhat between regions. Livelihoods, quality of life and access to woodlands are important, especially where woodland is planned in close proximity to population centres and expansion areas, social regeneration areas and local and national community forests. Economic objectives of woodland creation are also scored highly in regions where tourism might benefit, where derelict land needs to be restored, and for establishing plantations of high-yielding or high-quality timber.

Most new grants emphasise the potential environmental and conservation contributions of new woodland areas. Applications are more likely to be successful where they match local landscape guidelines, or fall within landscape-designated regions such as National Parks and AONBs, designed landscapes or areas with little cover. Woodland planting that enhances local biodiversity is also given high priority, such as planting to complement Habitat and Species Action Plans, extending ancient, semi-natural woodland with new native woodland, or restoring plantations on ancient woodland sites (PAWS), and developing 'floodplain' or riparian woods on land subject to seasonal flooding or in sensitive water catchments.

Geographical targeting of newly created woodlands is specifically encouraged in some regions, mainly to consolidate existing fragmentation. In some cases the targets are pre-defined clusters of existing semi-natural woodland or areas which have the greatest potential to form linked habitat networks, such as core and focal networks in Wales (Watts *et al.*, 2005a) and Forest Habitat Networks in Scotland (Moseley *et al.*, 2008). Planting within these envelopes may attract additional grant, with an extra premium in the case of native woodlands. Additional support may be available in some regions for planting to encourage species of conservation concern, such as declining birds or butterflies.

Support for new woodlands generally has four components: a) a woodland establishment grant, b) one-off additional contributions, for example where public access or nature conservation benefits can be achieved, c) annual payments to compensate for agricultural income forgone, continuing for a decade or more and d) support for planning and evaluation. Grant rates for planting or natural regeneration are determined according to the size of the area and the type of planting, i.e. whether for new native woodland, public woodlands or commercial forestry. Areas must normally exceed 0.25 ha and applicants are required to manage their woods in accordance with an approved five-year plan. For 'native' and 'community' planting schemes, relatively low tree densities are allowable (often with the condition that local stock is used), together with generous provision for open ground and shrub-planting. Such planting attracts higher rates of grant than commercial forestry schemes for which higher stocking densities are specified, where conifers may be used and the amount of allowable open ground is less. Finally, where newly created woodlands are open to the public and facilities for access are provided, grants may be available to offset the cost.

6.7.2 Other planting grants

Only a small proportion of the new woodland creation undertaken each year in Britain is either not funded, or supported by sources other than the Forestry Commission. Grants for small-scale planting – small areas of native trees, hedgerow trees, etc. – are available through a number of sources, such as local authorities, National Parks authorities, countryside projects and a range of non-government organisations and trusts. Other sources are the agri-environment schemes on farmland sponsored by the English, Welsh and Scottish Governments. For example, small areas of woodland creation to benefit wildlife (less than 1 ha, with a limit of 3 ha per holding) can also be part-funded through the Environmental Stewardship (Higher Level) Scheme managed by Natural England for the Department of Environment, Food and Rural Affairs. Within this scheme there is also provision for creating new wood-pasture and successional areas of scrub. Natural England also oversees the Energy Crops Scheme, which supports the costs of establishing short-rotation crops of willow, poplar and other broadleaved species.

7 DESIGNING A NEW WOOD AND SELECTING SPECIES TO PLANT

7.1 Designing a new wood

New woods will usually be created on land of low ecological value, and from the beginning will have impoverished floras and faunas, soils that may have been considerably altered by development or farming, and will lack stand heterogeneity and structure, dead wood or natural regeneration. Nevertheless it should be possible to design woodland that delivers for wildlife from the outset and over the long term. This will mean taking into account the context of the site within the local landscape, its relationship with existing woods and other semi-natural habitats, the presence of species of conservation importance; and the suitability of the soil and climate for growing the desired range trees and shrubs.

Key considerations for optimising wildlife potential will be:

- whether to plant or make use of natural regeneration
- which species to use, and their relative abundance and distribution in space
- the proportion of canopy trees to understorey and shrubs
- the amount of woodland cover relative to temporary and permanent open space
- how much 'edge' perimeter to include in rides, glades and scrub development
- whether to include ancillary habitat features such as pollards, ponds and riparian areas
- whether to introduce woodland ground flora or allow it to develop naturally
- how to create early structural diversity through management.

The complexity of the scheme will depend critically on its size. Avoid trying to include everything in small woods of one or two hectares. They will support some open space, but are simply not large enough to accommodate an extensive system of rides and glades, or a wide variety of species, and are less likely to cover a range of soil types, micro-topography, slopes and drainage gradients that can be exploited for biodiversity. Conversely, with larger schemes there is more opportunity to plan planting patterns to match site conditions, to incorporate more open space and secondary habitat features, and to manage robustly to develop age and structural diversity over time.

7.1.1 Making use of natural regeneration

Any prospect of natural regeneration will be determined by the position of the site relative to nearby seed sources. If it is distant from surrounding woods, trees or mature hedgerows, colonisation by trees and shrubs in the short term is unlikely, leaving little alternative but to plant if a quick tree cover is the objective. On the other hand, colonisation may be rapid where a site is adjacent to existing woods or relict hedgerows, making it worthwhile to consider setting aside some of the area for natural regeneration, saving on planting and allowing an extended age structure to develop over time. In Section 2.1 we described the exponential decline in seed rain with distance from the source, accepting that animal- and bird-assisted dispersal may carry seeds over very long distances. For wind-dispersed species such as ash, elm, willow, aspen, birch, hornbeam, field maple, lime and pine, a maximum dispersal gradient up to 100 m from sources might result in good seedling cover, although patchy and scattered towards the extremes, but if the objective is to deliver stocking densities similar to conventional planting practice it would be safer to assume a working distance of only 1–2 tree heights. In this case, natural regeneration could easily account for 80%–100% of the area of a 1 ha 'planting' site completely surrounded by woodland (depending on its shape), but

Natural regeneration including hornbeam, oaks, willows and birches in a former arable field adjacent to ancient woodland. Willows and birches are being browsed by cattle.

much less (30% for a square site) if the regeneration proceeds only from one edge, and falling off very rapidly as the designated area increases in size. Woodland regeneration grants usually allow only a fixed period, such as 5–10 years, to achieve satisfactory regeneration stocking, but in practice the process will often take much longer.

Predicting natural regeneration is a problem for managers, faced with a number of variables which may alternatively encourage or prevent success. The key factors are listed below:

Positive factors	Negative factors
Parent trees present	Seed sources absent or distant
Infertile subsoil, or stony soils	Loamy soils
Weak grass swards	Strong weed growth
Scarification to increase bare ground	Bramble and grasses
Burnt-over areas	Building and mature heather (but regeneration on lowland heaths should be discouraged)
Advance regeneration present	Dense bracken
Low grazing levels	High grazing levels
Small regeneration areas	Large regeneration areas
	Close proximity to undesirable, invasive tree and shrub species

after Harmer *et al.*, (1997); Thompson (2004)

The close proximity of seed trees has already been mentioned. An examination of advance regeneration, i.e. seedlings, saplings and scrub already present on the site (or at its periphery) will indicate which species are likely to colonise the site initially, and whether an acceptable level of cover is likely to be achieved. Some species are regular producers of seed, such as birch, ash, sycamore and Scots pine, while less regular species include beech, oak and chestnut. However in some years a tenfold increase over the normal quantity of seed may be produced in response to particularly favourable climatic conditions. During these so-called mast years up to 22 million viable seeds per ha (2,200 per m²) may be shed in Scots pinewoods, 3 million per ha in beech and 150,000 per ha in oak stands. The frequency of these events is typically 3–5 years in many broadleaves; in beech more than five years. For a manager wishing to make use of natural regeneration, regular inspections of the seed-bearing canopies of source trees, and timing the preparation of the site to coincide with a good seed year, will give the best results.

Another major pre-requisite for successful regeneration is a receptive seedbed. In general, seedbeds dominated by moss cover, decaying wood, thin litter layers or disturbed mineral soils are more favourable regeneration surfaces than thick, raw humus layers, matted grass, bracken, bramble, heather and shrub cover. Exceptions occur, for example where bramble or gorse patches may protect young seedlings from grazing. The extent of competition between surface vegetation and tree seedlings is also influenced by the site and soil type. In general, infertile soils (moist or dry) are better for regeneration than fine-textured soils with higher nutrient status,

Naturally regenerating alder on an ungrazed wet meadow bordered by riparian woodland.

where competition with other vegetation is likely to be a problem. The Ecological Site Classification soil grid can be used as a guide to predict favourable and unfavourable conditions (Thompson, 2004). Any treatments which disrupt or reduce surface vegetation and litter will aid the germination and establishment of regeneration by increasing seed contact with the mineral soil. Managers can use surface scarification, flailing, burning, herbicides, or close grazing prior to seeding. If the site is already partly bare, as in an arable field after harvesting or on some types of derelict land, no further action may be necessary, but creating a suitable seedbed where there is already established vegetation is rather more complicated. The point is considered further in Section 8.2 on artificial direct seeding as an establishment method.

Poor regeneration is often due to predation of seed and seedlings by domestic stock, deer, rabbits, hares, squirrels, pigeons, pheasants, voles, mice and slugs. Fencing or individual tree protection is part of the solution, at least during the critical establishment phase. Without this protection, red and fallow deer densities of 5–7 per km^2 are considered to be the maximum allowable for successful regeneration in European forests (although damage to the stand may still occur), or very low domestic stocking rates such as <5 cattle months per ha per year. Predation of seed is a particular problem at margins with existing woodlands, where small mammal populations are often abundant. Only in heavy mast years may the quantity of seed, or the following seedling regeneration, be sufficient to over-face the predator population and allow good establishment.

7.1.2 Limitations of natural regeneration

The diversity of colonising trees and shrubs may be limited and favour only a few species with the most efficient dispersal such as birch, willow and hawthorn. These pioneers can dominate a site for several decades, out-competing less efficient colonisers and even trees which have been deliberately planted. This may not be altogether welcome if the objectives of woodland creation are to accelerate the succession, maximise the variety of native trees and shrubs on the site, grow timber-producing species, or match the species composition of a mature community-type (or that of adjacent woodland). Having said this, natural regeneration has many advantages: it maintains genetic diversity in a given location, avoids fussy and over-formalised community stereotypes, creates rapid canopy cover and promotes early spatial and structural diversity. A balance therefore needs to be struck where some space is allowed within the overall scheme for natural regeneration to occur. For large, isolated sites where there is little hope of regeneration, planting will predominate. If, on the other hand, there are good seed sources nearby, planting in designated natural regeneration areas can be restricted to those species not likely to colonise naturally, while a proportion of the ground can be left to fill up naturally.

Pioneer willows in a former arable field adjacent to ancient woodland, effectively outcompeting hornbeam and oak seedlings which colonised the site at the same time.

Finally, when making use of natural regeneration, managers need to be aware of the risk that the seeds may have come from a small number of parent trees restricting genetic variation and limiting the adaptation of individuals to the new environment. With the climate likely to change quickly, natural succession may not always deliver the genetic diversity necessary if new ecological networks are to be established and functioning in time. Natural regeneration has a role to play in woodland creation or PAWS restoration, but in future may be seen as complementary to woodland creation projects relying primarily on planting to accelerate woodland development.

7.1.3 The value of open space in a woodland creation scheme

Rides and glades that are well designed and properly managed can significantly increase the wildlife value of new native woodland, particularly for insects, birds and bats. They offer sheltered open space, and can support a range of habitat types and plant communities, including scrub (woodland edge), species-rich grassland, heath and damp grassland. Larger woods may include an extensive ride network, whilst smaller woods of just a few hectares will support an internal ride or glade. Even relatively small areas of woodland open space can contribute to the conservation of open habitats in the wider landscape, support habitat networks, and thus provide opportunities for species to colonise or use them to move through the wider landscape.

Structural diversity is important for both a shrubby woodland edge and open ground vegetation. In a grassy ride for example, enhancing diversity with a range of 'microhabitats', from bare ground and short turf through to tall herb communities should produce habitat capable of supporting a diverse range of insects and their predators. This assumes that the diversity of plants in the community approaches that in semi-natural communities, and includes nectar sources for insects as well as food plants for their larvae.

TOP **Common fleabane along ride edges provides an excellent source of nectar for insects in mid to late summer.**

BOTTOM **Open areas in Denge Wood, Kent which are being managed specifically for Duke of Burgundy butterflies.**

Providing warm, sheltered open ground habitat encourages colonisation by woodland insects of conservation concern. This has been successful in mature woods in southern England where management and creation of open areas is benefiting now rare woodland specialist butterflies such as the Duke of Burgundy and small pearl-bordered fritillary. It is important that specialist habitat design advice is sought where rare species are involved. At the time of writing, few woodland creation schemes in Britain have been designed specifically to support species of conservation concern; but in certain circumstances, the opportunity could be seriously considered.

Butterflies and moths also illustrate very well some of the key ecological issues which underpin ride design and management in new native woodland. Most woodland butterflies rely on sheltered, sunlit rides and glades, with a plentiful supply of larval foodplants, and an abundant supply of flowers for nectaring. Open spaces offer protection from wind, and a warmer microclimate for species that like to bask, such as the comma, and in mature woodland, the fritillaries and white admiral. Exceptions include wood white and ringlet, which prefer 'light shade'; and green-veined white and speckled wood which will tolerate deeper shade. The adults of most species will use a wide range of flowers for nectaring, whilst their larvae are likely to feed on just a few species. This is particularly so for the woodland specialists such as white admiral, which feeds only on honeysuckle. Wider countryside species may also have a narrow range of foodplants, for example small tortoiseshell requires either nettle or small nettle. However, the presence of the right foodplant and an abundant supply of nectar is not always sufficient to allow a species to colonise a particular wood. The habitat and microclimate in which the foodplant is growing may be critical for breeding to take place. Some species such as the marbled white prefer tall grassy areas, whereas others such as the small heath require short vegetation. The pearl-bordered fritillary requires "plentiful leaf litter plus adequate violets without (too much) grass, plus tree/scrub seedling and re-growth development and over good spring weather" (Oates, 2004). If the grass is too long, the habitat becomes unsuitable, even with plentiful violets. This is the reason why pearl-bordered fritillary was lost from its last remaining woodland habitat in Kent in the early part of the 21st century.

White admirals are usually found in shady, mature woodland rides, but may visit sunny glades in new woodland to bask or nectar.

7.1.4 Designing rides and glades

Given a choice, and suitable design, east-west rides are the preferred option because they are sunnier for longer than north-south rides during the spring and summer months. In an east-west ride, the north side will be sunny and warm, whilst the south side will be cooler and moister. Sunny and warm areas will support nectaring and basking insects, whilst cool, shady conditions may be required for larvae of the same species. It is important that the sunlit areas of the ride contain some shorter vegetation that enables insects to bask. In addition to orientation, the extent of sun and shade in an east-west ride will be determined by ride width and tree heights along the southern edge. North-south rides can also be effective, but they are illuminated for a shorter period of the day. A detailed account of aspect and the duration of direct sunlight can be found in Ferris and Carter (2000).

Increasing the width of east-west rides will create more sunny areas, but there is a risk that they become wind funnels, particularly with prevailing westerly winds. This can be alleviated by:

- angling rides to the north or south near the edge of the wood,
- scalloping; creating bays along the edge that provide shelter and disrupt wind flows

A wide ride with scallops and 'pinch points' at frequent intervals is very valuable for wildlife.

- adding 'pinch points' where the tree canopy meets, to baffle the wind (also providing aerial routes for mammals such as dormouse to cross the open area – note this might be disruptive to the movement of bats, butterflies etc.).
- retaining some standard trees within the ride to baffle wind flows – adding a structural dynamic.

To allow sufficient light into the majority of the ride its width should be approximately one and a half times the height of the canopy trees along its edge. When planting new native woodland, it can be assumed that trees will grow to a height of 20 m; consequently rides should be at least 30 m wide. Narrower rides up to 10 m wide are often found in existing new woods – these will suffice in the early years, providing they are progressively widened to prevent shading. The width of north-south rides is not as critical, so if space is limited, they may not need to be widened to the same extent. They are likely to support a different flora to their east-west counterparts, which is more typical of light woodland shade; consequently they provide important habitats in their own right. As woodland grant schemes usually allow areas of up to 40% open space, then any wood larger than 2 ha should comfortably support a ride, or network of rides. Even small woods of approximately one hectare will support some open space in the form of glades, or perhaps a short ride, depending on the shape of the wood.

The ideal ride management system for an east-west ride is a three-zone system (Warren and Fuller, 1993), designed for mature woodland, but also suitable for new woodland (Figure 7.1).

Figure 7.1 Profile of a three-zone ride management system.

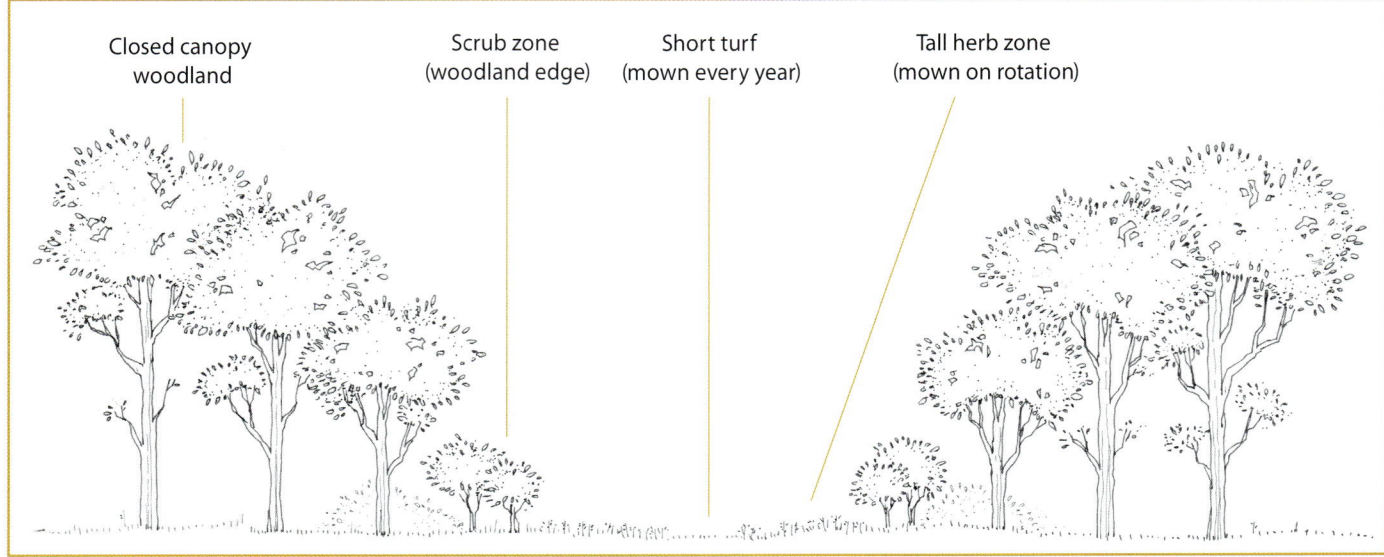

Both internal and external woodland edges should be diverse in both structure and species.

Zones or strips of differing habitat are created, from a central track of short dry turf with bare areas, through tall herb swards rich in wild flowers and grasses (sedges and rushes where damp), to the graduated scrub and coppice zone of the woodland edge. Such designs must be maintained by appropriate mowing and cutting regimes to enhance and retain biodiversity. Ideally, cuttings should be removed to avoid damage to the habitat through soil enrichment.

The central zone of the ride should be at least 2 m wide to accommodate management machinery (e.g. forwarders and tractors) and mown once or twice a year to create areas of short turf and maintain access. Occasional patches of bare ground, which occur naturally in woodland glades, will add significantly to the value of this area, particularly along south-facing woodland edges. In sunny positions, bare ground warms up rapidly, and on hot days may be up to 10°C higher than the surrounding vegetation.

Bare ground is important because it supports a rich and characteristic insect fauna (Key, 2000). Ants, flying insects and some spiders for example scavenge, hunt or ambush their prey on bare ground. Predatory beetles such as adult green tiger beetles, use bare ground in heathland areas for hunting; their larvae ambush prey from burrows in bare areas. Many species of solitary bees and wasps also burrow in bare ground to make nests. Purple emperor butterflies descend to bare ground to probe for salts from minerals or animal dung. Other butterflies simply use bare ground for basking. Reptiles such as lizards and snakes also use bare ground for basking. In the past, bare ground would have been created by large herbivores grazing woodland glades, but today such areas may be created by horses, human traffic, timber extraction or accidentally during mowing.

Male purple emperor probing for salts on bare ground in a woodland glade.

In larger woodland creation schemes there is also an opportunity to create glades, which are defined as permanent open areas, non-linear,

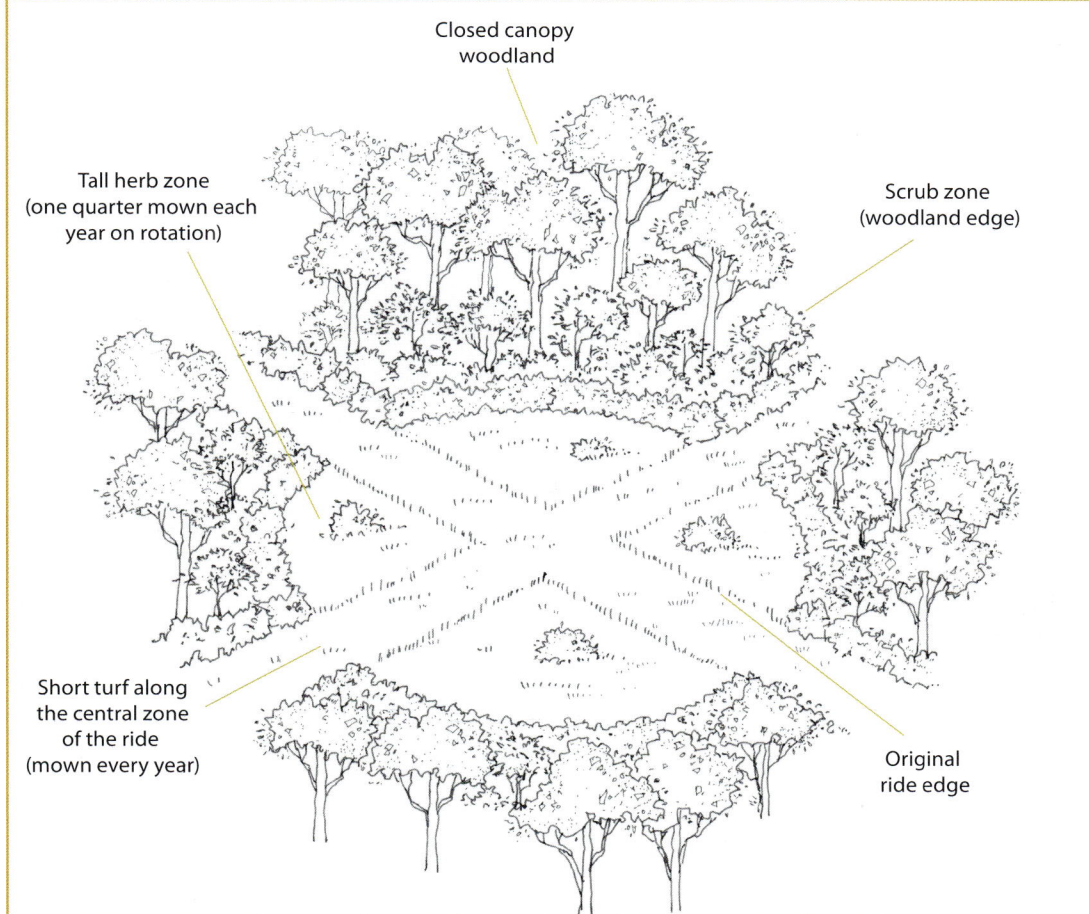

Figure 7.2 Creating a glade at the intersection of two rides.

with few or no trees (Warren and Fuller, 1993). They provide additional opportunities for wildlife of open grassland, heath or marshy areas, due to their size and shape, typically 0.25–2.0 ha in size. Glades are usually incorporated into the ride network, but they can be located in a wooded area some distance from a ride. Glades can be created in smaller woods by enlarging the opening areas where two rides intersect, known as box junctions. Such glades have the added advantage of benefitting from species dispersal along the ride network. The glade illustrated in Figure 7.2 covers approximately 0.25 ha, and would be suitable for smaller woods of around 2.0 ha (amounting to 12.5% of the area).

7.1.5 Managing rides and glades

Twenty-five percent of the tall herb zone, between the shorter turf and the shrubs of the woodland edge, should be mown each year with a flail, on a rotational basis. This will create a mosaic of tall grasses and herbs of four different ages, sufficient to maintain viable populations of insects remaining in uncut, taller vegetation. The shrubby ride edge should be cut (coppiced) on rotations of 8–20 years to create a mosaic of structural diversity and different-aged shrubs. The age will to some extent depend on the growth rates of the species concerned and whether it will be marketed, say, for woodfuel. If small trees and shrubs have been planted fairly close together, they should be cut more frequently to maintain a thicket; some species, like dogwood and blackthorn, will respond by suckering. If the woodland edge has regenerated naturally, it may have a lower density of trees and shrubs and therefore require less frequent cutting.

TOP LEFT **Dragonflies and damselflies such as this azure damselfly use new woodland rides to bask and hunt.**

TOP RIGHT **Common whitethroats are attracted to scrubby areas in new woodland.**

BOTTOM LEFT **Meadow brown nectaring on wild marjoram in a new woodland ride.**

BOTTOM RIGHT **Hazel nuts are attractive to small mammals, particularly dormice.**

Rides with 'three-zones' can be further enhanced by incorporating a scalloped woodland edge, effectively widening them further. Scallops may be up to 20 m long and 20–50 m deep, providing bays that offer more shelter from the wind (Warren and Fuller 1993). Scalloping replaces straight ride edges with more natural, diffuse ones. It increases the total amount of ride edge and helps to diversify wildlife habitats. Some scalloped areas may be coppiced, with others maintained as tall herbs or grassland. Gently curving rides also provide an alternative to long, straight rides.

Glades should also be managed if they are to remain open and structurally diverse. They should be divided into a number of sectors, depending on their size, which should be mown on rotation to achieve the desired variation in vegetation height. In the glade illustrated in Figure 7.2 for example, each individual quarter could be mown on rotation, once every four years or more. Cuttings from the glade should always be removed. Areas of short turf would be mown annually, after seed set. The shrubs along the woodland edge should also be cut on a longer rotation, or managed as coppice. Naturally regenerating trees and shrubs in the open areas should be cut back as necessary.

7.2 Selecting trees and shrubs

One of the more interesting aspects of woodland creation is the selection of trees and shrubs for planting. Information acquired during the landscape evaluation exercise (Chapter 6) should provide the necessary background to undertake this task; the following steps are recommended:

Step one: identify the most appropriate woodland communities for the site
Step two: select the canopy and understorey species for the core woodland areas
Step three: select woodland edge mixes with the emphasis on diversity
Step four: determine the planting percentages.

Step one: identify the most appropriate woodland communities for the site

We suggest using the National Vegetation Classification (NVC) as a guide, alongside information on the trees and shrubs characteristic of reference woodland communities in the local landscape (Section 6.4). It is important to emphasise that every semi-natural wood is unique; made up of a mosaic of vegetation communities which differ subtly, or more significantly from each other, depending on soil and other conditions, sometimes within relatively small areas. So the temptation to follow a prescription entirely based on an NVC type, or to try to mimic a specific community found in local reference woodlands, should be resisted. Some categories, such as lowland ash and oak woods (W8 and W10) are very broad, making it difficult to predict a precise relationship between the site and any theoretical sub-community.

Gatekeeper basking along the shrubby edge of new woodland.

What is more important is that the planting mix takes account of local variations in the appropriate NVC type or types, and that a diverse range of shrubs relevant to these communities is included. This should prove attractive to wildlife and lead to good structural diversity in the canopy. If there is no appropriate reference woodland in the local landscape, soil and site characteristics become the primary selection criteria; species selection may then be based loosely on NVC prescriptions, with reference to literature on the trees and shrubs in semi-natural woodland outside the local landscape. Another approach would be to examine any vegetation present as 'optimal precursors' (indicators) of site conditions, matched to a designated NVC woodland type (Rodwell and Patterson, 1994); but again no precise relationship can be assumed or proved.

Step two: select the canopy and understorey species for the core woodland areas

Published floristic tables provide complete lists of species and their frequencies in NVC woodland types, and their sub-communities (Rodwell, 1991). More accessible descriptions of NVC woodlands communities and sub-communities can be found in the Joint Nature Conservation Committee's *National Vegetation Classification: Field guide to woodland* (Hall *et al.*, 2004) (see also Section 1.2). Based on the information in the literature, and species lists from the local landscape evaluation (Chapter 6), it should be possible to draw up a putative planting list.

For many NVC communities, the list will include too many species to contemplate planting them all. In the case of ash-maple woodland (W8) for example, 35 native woody perennials are listed (Rodwell, 1991), many of which occur at low frequencies. However, even 20-species mixtures are probably impractical and not particularly 'natural', especially at the scale of a small wood; simpler models have a greater chance of success (Hodge, 1995). In practice, we might expect to find at least four major species and 10 minor ones present in the canopy and understorey in W8, W10 and W12 communities; in upland oak woods and birch woods (W11 and W17) two major, and up to four minor species, would be more realistic. In general, the more extreme are the site conditions in terms of low fertility, exposure or wetness, the more impoverished the species list becomes.

Local survey data may reveal the main and sub-communities present in local reference woodland. Referring from this to the NVC floristic tables (Table 7.1), the dominant canopy and understorey species can be selected to form the new core woodland, together with some of the species present at lower frequencies. As woodlands are rarely homogeneous, it is important to consider introducing some variation in the canopy and understorey communities within the new wood, especially if the wood is greater than a few hectares.

TOP **Spindle provides an autumn and early winter fruit resource.**

LEFT **Common whitebeam fruit ripens in late summer.**

RIGHT **Rowan fruits are particularly favoured by winter thrushes.**

Table 7.1 Examples of native woody perennials and their frequency values in selected NVC woodland sub-communities (after Rodwell, 1991)

A: Woodland community species components

Species	Frequency		
	W8a	W10a	W17b
Constants of the community			
Alder		●	
Ash	●●●●		●
Aspen		●	
Beech	●	●	●
Crab apple	●		
Downy birch	●	●	●●●
Field maple	●●		
Goat willow	●		
Grey willow	●		
Holly	●	●	
Hornbeam		●	
Lime		●	
Pedunculate oak		●●●	
Rowan	●	●	●
Sessile oak			●●●●●
Silver birch		●●●	
Small-leaved lime		●	
Wild cherry	●	●	
Yew	●	●	
Characteristic of the sub-community			
Ash		●	
Aspen	●		
English elm	●		
Hornbeam	●●		
Pedunculate oak	●●●●		●
Sessile oak		●●●	
Silver birch	●●		●
Small-leaved elm	●●		
Small-leaved lime	●●		
Wild service-tree	●		
Others			
Blackthorn	●	●	
Broom		●	
Crab apple		●	
Dogwood	●●		
Elder	●	●	
Field maple		●	
Goat willow			●
Guelder-rose	●	●	
Hawthorn	●●●	●●●	●●●
Hazel	●●●●●	●●●	●
Holly			●●●
Midland hawthorn	●	●	
Sessile oak	●		
Spindle	●		
Wayfaring-tree	●		

A: Woodlands W8a (ash-maple wood, primrose-ground ivy sub-community);
W10a (lowland oak wood, typical sub-community); and
W17b (Atlantic oak wood, typical sub-community).

B: Scrub community components

Species	Frequency	
	W21	W24
Constants of the community		
Ash sapling*	●●●	●
Beech sapling*	●	●
Blackthorn	●●●	
Buckthorn	●	
Dog-rose	●●●	
Field-rose	●	
Grey willow	●	
Hawthorn	●●●●●	
Hazel	●●	
Holly	●	
Silver birch sapling	●	
Spindle	●	
Others		
Blackthorn		●
Common juniper	●	
Crab apple	●	
Dogwood	●	
Elder	●●	●
Field maple	●	
Hawthorn		●●
Hazel		●
Midland hawthorn	●	
Wayfaring-tree	●	
Wild privet	●	
Yew sapling	●	

B: W21 (hawthorn-ivy scrub, typical sub-community); and
W24 (bramble-Yorkshire-fog scrub, typical sub-community).

(* – for scrub and shrubby woodland edge, high forest trees would not be planted)

Frequency values (how often a plant is found on moving from one sample of vegetation to the next):
●●●● and ●●●●● – community constants (61–80% = IV, 81–100% = V)
●●● – common or frequent species (41–60%)
●● – occasional (21–40%)
● – rare (1–20%)

LEFT **Hawthorn fruits are consumed by a wide variety of birds.**

RIGHT **Wayfaring-tree fruit are consumed in autumn by warblers prior to migration.**

For the communities that are relatively species-poor, devising a planting mix will be much more straightforward. For example, only 11 native woody species are listed by Rodwell (1991) for the Atlantic oak woods (W17) confined to acid soils in the cool, wet north-west of Britain (Table 7.1). The native pinewoods of the Central and North West Highlands of Scotland are similarly species-poor, presenting fewer problems for selection.

Should rarer species be planted?

At the national level, it is important to respect the natural ranges of different trees and shrub species in new native woodland schemes in order to protect their genetic integrity, even though they may grow well elsewhere (Soutar and Peterken, 1989). Species such as small- and large-leaved lime, wild service-tree, box, Midland hawthorn and the rare whitebeams come into this category. Locally, semi-natural distributions of species within woods are also highly variable, with some strongly gregarious species such as hornbeam, small-leaved lime, sessile oak and alder forming large clumps, or clonal patches in the case of suckering elm, wild cherry and aspen (Rackham, 1992). Other, non-gregarious species are less frequent and are often widely dispersed within or between woods, as are Midland hawthorn, wild service-tree and crab apple in the lowlands. In semi-natural woods the result is a mosaic of different species of varying patch sizes, the scale of the pattern depending on species characteristics and the degree of environmental variation.

Consequently, rare species, or those with limited distributions, are not generally considered appropriate for planting outside their natural range because their native distribution patterns are of intrinsic importance. More information may be found in local and national floras.

Should species likely to colonise naturally be planted?

Avoid planting species which are likely to colonise naturally, such as birches, willows, bramble and ivy (Section 7.1). Bramble will almost certainly colonise and may need to be controlled when the trees are establishing, although patches should be retained as they are important for wildlife: bramble flowers support nectaring butterflies and other insects in mid/late summer; dead stems provide nest sites for some woodland solitary bees and wasps; dormouse, and birds such as nightingale and common whitethroat nest in bramble; it is particularly attractive to insectivorous birds such as warblers; and its fruit attracts a wide range of birds and small mammals, including dormouse.

Ivy is also a natural colonist of the woodland edge: late autumn flowers are an important nectar source for insects overwintering as adults; it is the food plant of the holly blue butterfly; its late winter/early spring fruits are an important resource as other fruits are exhausted; and older climbers can support insects, bat roosts and nesting birds such as spotted flycatcher.

Step three: select woodland edge mixes with the emphasis on diversity

Selecting species to plant along the woodland edge, including rides and glades is one of the key stages in the whole planning operation. Any areas of scrub would also come into this category.

Too many smaller woods have been planted with a narrow range of trees, and very few shrubs, and are the poorer for it. Reference should again be made to local survey data and NVC floristic tables to select shrubs and small trees. As with the canopy and understorey, some variation should be introduced to woodland edge and scrub mixes, for both species and structural diversity. For the more diverse shrub communities where there is greater choice of planting material, such as those found in ash-maple woodland (W8), chalk beech woods (W12) or hawthorn-ivy scrub (W21), one should also be aware of the resources which they provide for wildlife. Consequently, when selecting shrubs and small trees, some consideration should be given to the following questions:

- **How will the planted species contribute to the desired vegetation structure?**

Canopy cover and density affect light conditions and hence colonisation a range of shade-tolerant plants; diversity of cover along the woodland edge is important for insects and the feeding and nesting of a range of woodland birds. With a good range of small trees and shrubs matching the conditions, and an appropriate design, structural diversity should be assured.

- **How valuable is the species to wildlife?**

The woodland edge and areas of scrub can host diverse insect communities. Foliar, sap, nectar, pollen and fruit feeding insects are very important constituents of woodland biodiversity. They also provide an essential source of food for bats, and the majority of woodland birds during the breeding season, including the critical post-fledging period.

- **Are fruits available throughout the year?**

For some woodland edge and scrub communities, the mix of small trees and shrubs can include some selected to provide an almost year-round supply of fruit. Fruit is a vital food for many mammals, insects and woodland birds, particularly in the post-fledging period, and throughout the autumn and winter months. Whilst many species bear fruit in the autumn, far fewer have fruit in late winter, spring and early summer, so it is well worth checking (Box 7.1). Climate change is already affecting fruiting phenology of some plants; hawthorn and bramble for example may flower and fruit several weeks earlier than in the recent past. If these fruits are consumed early, then this may have serious implications for birds and animals which rely on them later in the winter. Therefore, where appropriate, make sure that species which naturally fruit or seed in late winter, such as guelder-rose, crab apple and holly are well represented.

Step four: determine the planting percentages

Finally, the numbers of trees and shrubs of each species to be planted in the various woodland communities must be determined. Published NVC tables provide averaged frequencies and cover values for different trees and shrubs for each community type, although direct reference to the mosaic found in local ancient woodlands is probably a more reliable guide. Examples for five different communities are given in Table 7.1, including scrub communities to guide the planting of woodland edge and areas of scrub. This information, together with data on the frequencies of trees and shrubs in reference woodland communities (Section 6.4) can be used as a guide to calculating planting mixes. In large woodland planting schemes, it is best to avoid homogeneity across large areas by varying the mix of species to reflect natural variation that is found in native

LEFT **Midland hawthorn flowers provide an important early season source of nectar for insects.**

RIGHT **Elder fruits are quickly consumed by birds and small mammals in late summer.**

Box 7.1 Summary of the value to wildlife of some of the shrubs and small trees which might be planted along the edge of more diverse lowland mixed deciduous woodland (W8 and W10), or in associated scrubby areas

Species	Key value to wildlife
Blackthorn:	characteristic of the woodland edge and an important species for wildlife; supports a very high diversity of insects; provides a very important early spring nectar source for insects; fruit consumed by birds and small mammals in the autumn/winter, which disperse seeds; dense cover important for nesting and roosting birds
Broom:	occurs infrequently in oak woods; supports a wide range of insects; dense foliage provides valuable nesting sites for birds
Buckthorn:	occurs infrequently in hawthorn-ivy scrub; supports a smaller range of feeding insects; foodplant of the brimstone and green hairstreak butterflies; berries consumed by birds in early winter, which disperse seed
Cherries:	widely distributed in oak and ash woods; supports a wide range of insects; important nectar source for insects; summer fruits consumed by many birds
Common whitebeam:	occurs naturally in southern calcareous ash woods; supports a range of feeding insects; provides late summer/early autumn fruit for birds
Crab apple:	occurs infrequently in oak and ash woods; important late-winter fruit resource when other fruit becomes scarce; supports good diversity of insects
Dogwood:	occurs infrequently in ash woods; supports a range of feeding insects; early winter fruit valuable for many birds, which disperse seeds
Elder:	occurs infrequently in oak and ash woods and an important species for wildlife; fruits for a short period in late summer when few other shrubs are in fruit; consequently fruit consumed quickly and seeds dispersed by many birds and small mammals; foliage and flowers attract relatively few insects
Field maple:	characteristic of ash woodland edge, infrequent in oak woods; may be rapidly colonised by lichens; supports a range of feeding insects
Gorse:	occurs infrequently in oak woods; supports a range of feeding insects; foodplant of the holly blue and green hairstreak butterflies; good cover for nesting and roosting birds
Guelder-rose:	occurs infrequently in oak and ash woods; supports a range of feeding insects; an important mid- to late-winter fruit resource, consumed and seeds dispersed by birds
Hawthorns:	characteristic of the understorey and woodland edge and an important species for wildlife; supports a very high diversity of insects; very important early season nectar source for insects; important foodplant for moth larvae; attractive to insectivorous birds; fruit consumed and seeds dispersed by birds in the autumn/winter, especially winter thrushes; important cover for nesting and roosting birds
Hazel:	characteristic of the understorey and woodland edge; supports a high diversity of insects; important foodplant for moth larvae; attractive to insectivorous birds; nuts are an important autumn food source for the dormouse
Holly:	characteristic of the understorey and woodland edge; fruits from October, becoming an important late-winter fruit resource when other fruit becomes scarce; fruits consumed and seeds dispersed by birds; foodplant of the holly blue butterfly
Honeysuckle:	characteristic of the understorey and woodland edge of oak woods, occurs infrequently in ash woods; fruits briefly in late summer – berries attract a range of frugivorous birds, including bullfinch and marsh tit; used as a source of nesting material by dormice
Rose species:	occurs infrequently in oak and ash woods; late summer flowers of rose species provide valuable nectar sources for insects; fruits consumed by birds and mammals in the autumn
Rowan:	occurs infrequently in oak and ash woods; an important food source for insects; late summer to early winter fruits important for warblers and favoured by winter thrushes
Small-leaved elm:	now rare in ash woods due to Dutch elm disease; intrinsic conservation value; elms support wide variety of moth larvae; foodplant of the white-letter hairstreak
Spindle:	occurs infrequently in ash woods; intrinsic conservation value; provides an autumn and early winter fruit resource
Wayfaring-tree:	occurs infrequently in oak and ash woods; late summer/early autumn fruits important for warblers prior to migration
Wild privet:	occurs infrequently in oak and ash woods; mid-summer nectar source; valuable winter source of berries for birds
Willows:	generally occur infrequently in ash woods; very high diversity of insects, many feeding exclusively; important foodplants for moth larvae; flowers provide valuable early source of nectar; thicket stage provides important nesting habitat for a range of specialist birds, including willow tit
Yew:	occurs infrequently in oak and ash woods; autumn/winter source of berries for birds; provides good shelter in winter

Box 7.2 Selection of trees and shrubs for the planting of Victory Wood, at Lamberhurst Farm in Kent

Step one: identify the most appropriate woodland communities for the site

The landscape character assessment and ecological assessment criteria supporting the planting of Victory Wood was presented in Section 6.5.1. Essentially, the site is bordered by two ancient woods, Ellenden Wood and Blean Wood. These woods are dominated by lowland sessile oak wood (W10a), with some ash-maple woodland (W8a) along a stream gully; and small patches of rare acid sessile oak-beech (W15) distributed through Ellenden Wood. Soil analysis established that, since the clearance of North Blean Wood in the 1960s, liming and fertiliser use had raised the pH and the phosphorus index in some areas; but the site was still low in nitrogen. Sessile oak wood was still considered generally appropriate, but one area with a higher base status was considered suitable for an ash-maple community, adding some variety to the planted woodland.

Step two: select the canopy and understorey species for the core woodland areas

The 'closed canopy' planting mixes for Victory Wood were based on the NVC floristic tables for W8a and W10a communities (Table 7.1) and the species known to be present in the reference woods. Due to the rarity of the acid sessile oak-beech community in the reference woods, no attempt was made to create this community in the planted woodland.

Lowland sessile oak woodland mix:
NVC floristic tables show the most frequent species to be sessile oak, pedunculate oak, silver birch and hazel. Sessile oak was dominant in the reference woods, so it was reflected in the planting mix (see below), but some pedunculate oak was also included as it was considered less likely to be disadvantaged by climate change in the South East. Silver birch may colonise the site naturally, but it was included for its wildlife value in the planting mix to ensure its presence early on. Other trees selected as characteristic of the reference woods included: beech, downy birch and hornbeam. Four shrubs frequent in the understorey of the reference woods were also included: hawthorn, holly, hazel and Midland hawthorn. Wild service-tree is not listed in the W10 floristic table, but was widely scattered in the reference woods, justifying its inclusion. The diversity of shrubs was increased in the woodland edge mixes (see below).

Ash-maple woodland mix:
NVC floristic tables show the most frequent species to be ash, pedunculate oak, hazel and hawthorn. Other trees selected as characteristic of the reference woods included: sessile oak, beech, hornbeam, small-leaved elm and field maple. Midland hawthorn was added as it dominated the shrub layer of the reference woodland. Sessile oak was again the dominant oak in the reference woods, so was reflected in the planting mix. Hornbeam was also characteristic and was consequently included as an important forest species. A small number of small-leaved elms, which are in recovery at this site following the ravages of Dutch elm disease, were included for their intrinsic wildlife value. Planting a small number should at least enable a continued turnover of elm trees in the understorey. The diversity of shrubs was increased in the woodland edge mixes (see below).

Step three: select woodland edge mixes with the emphasis on diversity

Woodland edge and shrubby areas were poorly represented in the reference woods for Victory Wood, consequently the woodland edge planting mixes were based primarily on the NVC floristic tables for W8a and W10a communities; their associated scrub communities (W21 and W24 respectively) (Table 7.1); and their value for wildlife (Box 7.1; Tables 7.2 and 7.3). However, species were only chosen which occurred naturally in the wider landscape.

Lowland sessile oak woodland edge mix:
The woodland edge mix comprised 12 species, of which eight were not included in the closed canopy woodland. These were: blackthorn, field-rose, elder, honeysuckle, wayfaring-tree, guelder-rose, gorse and broom. The other species in the mix included: hawthorn, Midland hawthorn, holly and hazel.

Ash-maple woodland edge mix:
To reflect the greater diversity in ash-maple woodland, the edge mix comprised 14 species shrubs and small trees, of which 10 were not included in the closed canopy woodland. These are: wild cherry, grey willow, goat willow, blackthorn, dog-rose, elder, honeysuckle, spindle and crab apple. The other species in the mix included: hawthorn, Midland hawthorn, holly, hazel and field maple.

Step four: determine the planting percentages

The planting percentages for the oakwood mixes are given as an example. The key reference wood for Victory Wood was Ellenden Wood, a sessile oakwood which comprised several distinct woodland communities; to reflect this, three planting mixes were devised for the sessile oakwood areas. Each was made up of 80% canopy species and 20% understorey species; sessile oak dominated the canopy mix and all three comprised the same understorey mix. They differed in the make-up of the canopy species: the main mix represented a more 'typical' community; the second a community where hornbeam is absent and beech is more prominent; and the third a community where beech is absent.

Sessile oakwood canopy tree mixes (80% of planting mix):

	Main mix (%)	Variation 1 (%)	Variation 2 (%)
Sessile oak	45	50	50
Pedunculate oak	5	5	5
Beech	5	20	
Downy birch	2.5	2.5	2.5
Silver birch	2.5	2.5	2.5
Hornbeam	15		20
Wild service-tree	5		

Woodland edge
The species mix, density of planting and spacing were varied to create structural diversity, provide some limited opportunities for natural regeneration and attract wildlife. Fifteen of the 20 species planted in the ash-maple and oak wood edges were not included in the core woodland areas. They were selected primarily for their attractiveness to wildlife (Box 7.1); in addition, the density of planting and spacing was also varied. This was achieved by planting the trees and shrubs randomly along the edge at a minimum 2 m spacing, but varying the stocking density from 100% down to 50%.

Fallen acorns ready to be collected in a mast year.

woodland (Section 6.4 and Box 7.2). This is particularly important along the woodland edge, where the species mix, density of planting and spacing will create structural diversity and provide opportunities for natural regeneration. Attempts to precisely reproduce distinct groupings of species within local reference woods should be avoided.

7.3 Sourcing seed of trees and shrubs

It was argued earlier (Section 4.3) that sourcing seed from the local Forestry Commission seed zone(s) alone may become increasing untenable as the climate changes. The consequence of this is that planting stock would be sourced from several locations, of both local and non-local provenance. However, in the absence of detailed knowledge on the genetics of most British trees and shrubs, even defining the limits of 'local' areas for collecting plant material must rely to some extent on guesswork and best estimates. There are several default positions:

- to accept the prescribed Forestry Commission seed zones until a better knowledge-based system has been produced;
- to match the environmental conditions at the planting site as closely as possible with the collection location, using Natural England's Natural Areas, or their equivalents in Scotland and Wales;
- to collect plant material from the nearest available semi-natural woods, provided this is logistically and economically feasible.

For sourcing seed of native trees and shrubs, a strategy based on the composite provenancing method (see Section 4.3) could be adopted, and specified to seed suppliers as follows:

The bulk of seed should ideally be collected from semi-natural stands that are continuously maintained by natural regeneration in the local landscape close to the planting site. If this is not possible, the local seed zone could be used, making sure that collections were made under the Voluntary Scheme for the Certification of Native Trees and Shrubs, endorsed by the Forestry Commission; but in England, a more attractive alternative would be to source seed from the local Natural England Natural Area which is based on geomorphological features rather than political boundaries.

Mixes for each species could be augmented with seed collected from eco-matched sites to the south of the planting area, and could contain up to 25% of this material; in northern Britain, this could be from southern England; in southern England it should be from areas in Europe with a similar maritime climate, not more than 2° south of Britain, avoiding continental seed sources.

Once the sources have been chosen, seed should be collected from sufficient parent trees in semi-natural stands to capture a wide range of genetic diversity, whilst avoiding over-collection from individuals or a population as a whole. Whether providing a specification to seed suppliers, or collecting one's own seed, it is important therefore to ensure that a few basic guidelines are observed:

- species with self-pollination mechanisms, limited seed dispersal and localised populations, may be collected over a narrow range; for many wind- or insect-pollinated tree species with wind or animal seed dispersal, collection at a wider, intermediate to regional scale should be adequate to capture sufficient genetic variation.
- collect from healthy, viable populations of interbreeding trees in well-authenticated semi-natural stands, such as ancient woodland; if possible, isolated from other stands containing non-native or improved native genotypes of the same species.
- conditions at the collection site should be matched as closely as possible to the characteristics of the planting site in terms of the local climate, topography, soil and vegetation type.

- the number of parents should ideally optimise genetic variability in the progeny; guidelines on parent number varies with authority, but many suggest 20–30 individuals.
- sample the range of morphological variation, collecting from genetically unrelated plants; avoid selecting for particular traits. As neighbouring trees are more likely to be closely related, collect from widely-spaced individuals: distances of 50–100 m are a useful guide. Collect similar quantities from each individual and no more than 20% from any individual plant.
- avoid collecting from reproductively isolated plants in remnant populations, but if unavoidable, bulk the seed with that of other local plants.

7.4 Planting patterns

As different tree species grow at different rates, even-aged mixtures soon suffer competition between the species components, resulting in the shading out of the slowest-grown by the quickest. This is an important issue when new native woodland is being planned. Foresters address the problem either by seeking to combine species with compatible growth rates or characteristics, such as planting shade-tolerant together with light-demanding species, or spatially separating the different species from each other by grouping them in some geometric layout or pattern (Box 7.3).

7.4.1 Designs for new native woodland

For new native woodlands, perhaps closest to the naturalistic patterns in semi-natural woods are variations of the group system, segregating species into group sizes that reflect their more-or-less gregarious tendencies.

Group sizes in turn can be based on frequencies of each species typical of the target communities, adjusted according to those frequencies found in the local woodlands. No particular formula is advocated here for varying the size or composition of the groups according to the woodland community type, or to take account of the overall size of woodland creation scheme. For large-scale schemes, the major difference compared with smaller schemes would

---

Box 7.3 Planting mixture designs in forestry

Group system planting

Group system planting in forestry locates each species in its own small 'pure' block, reducing competition between slow and quick-growing species (except at the edges of the groups). Within the groups themselves, the similar performance of the trees forces them to grow tall and straight, improving the prospects for timber production. In much forestry practice, groups are planted either as regular and staggered sequences or randomly, usually in small blocks of 9–25 trees: in practice the larger groups are easier to manage and will suffer less from edge effects. From an ecological point of view, groups growing at different rates will begin to develop some variation in canopy structure and might be expected to create a patchier environment than intimate mixtures, with longer light and litterfall gradients between blocks. Later thinning should extend this patchiness, although this is also true of some other mixture types.

Species intended to form the eventual canopy dominants can also be planted as groups within a matrix of other species that will be thinned out earlier. These target groups are located at a suitable distance apart that will eventually allow their expanding canopies to coalesce before final felling. Groups of nine trees at 10–12 m spacing between groups are commonly used, resulting in a final crop spacing of 70–100 trees per ha. The technique was often used with conifer- broadleaved mixtures, planting small groups of broadleaves within a conifer matrix in a 25:75% ratio. In urban and community forests planted for amenity and conservation purposes, all-broadleaved mixtures are common, comprising a matrix of shrubs and 'nurse' species such as alder and birch. These nurse species are designed to be progressively thinned around longer-term groups of canopy species.

Intimate mixtures

The suppression of one or more species will surely follow unless heavy thinning is continually employed to favour the slower-growing 'losers': hence such an arrangement is not often employed commercially, although it was once common in farm woodland and urban plantings. 'Averaging' of the light conditions created by the composite canopy tends to produce uniform conditions in the understorey. If no corrective management is carried out the slower-growing species will quickly be lost, resulting in even greater uniformity of the canopy. Intimate mixtures are diverse at the individual level but appear homogeneous at the stand level.

be a greater availability for the deployment of rides, open spaces and other features. The spatial arrangement of the groups themselves can be carried out in a number of ways, both by allowing unplanted space between groups and altering the density of planting within groups, allowing for natural colonisation to take place. Spacing between individuals, ranging from 1.5 m apart to 10 m or more, will promote gradients within and between species groups and to some extent mirror the patchiness of naturally regenerated stands (Rodwell and Patterson, 1994). Clumps of trees may be single species, or mixed clumps of two or three species, providing the growth rates are well matched (Figure 7.3A). The clump size itself may be varied, as it is in forestry practice (Figure 7.3B), with clumps ranging in size from nine trees to as many as 64 in larger plantings. Varying the space between clumps (Figure 7.3C) will create greater structural diversity, and provide an opportunity for natural colonisation. Spaces of about 5 m will quickly become shaded as the canopy closes, but larger spaces up to 20 or 30 m could be created in larger woods, which may develop into open glades. Variation can also be introduced by varying the spacing between clumps (Figure 7.3D); this again adds to the structural diversity of the wood, and avoids the traditional regimented planting in straight lines.

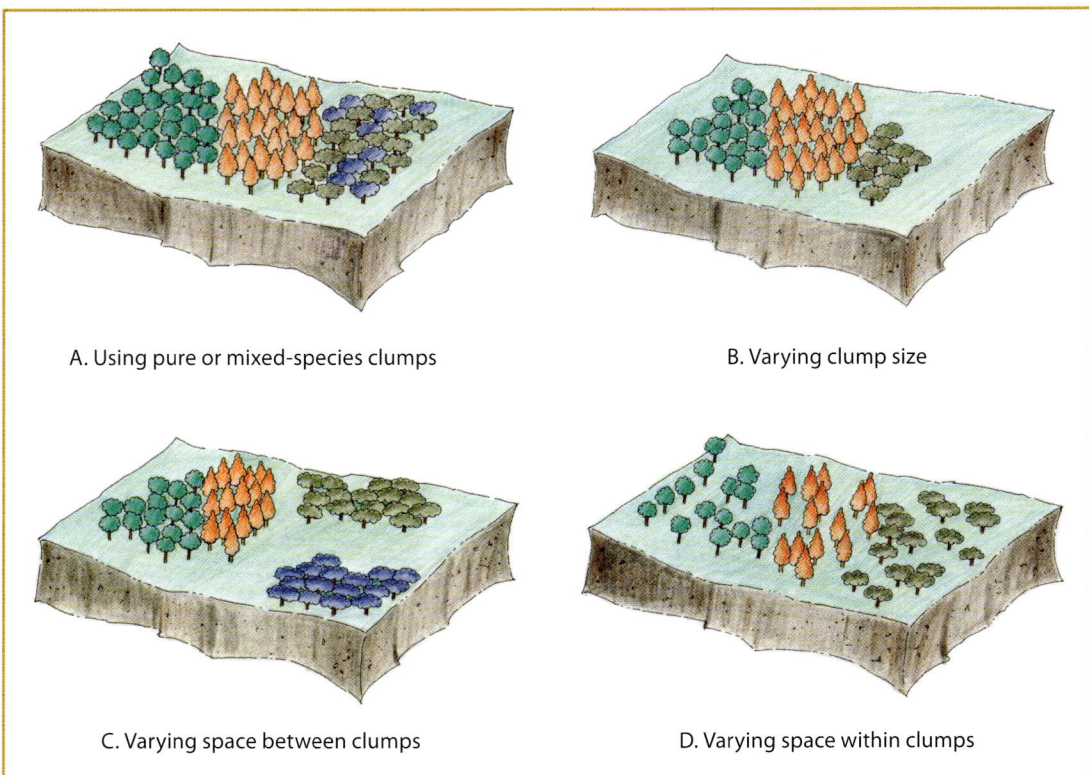

Figure 7.3 Sketches of differing spacing and group sizes used to guide tree planting programmes.

A. Using pure or mixed-species clumps

B. Varying clump size

C. Varying space between clumps

D. Varying space within clumps

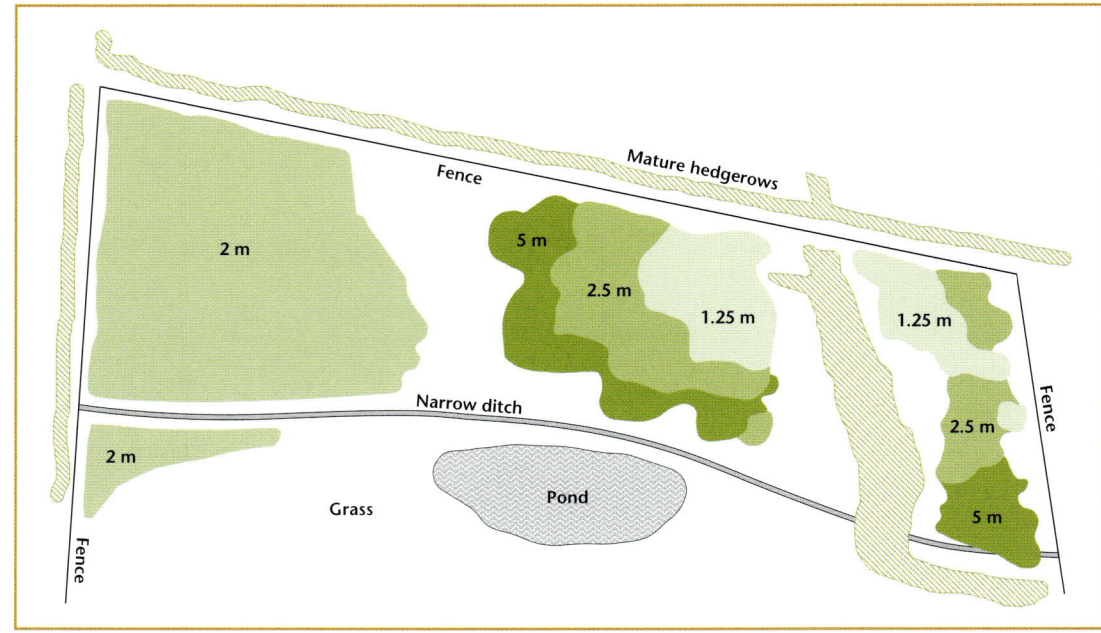

Figure 7.4 The demonstration new native woodland planted at Desford, near Leicester on a heavy, moisture-retaining site. The species mixture was a simplified version of NVC W8, in which tree species were planted as individual species groups in blocks of 5x5 m. Within the blocks, trees were spaced at 1.25, 2.5 and 5 m spacing, creating gradients of different planting density across the site. (Source: Harmer, 1999b; © Crown copyright, reproduced with the kind permission of the Forestry Commission).

Figure 7.5 Carrifran Wildwood, a 650-ha site in the Southern Uplands of Scotland, in which about half of the area is being converted to new native woodland. The overall design was based on varying site conditions across the site, matched to six main NVC communities (W4, W7, W9, W11, W17 and W19), each of which was planted as a mosaic of single-species clumps at variable spacing (reproduced with kind permission from Philip Ashmole, Borders Forest Trust). © Crown copyright and/or database right. All rights reserved. Licence number 100049759.

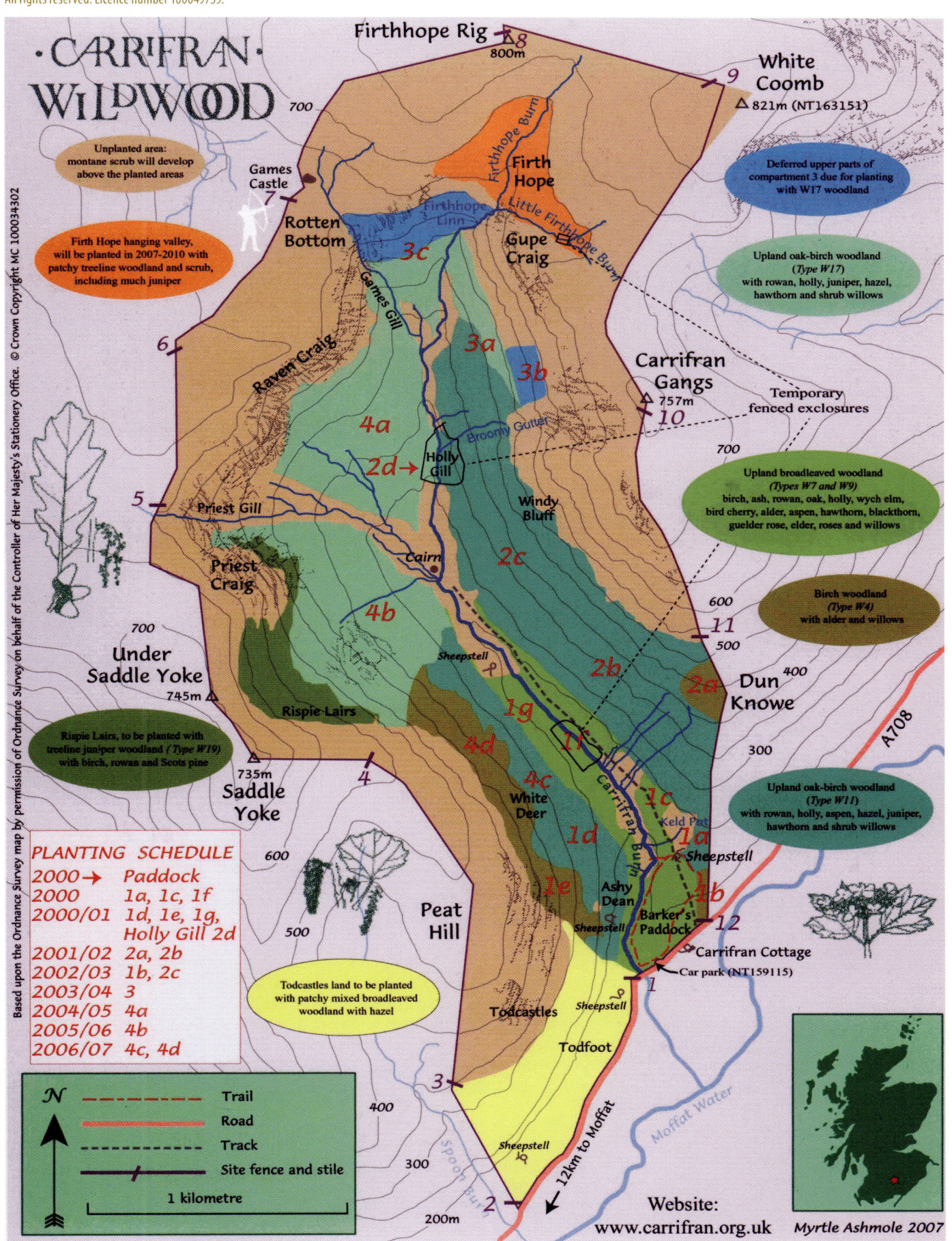

The Carrifran Valley from Brodesbeck High, looking north. The surrounding hills have virtually no remaining native woodland cover and are extensively grazed, apart from scattered plantations of non-native spruce and larch (see to the right of the photograph). (Reproduced with kind permission from Philip Ashmole, Borders Forest Trust).

Two practical examples in new native woods also illustrate different types of planting layout. In the first, a neglected 1 ha agricultural field at Desford, near Leicester, was planted with a simple eight-species mix, based on an ash-maple woodland (NVC W8) (Harmer, 1999b). The trees were planted as single-species plots, 5x5 m square, with variable spacing within the plots, giving 25, nine and four trees per plot, with shrubs planted in patches throughout (Figure 7.4). In two areas different spacing was employed to give gradual gradients of tree density across the site. In the second example at Carrifran Wildwood (Figure 7.5), an upland site near Moffat on the Scottish Border, the much larger site of 650 ha encompassed a wide range of altitude, topography and soils (Ashmole and Ashmole, 2009). The varying site conditions meant that a much wider portfolio of appropriate NVC communities could be selected. Large areas of the site were left unplanted, and the trees and shrubs were again planted as single-species groups at variable spacing.

7.5 Creating plant communities in rides and open spaces

A more challenging task in many respects is to aid the development of 'semi-natural' vegetation communities in woodland rides, glades and open spaces, which will attract diverse insect populations. This is an aspect of woodland creation which has often been neglected in the past, and yet can make a huge difference to the value of a new wood for wildlife. Open spaces have traditionally been sown with agricultural grass seed mixes, or allowed to colonise naturally. In both cases, regular cutting may produce a 'neat and tidy' appearance, but the value to wildlife is usually very limited, except in rare circumstances where the site is on soil of low fertility, and/or adjacent to unimproved semi-natural grassland.

Grassland or heathland communities in woodland open spaces should resemble semi-natural habitats in the wider landscape, so species mixes should be based on these. The first step therefore is to identify the most appropriate grassland/heathland community for the open areas in the new woodland. However, finding suitable reference sites can be difficult, particularly in the lowlands, where unimproved grassland has declined dramatically and is now rare. If this is the case, the National Vegetation Classification (NVC) is useful as a guide, alongside any published information on the plants characteristic of local grassland or heathland communities on similar soil types (Section 6.4).

Ideally, reference sites could act as donor sites, providing harvested seed for sowing or green hay for spreading in rides and glades. As this is rarely possible, species mixes could be designed by the practitioner, based on these semi-natural communities, although this is significantly more expensive. Alternatively seed mixes of the particular vegetation community could be harvested from matched sites in the wider area, although these can also be difficult to obtain.

PART TWO WOODLAND CREATION PRACTICE – **DESIGNING A NEW WOOD AND SELECTING SPECIES TO PLANT**

Whilst these are the best options for creating diverse communities in woodland rides and open spaces, an alternative widely used in habitat creation is to sow commercially available generic wildflower or grass seed mixes which are designed for a limited number of different situations such as soil type. Some species are sold as potted seedlings or plugs, although these are relatively expensive and require extra care to ensure their survival. Care must be exercised, where purchasing from commercial suppliers, to avoid inappropriate species and cultivars. A final option is to consider natural regeneration, especially for new woodland in close proximity to unimproved grassland or heathland, from where some natural colonists may arrive in the longer term. In this case, colonisation might be accelerated through the movement of livestock, local provenance is assured and the method is a low cost option in comparison to seeding.

The main considerations when deciding upon the method of creating grassland or heathland in woodland rides are glades are summarised in Tables 7.2 and 7.3. Each method can be used on ex-arable land or pasture given appropriate site preparation. Most success will be achieved on less fertile land with a phosphorus (P) Index of 0-1; levels of 2 may be marginal in some cases. Where soil fertility is high, a robust grassland type containing a range of competitive herbs, such as a neutral hay-meadow mixture, will provide a variety of wild flowers if maintained with a suitable mowing regime.

Natural colonisation of a chalk bank along the margins of a new wood.

7.5.1 Formulating seed mixes

Formulating seed mix requires more thought, but the pleasure of watching a meadow or heathland develop may ultimately be more rewarding than, for example sowing a generic seed mix. The advantages of specifying the composition of the seed mix are that factors such as topography, geology, soils (including fertility) and the species composition of unimproved grassland or heathland in the local landscape can be taken into consideration. The main

Table 7.2 The limitations of commercially available generic seed mixes or plug plants used for establishing grassland in woodland open spaces

Methods	Limitations
Sowing a generic meadow mix	• Mix may contain species uncharacteristic of local grassland communities • Provenance can be difficult to ascertain, and unlikely to be local • Non-local seed should not be sown close to unimproved semi-natural grassland • May be more cost effective than using locally sourced seed
Sowing a generic grass seed mix	In addition to the issues relating to sowing a generic meadow mix listed above: • Ensure mix does not contain persistent and highly competitive agricultural or amenity cultivars • Simple grass mix increases the chances of success • Absence of wildflowers makes this more cost effective • Any natural colonisation of herbs from adjacent species-rich habitat likely to be slow • Species-rich hay spreading, slot seeding or oversowing can be undertaken after 3 years or so to introduce wildflowers, following scarification or spraying
Potted seedlings or plugs	• Plant in bare ground or sward • Target species can be planted into an existing species-rich sward eg. butterfly foodplant or insect nectar plant • Introduce species difficult to propagate through seed • Expensive and mortality can be high • Requires careful planting and aftercare until established • Plants can be swamped by existing vegetation, but may still be more robust than developing seedlings • Provenance can be difficult to ascertain

disadvantages are that it may be more expensive than purchasing a generic seed mix or, if available, seed harvested from a local meadow (Table 7.3). Furthermore, if purchased from a seed company the individual species may not all be collected locally or from an eco-matched site. Ensuring local collection of all species in the mix will add to the expense.

Published floristic tables provide complete lists of species and their frequencies in NVC open ground communities and sub-communities (Rodwell, 1992). Based on the information in the literature, species lists from local reference sites (Section 6.4), and local knowledge of plant communities, it should be possible to draw up a putative planting list. The list will almost certainly include far too many species to contemplate planting them all. However, it should be possible to choose species most characteristic of local grassland communities (Table 7.4). Furthermore, specifying which species are included in the mix allows the value of plants for insects to be considered (Box 7.4), and how they might contribute to a diverse vegetation structure. This is particularly relevant to species-rich grassland. To help with this process, some of ways in which a diverse grassland flora in rides and glades can attract wildlife are considered below.

Wild marjoram may persist in the seedbank of ex-arable on chalky soils.

Planting rare species or those likely to colonise naturally

Species such as wild marjoram may not require planting if they are likely to colonise naturally; slow colonising species might be included in more isolated woodland open spaces. Species which are rare, or have a limited distribution are not considered appropriate for planting because their native distribution patterns are of intrinsic importance and they may require specialised habitat management. Information may be found in local and national floras.

Table 7.3 Options for establishing grassland in woodland open spaces using seed harvested from local meadows, or a seed mix designed by the practitioner, based on the flora of local meadows

Methods	Key issues	Practical considerations
Sowing species-rich grassland mixes harvested from local donor habitat	• Local provenance • Sourced from matched communities • Potentially rapid establishment of a diverse sward • Early introduction of wild flowers will enhance value woodland for insects and other wildlife • Some control over species sown, though not over establishment • Cost effective for relatively small areas of woodland open space	• Finding a suitable source can be difficult • Species introduced determined by diversity and abundance in source meadow • Weed burden must be reduced prior to sowing on ex-arable or pasture • Some ground preparation e.g. rotovation and scarification required to open-up sward in existing pasture • May prove expensive for larger areas • Hay may need to be removed on sites with high fertility • Will need after care to control residual weeds and manage competition
Spreading species-rich green hay from local donor habitat	• Local provenance • Sourced from matched communities • Potentially rapid establishment of a diverse sward • Rich sward more likely • Fresh seed – high viability • Lower cost than bulking seedlots	• Finding a suitable source can be difficult • Hay should be spread within a few hours of cutting, and subsequently removed • Sward likely to be dominated by grasses if hay allowed to dry out • No guarantee of which species will be viable in the mix • Weed burden must be reduced prior to spreading • Ground preparation required e.g. rotovation and scarification, and grazing or light rolling after strewing • Will need after care to control residual weeds and manage competition
Sowing mixes designed by the practitioner to match local grassland communities	In addition to the generic issues relating to sowing seed mixes listed above: • Mix should match target communities • Appropriate species can be sourced to match target vegetation communities	• Provenance can be difficult to ascertain, and may not be local • Local seed could be very costly to obtain • Cost could limit the area sown • Rare species should generally be avoided

Determining the planting percentages in formulated seed mixes

Once the make-up of the final planting mixes have been decided, determine the percentages of grasses and wildflowers of each species to be sown in consultation with the frequency tables in Rodwell (1992). Conventional wildflower seed mixtures are commonly supplied in the ratio of 80% grass to 20% of herbs. This reduces the cost of the mixture, as grasses are cheaper to produce and are often the same cultivars that are used in bulk for amenity and sports turf, rather than 'native' varieties from semi-natural situations. There is therefore a danger that on fertile sites the grasses will out-compete the herbs, which are already in a minority. One approach is to omit the grasses entirely, sowing only herbs, or to reduce the proportion to a lower level, such as 10–50%. Grasses will quickly invade the site of their own accord and some will almost certainly be present in the soil seed bank.

Table 7.4 Characteristic species of grassland communities based on the NVC for a) species-rich, neutral grassland (MG5), chalk grassland (CG2) and acid, montane grassland (U4) (frequency values after Rodwell, 1992). Whereas most constant species are usually obtainable in standard commercial seed mixes, many frequent species may be more expensive or not available

Species	Frequency		
	MG5	CG2	U4
Constants			
Common bird's-foot-trefoil	●●●●●	●●●●	
Cock's-foot	●●●●		
Common bent	●●●●		●●●●●
Common knapweed	●●●●		
Crested dog's-tail	●●●●●		
Crested hair-grass		●●●●●	
Fairy flax		●●●●	
Glaucous sedge		●●●●●	
Heath bedstraw			●●●●
Meadow oat-grass		●●●●	
Mouse-ear-hawkweed		●●●●	
Quaking-grass		●●●●	
Red clover	●●●●		
Red fescue	●●●●●		
Ribwort plantain	●●●●●	●●●●	
Rough hawkbit		●●●●	
Salad burnet		●●●●●	
Sheep's-fescue		●●●●●	●●●●●
Small scabious		●●●●	
Sweet vernal-grass	●●●●		●●●●●
Tormentil			●●●●●
White clover	●●●●		
Wild thyme		●●●●	
Yorkshire-fog	●●●●		
Frequent species			
Common bird's-foot-trefoil			●●
Black medick		●●	
Bulbous buttercup	●●●	●●	
Burnet-saxifrage		●●	
Cat's-ear	●●●		
Cock's-foot		●●●	
Common dog-violet			●●●
Common mouse-ear	●●		●●
Common rock-rose		●●●	
Common sorrel	●●●		●●
Cowslip	●●	●●	

Species	Frequency		
	MG5	CG2	U4
Frequent species cont'd			
Daisy	●●		
Devil's-bit scabious		●●	
Downy oat-grass		●●	
Dropwort		●●	
Dwarf thistle		●●●	
Eyebright		●●	
Harebell		●●●	
Heath wood-rush			●●
Heather			●●
Horseshoe vetch		●●	
Lady's bedstraw	●●	●●●	●●
Lesser trefoil	●●		
Meadow buttercup	●●●		●●
Meadow vetchling	●●		
Oxeye daisy	●●		
Quaking grass	●●		
Red clover		●●●	
Red fescue			●●●
Ribwort plantain		●●●	●●
Rough hawkbit	●●		
Rye-grass	●●●		
Self-heal	●●●	●●●	
Smooth meadow-grass			●●
Squinancywort		●●	
Upright brome		●●	
Wavy hair-grass			●●
White clover		●●	●●
Yarrow	●●●		●●
Yellow oat-grass	●●●		
Yellow rattle	●●		
Yorkshire-fog		●●	●●

Frequency values (how often a plant is found on moving from one sample of vegetation to the next):
●●●● and ●●●●● – community constants (61–80% = IV, 81–100% = V)
●●● – common or frequent species (41–60%)
●● – occasional (21–40%)
● – rare (1–20%)

Box 7.4 Attracting wildlife to woodland open spaces

Plants which attract insects

A range of pollen, nectar sources and foliage will attract insects of meadows and woodland open spaces, which in turn provide an important food resource for foraging birds, bats and other fauna. Saproxylic species from the woodland interior will also benefit from nectaring opportunities in rides and glades. The daisy (Compositae) and carrot (Umbelliferae) families are particularly attractive to insects, and many species can be found on a range of soil conditions. Composites such as yarrow, goldenrod, thistles and ragworts attract insects with long tongues, such as butterflies and moths. Umbellifers, such as hogweed and wild angelica, are more suited to insects with smaller mouthparts, such as beetles and flies. Bumblebees forage for nectar and pollen from a wide range of flowers, although there are believed to be individual preferences amongst species. Nectar-feeding butterflies and other insects common in the wider countryside also visit a variety of flowering plants. Some of these species should be in the planting mix, others such as common fleabane and wild marjoram may invade naturally; thistles and ragworts may also colonise, and be unwelcome.

Flowering period is also an important consideration. Butterflies, moths and bumblebees for example require an abundant supply of flowering plants throughout their flight season – which extends from March through to late October – particularly in the peak summer season (see table opposite). If formulating seed mixes, select a few species which flower early, and late in the season.

Foodplants of butterfly and moth larvae

The larval foodplants of most wider-countryside butterflies (Table 7.5) grow on a wide range of soil pH (Tables 7.6 and 7.7). Most of these plants also host some macromoth species, whilst some support very large numbers (Table 7.8, sourced from Crafer, 2005). In many lowland situations, particularly on neutral or chalk grassland, mixes harvested from meadows, and especially formulated seed mixes, provide food plants for the larvae of a diverse range of macromoths and most of the wider countryside butterflies. Other habitats, such as acid grassland and heathland have less plant diversity, and will naturally support a much lower diversity of butterflies and moths. Whatever plants are introduced, establishment of larval foodplants does not guarantee colonisation by butterflies, moths or any other insects. Continued management is essential to provide the necessary variety of sward heights and densities to suit different species.

Benefits of a diverse vegetation structure

Woodland rides and glades should provide a transition from high forest, through scrub and taller herbs to short grassland. Insects have differing ecological niches within grassland and heathland, and for some, these will vary as the insect moves through its life cycle: larvae may develop in the soil, herb vegetation, leaf litter or deadwood, whilst adults require open structured flowers for nectar, such as umbellifers and composites. Factors of importance to all insects include:
- plant structure
- plant abundance
- sward height
- flowering phenology for the supply of nectar and pollen
- location of the plants with respect to temperature, light and shade
- competition from other herbs.

The size and visibility of a plant, or whether it is growing in isolation or as part of a small colony may determine its suitability for egg-laying. There is considerable variation in the use of species by insects. Some species, such as the speedwells are little used, whilst others such as thistles and knapweeds have a high insect diversity associated with them. Specially formulated mixes give an opportunity to introduce a broad mix of plants to create a structurally diverse sward of grasses and herbs. This will support the varied food and niche requirements of a diverse range of insects.

Flowering times of plants providing nectar for insects.

Species	M	A	M	J	J	A	S	O	N
Sallows	■	■							
Colt's-foot	■	■	■						
Primrose	■	■	■						
Dandelion	■	■	■						
Bluebell		■	■						
Bugle		■	■	■					
Cuckooflower		■	■	■					
Cow parsley		■	■	■					
Broom			■	■					
Ragged-robin			■	■	■				
Oxeye daisy			■	■	■	■			
Tufted vetch				■	■	■			
Red campion			■	■	■	■	■		
Clovers			■	■	■	■			
Violets			■	■	■	■			
Bird's-foot-trefoil			■	■	■	■			
Bramble			■	■	■	■	■		
Hogweed				■	■	■			
Wild privet				■	■				
Ground-elder				■	■				
Red valerian				■	■	■			
Meadowsweet				■	■	■			
Sow-thistles				■	■	■	■		
Betony				■	■	■			
Tormentil				■	■	■	■		
Wild carrot				■	■	■			
Ragworts				■	■	■	■		
Devil's-bit scabious					■	■	■		
Small scabious					■	■	■		
Yarrow				■	■	■	■	■	
Wild thymes				■	■	■			
Wild teasel				■	■	■			
Hemp-agrimony					■	■	■		
Knapweeds				■	■	■	■		
Wild marjoram					■	■	■		
Watermint					■	■	■	■	
Thistles				■	■	■	■		
Wild angelica					■	■	■		
Common fleabane					■	■	■		
Ivy							■	■	■

Table 7.5 Larval foodplants of butterflies which may occur in new native woodland

Species	Main foodplants
Wider countryside species	
Small skipper	Yorkshire-fog; rarely other grasses such as Timothy, false brome
Essex skipper	Cock's-foot, but may use other grasses such as creeping soft-grass, Timothy, false brome, meadow foxtail, tor-grass, common couch
Large skipper	Cock's-foot; occasionally purple moor-grass and false brome
Brimstone	Buckthorn, alder buckthorn
Large white	Wild or cultivated crucifers
Small white	Cultivated crucifers; sometimes wild crucifers, including wild cabbage, hedge mustard, charlock, wild mignonette
Green-veined white	Wild crucifers, including wild cabbage, hedge mustard, large bitter-cress, cuckooflower, charlock
Orange tip	Cuckooflower and garlic mustard; occasionally large bitter-cress, charlock, winter-cress, hedge mustard, turnip, hairy rock-cress
Purple hairstreak	Oaks
White-letter hairstreak	Wych elm, English elm, small-leaved elm
Small copper	Common sorrel, sheep's sorrel; occasionally broad-leaved dock
Brown argus	Crane's-bills
Common blue	Common bird's-foot-trefoil; others include greater bird's-foot-trefoil, black medick, lesser trefoil, white clover, common restharrow
Holly blue	Holly, ivy; others include a wide variety of shrubs such as dogwood, bramble, spindle
Red admiral	Common nettle; sometimes small nettle
Painted lady	Thistles (*Carduus* spp. and *Cirsium* spp.); wide range of other plants including mallows, common nettle, viper's-bugloss
Small tortoiseshell	Common nettle, small nettle
Peacock	Common nettle
Comma	Common nettle; others include hop, willows, currants
Speckled wood	Cock's-foot, false brome, Yorkshire-fog, common couch and other grasses
Scotch Argus	Purple moor-grass (Scotland), blue moor-grass (England)
Marbled white	Red fescue; possibly supplemented with sheep's-fescue, Yorkshire-fog, tor-grass
Gatekeeper	Fine-grasses, including bents, fescues, meadow-grasses
Meadow brown	Fine grasses including bents, fescues, meadow-grasses; coarse grasses including cock's foot, false brome
Ringlet	Meadow-grasses, coarse grasses including cock's foot, false brome, common couch, tufted hair-grass
Small heath	Fine grasses including bents, fescues, meadow-grasses
Habitat specialists	
Dingy skipper	Common bird's-foot-trefoil; occasionally horseshoe vetch, greater bird's-foot-trefoil
Green hairstreak	Gorse, broom, Dyer's greenweed, buckthorn, dogwood; common rock-rose, common bird's-foot-trefoil on chalk grassland, possibly in woodland.
Brown hairstreak	Blackthorn, occasionally other *Prunus* spp.
White admiral	Honeysuckle

Table 7.6 Plants providing nectar and pollen for insects: their soil requirements, regeneration strategies and colonisation potential

Species	*Regeneration strategy	Colonisation potential
Acid-neutral-basic		
Betony	V,S	Poor
Bird's-foot-trefoils	Bs	Poor
Bluebell	V,S	Poor
Clovers	V,S,Bs	Moderate
Colt's-foot	W	Good
Common fleabane	W	Good
Cow parsley	S	Good
Cuckooflower	V,Bs	Poor
Dandelion	W	Good
Goldenrod	W	Good
Hogweed	S	Good
Knapweeds	V,S	Moderate
Ragged-robin	W	Moderate
Ragworts	W,Bs	Good
Red campion	Bs	Moderate
Sow-thistles	W,Bs	Good
Thistles	W,Bs	Good
Watermint	V,Bs	Poor
Wild angelica	S	Poor
Wild teasel	S	Moderate
Yarrow	V,S	Moderate
Acid		
Broom	Bs	Poor
Devil's-bit scabious	S	Poor
Tormentil	V,Bs	Poor
Acid-neutral		
Bugle	V,Bs	Poor
Neutral-basic		
Meadowsweet	V,Bs	Poor
Oxeye daisy	S,V,Bs	Good
Primrose	V,Bs	Poor
Basic		
Hemp-agrimony	W	Good
Red valerian	W	Good
Small scabious	S	Poor
Violets	S,V	Poor
Wild marjoram	V,Bs	Moderate (local)
Wild privet	S,V	Moderate
Wild thyme	V,Bs	Poor

* Natural regeneration strategies (Grime *et al.*, 1990):
V – Vegetative expansion: new shoots remain attached to parent until well established
S – Seasonal regeneration: seeds or vegetative propagules produced in a single cohort
Bs – Persistent seed bank: viable, but dormant seeds present throughout the year
W – Numerous, widely dispersed seeds: wind-dispersed widely, but may be of limited persistence

Table 7.7 Larval foodplants of wider countryside butterflies and some macromoths: their soil requirements, regenerative strategy and colonisation potential

Species	Regeneration strategy*	Colonisation potential
Acid-neutral-basic		
Annual meadow-grass	S,Bs	Good
Broad-leaved dock	Bs	Good
Common bird's-foot-trefoil	Bs	Poor
Common couch	V,Bs	Poor
Common nettle	V,Bs	Good
Common stork's-bill	S,Bs	Moderate
Creeping bent	V,Bs	Good
Cuckooflower	V,Bs	Poor
Garlic mustard	S,Bs	Good
Red fescue	S,V	Good
Rough meadow-grass	V,Bs	Good
Sheep's-fescue	S,V	Poor
Yorkshire-fog	S,V,Bs	Good
Acid		
Purple moor-grass	V,Bs	Moderate
Sheep's sorrel	V,Bs	Moderate
Velvet bent	V,Bs	Good
Acid-neutral		
Common sorrel	S,V	Poor
Neutral-basic		
Cock's-foot	S	Good
Dove's-foot crane's-bill	S,Bs	Moderate
Dyer's greenweed	S	Poor
False brome	S,V	Moderate
Giant fescue	S	Moderate
Smooth meadow-grass	Bs	Moderate
Spreading meadow-grass	V,Bs	Good
Tall fescue	S,V	Moderate
Wood meadow-grass	V	Poor
Basic		
Blue moor-grass	S	Moderate
Common rock-rose	Bs	Poor
Narrow-leaved meadow-grass	V,Bs	Good

* natural regeneration strategies (Grime et al., 1990):
V – Vegetative expansion: new shoots remain attached to parent until well established
S – Seasonal regeneration: seeds or vegetative propagules produced in single cohort
Bs – Persistent seed bank: Viable but dormant seeds present throughout the year

Table 7.8 Use of butterfly foodplants (herbs and grasses) by macromoth larvae (source: Crafer, 2005)

Foodplant	Number of moth species
Annual meadow-grass	36
Bents	2
Blue moor-grass	0
Chickweeds	56
Creeping soft-grass	1
Cock's-foot	3
Common bird's-foot-trefoil	20
Common nettle	30
Common sorrel	13
Common stork's-bill	1
Couches	17
Crane's-bills	3
Cuckooflower	1
Dandelions	66
Docks	95
Dyer's greenweed	8
False brome	1
Garlic mustard	1
Groundsels	33
Plantains	66
Purple moor-grass	8
Red fescue	4
Rock-roses	7
Rough meadow-grass	3
Sheep's-fescue	7
Sheep's sorrel	8
Smooth meadow-grass	2
Tall fescue	4
Thistles	7
Tor-grass	0
Wood meadow-grass	4
Yorkshire-fog	3

Lowland species-rich meadow created in the open space of new native woodland.

Box 7.5 Selection of herbs and grasses for sowing rides and glades in Victory Wood, at Lamberhurst Farm in Kent

The landscape character assessment and ecological assessment criteria supporting the planting of Victory Wood was presented in Section 6.5.1. Soils in the adjacent ancient woodland are acidic, but farming practices have increased the soil pH on the planting site to 5.7 to 7.2. Most of the rides and glades on the site would now support a species-rich neutral grassland community. However, there was one area adjacent to Ellenden Wood where the soil pH was 5.7: re-establishing a more acid grassland community could be a longer term aim for this area.

Vegetation surveys on the site two years after the cessation of arable cropping revealed species-poor swards along the field margins, dominated by soft-brome and black-grass, with occasional false oat-grass, Italian rye-grass, thistles, willowherbs, cut-leaved crane's-bill, common bird's-foot-trefoil, meadow grasses, bristly oxtongue, common fleabane, creeping buttercup, bramble, ragwort and sow-thistles. The fields themselves were dominated by black-grass, soft-brome and broad bean. The surveys concluded that the weed burden should be reduced by herbicide treatments prior to any attempts to create species-rich grassland.

The preferred seed options were seed mixes harvested from local meadows, but no seed was available. The choice was therefore between a commercially available generic meadow mix or seed mixes designed for the site. For the woodland rides, the following seed mixes were proposed:

Neutral grassland areas

In the absence of suitable neutral grassland reference sites, the species mix proposed for the bulk of the rides was based on MG5 NVC floristic tables (Table 7.4) and general knowledge of species characteristic of neutral meadows in Kent. With the exception of Yorkshire-fog, all MG5 community constants were selected to provide the foundation for the open areas. Yorkshire-fog is likely to colonise rapidly, or arise from the seedbank; it is also highly competitive, so for this reason it was not included in the mix.

Other plants characteristic of unimproved neutral grassland in Kent were then selected for their value for wildlife (Tables 7.5–7.8; Figure 7.7). For example, the 22 plants selected provide resources for the larvae of at least 11 wider countryside butterflies. Cut-leaved crane's-bill could also be included to support an existing colony of brown argus butterflies. Site disturbance at planting would almost certainly result in a greater range of thistles, sow-thistles, hogweed and bramble in some abundance, which would provide important additional nectar sources for insects.

Acid grassland areas

Where the pH of the soil was below 6, the development of a more acidic community could be a longer term aim, as progressive leaching of bases would further acidify the surface horizon over time. Unimproved acid grassland communities in Kent are typically represented by the sheep's-fescue-common bent-sheep's sorrel community (U1). These species also comprise the three community constants, and all were included in the proposed mix. Other species characteristic of unimproved U1 acidic grasslands were chosen from the NVC floristic table, with reference to the tables describing wildlife value (Tables 7.5–7.8). For example, the larval foodplants of several wider countryside butterflies typical of acid grassland are included in the mix; Yorkshire-fog and cock's-foot for small skipper and Essex skipper respectively; sheep's sorrel for small copper; and bents and fescues for gatekeeper, meadow brown and small heath.

The grass component of the proposed species-rich neutral grassland mix is dominated by crested dog's-tail, common bent and red fescue; other grasses are included at much lower percentages (2.5–5.0%). The wild flower component of the mix was divided fairly evenly between the various species.

The grass component of the proposed acidic grassland mix is dominated by sheep's fescue and common bent; other grasses are included at much lower percentages. The wild flower component of the mix is dominated by sheep's sorrel, with the remainder of the mix divided fairly evenly between the other species.

Neutral grassland sowing mix

Sowing mix	
Grasses	**% by weight**
Common bent*	5
Sweet vernal grass*	2
Crested dog's-tail*	6
Cock's-foot*	0.5
Meadow fescue	0.5
Red fescue*	5
Smooth meadow-grass	1
Total	20
Wild flowers	
Yarrow	4
Garlic mustard	4
Cuckooflower	4
Common knapweed*	12
Meadow vetchling	8
Autumn hawkbit	4
Oxeye daisy	4
Common bird's-foot-trefoil*	12
Ribwort plantain*	4
Meadow buttercup	4
Bulbous buttercup	4
Yellow-rattle	4
Common sorrel	4
Red clover*	4
White clover*	4
Total	80

* constants of an MG5 community

Acid grassland sowing mix

Sowing mix	
Grasses	**% by weight**
Common bent	7
Sweet vernal-grass	0.5
Cock's-foot	0.5
Wavy hair-grass	2
Sheep's-fescue	7
Yorkshire-fog	0.5
Annual meadow-grass	2
Timothy	0.5
Total	20
Wild flowers	
Yarrow	4
Common mouse-ear	4
Cat's-ear	4
Common bird's-foot-trefoil	8
Sheep's sorrel	40
Mouse-ear-hawkweed	4
Ribwort plantain	4
Tormentil	4
Lesser trefoil	8
Total	80

8 ESTABLISHING NEW NATIVE WOODLAND

Site preparation and tree planting methods are well documented in the literature and many techniques are standard practice (e.g. Williamson, 1992; Van Lerberghe and Balleux, 2001; Agate, 2000 and 2002). Consequently these methods are not repeated in detail here, but general issues relating to the management of new native woodland for wildlife are discussed.

8.1 Planting trees and shrubs

8.1.1 Planting stock

New native woodlands are best planted with bare-rooted seedlings, undercuts or transplants, depending on how they have been grown in the nursery. These are usually 30–100 cm high and 1–3 years old, and are usually competitively priced. Transplants spend their first year in seedbeds before transplanting into lines for growing on, while in undercuts the roots are severed by a mechanical blade drawn beneath the nursery bed at 8–10 cm, usually in their second growing season. Both techniques produce a good fibrous root system, allowing the plants to establish well and grow rapidly. Planting of bare root stock is usually undertaken in the winter months when the trees are dormant. A more expensive option is to grow seedlings in root-trainers, i.e. plastic modules containing compost, into which the seed is directly planted. These benefit from the protective compost around the root system when introduced to the planting site, and like other container-grown plants, may establish better than bare-root material, and can be planted earlier, in late summer or autumn.

Older trees, such as feathered trees and standards up to 3 m tall and 3 cm diameter at one metre above ground, are generally avoided because they are more expensive and require staking. Their high shoot to root ratio means that the roots may not initially be able to deliver enough water to the transpiring leaves, often resulting in poor survival and long establishment times.

Once lifted, the roots of bare-rooted seedlings, undercuts and transplants are vulnerable to desiccation, so they should be supplied in sealed plastic sacks which are white on the outside and black on the inside, to protect them from excessive heat and frost. At all times up to

Bare root trees delivered to a site for immediate planting.

planting, the sacks must be handled carefully to avoid damaging the root systems. Sacks may be stored for a few weeks in a cool, dark building or the trees can be removed and the roots buried in a shallow trench for protection, known as 'heeling-in'.

8.1.2 Protection after planting

Young trees and shrubs are likely to require protection immediately after planting. This is to protect them from mammals such as voles, rabbits and deer, and in some cases from humans. On many sites, the likely pests will have been identified, especially if an ecological assessment has been carried out beforehand (Section 6.2).

Rabbits can occur in high numbers, and are able to damage the bark of young trees up to 75 cm above ground level. For larger sites, fencing is the best option, whilst individual tree protection may suffice on smaller sites. Brown hares (now a UK BAP priority species) rarely pose a serious threat to young trees, especially as their numbers have declined in recent years.

Bank and field voles are ubiquitous and are always liable to cause damage by gnawing the basal 20 cm of the tree. Voles inhabit the tall grass and weedy vegetation typical of many new woodland schemes during the establishment phase and before canopy closure. An effective method of protecting trees against voles is to maintain an area of bare ground around the base of the stem. Some mulch materials however may have the opposite effect, as the animals may be able to use the mulch as cover to approach the base of the tree. Encouraging barn owls and kestrels through the provision of nesting boxes may provide some natural pest control.

Squirrels pose a serious threat to older trees, as they begin to close canopy. At this stage, they can do considerable damage by stripping bark, particularly of smooth-barked species such as beech, but they will attack other species such as oak and willows. Deer are also a very serious threat to young trees, browsing new shoots up to 2 m above ground. If deer are present at threshold densities that are likely to cause damage, and there is no provision for population control in the vicinity, the erection of deer fences may be essential. The minimum fence height for roe deer is 1.2 m for areas <2 ha, and 1.5 m for areas >2 ha; for muntjac and fallow deer, 1.5 m is recommended, rising to 2 m for red and sika deer. Detailed instructions on fence construction can be found in a Forestry Commission Practice Note on deer fencing (Pepper, 1999).

Example of a 1.2 m deer fence.

The following factors should be considered before choosing between fencing and individual protection:

- the scale, density and shape of the planting scheme: for large planting areas, it is more cost-effective to use fencing to protect young trees from most mammals except voles. Individual protection means a fixed cost per tree, but for small planting areas (1–3 ha) this may be more economical, depending on the grazing/browsing animals present and the planting density employed. Enclosure shape is particularly significant when the planting area falls below 1 ha, when the perimeter:area ratios may vary widely. The most efficient enclosures are circular, with increasing perimeters relative to areas required for other shapes, in the following order: squares < 2:1-sided rectangles < right-angle triangles < 4:1-sided rectangles. However, the ultimate shape will also be driven by other factors besides cost, such the landscape planting strategy adopted (Section 5.2) and how it fits in with any prescribed ecological networks (Section 4.4).

- risk: a damaged fence puts all trees at risk, whereas if a tree shelter is removed, only one tree is at risk

- access: fencing requires special access provision to the site, which is not an issue for tree shelters

- effect on local wildlife: fencing blocks the movement of mammals such as badgers, so this may need to be taken into account, for example through the provision of badger gates.

The two main types are of individual tree protection are spiral guards and tree shelters. Chemical repellents applied to individual trees are another possibility, but most products have a short life-span and some are virtually ineffective. Spiral guards are wrapped around trees to reduce bark stripping primarily by rabbits and voles. Trees must be sturdy and at least 75 cm high to avoid any inhibition of growth. Canes may also be needed to provide additional support.

Tree shelters come in a range of brands and heights, depending upon the nature of the protection required. The translucent polypropylene tubes modify the microclimate around the young trees, while at the same time providing protection from browsing animals and small mammals. Conveniently, they also provide some protection for trees from herbicide sprays (important as the shelters confer no immunity from weed competition) and allow the trees to be then easily found during weeding operations. Tube height should be selected according to the browsing reach of the target animal: 0.6–0.75 m for rabbits and hares, 1.2 m for roe deer and some sheep breeds, 1.8 m for red, fallow and sika deer, and up to 2.2 m for cattle and horses. Tube diameter is less critical – usually 8–12 cm – but the shelter effect declines with increasing diameter, due to turbulence over the open surface.

Shelters act as miniature greenhouses, raising day temperatures inside the tube, while the humidity inside is increased by leaf transpiration and the lack of air movement. Shorter and wider tubes produce correspondingly less of a greenhouse effect. Because the drying power of the air inside the tube is less than that outside, the leaf stomata tend to stay open for longer, thereby prolonging periods of photosynthesis and encouraging rapid shoot development. In very shaded planting situations, however, the polypropylene material (and its additional colour tint) may reduce light levels below a critical level, to the detriment of tree establishment.

Trees generally grow taller in shelters than in the open, strongly reducing the stem diameter to height ratio. The best responses in height increment to shelters have been found in oak, beech[1], lime, sycamore, birch, sweet chestnut and other broadleaves; responses are generally less marked in conifers (Potter, 1991). The resulting tree form is much more columnar than unsheltered trees (which tend to be more conical in shape) but, once the trees have grown out of the tubes, there is no evidence that this effect persists. The slender stems may not support foliage weight and the removal of the shelters after three to four growing seasons can result in the bending or collapse of the shoot, causing the stem to deform and grow horizontally. Experiments have shown that this effect is most pronounced in taller shelters. Shorter tubes will produce less columnar growth and allow the development of a low-level thicket that creates good nesting and feeding habitat for birds.

A survey of shelter use in England in 1992 showed very high tree survival – 89%, but there was much evidence of poor maintenance, with weed control inadequate on 60% of sites – either

---

1 Although beech normally responds well, in some instances shelters have been found to encourage colonisation by woolly aphids *Phyllaphis fagi*, sooty moulds and mildews, reducing survival.

none, or just mowing (Kerr, 1995). On many sites inadequate browsing protection was given because the wrong shelter height had been selected. Poor staking was general, with larger shelters needing thicker stakes. Gradual breakdown of tree shelters was significant in the older plantings (6–11 years), but nearly 50% of these showed none, suggesting that biodegradation rates are slow.

In summary, the main advantages conferred by shelters are improved tree survival rates and accelerated height growth, the latter leading to rapid canopy development and the domination of weed growth. Shelters can also be used to 'select' and protect individuals resulting from natural regeneration, and to short-circuit the nursery production process by sowing seeds, especially those of large-seeded species such as oak, directly into the tubes. Disadvantages are the visual 'graveyard' effect of geometric planting, and the narrow stems that are susceptible to deformation and wind damage.

Removal of tree protection

Individual tree protection will have served its purpose (given reasonable tree growth) in 5–7 years. Tubes or spirals left in place after this can restrict tree growth. Spiral guards may spontaneously uncoil themselves and are fairly easy to remove. Removal of tubes may result in stem failure if done too late. If the tubes have been left on and the trees would otherwise collapse if they were removed, the shelter can be strongly staked until the stem thickens sufficiently to support the crown – although at considerable cost. Another technique is to slit the tubes halfway down to allow some stem movement and to encourage stem thickening prior to complete removal in the following year. Deer fencing will probably be required for 10–15 years as trees will be vulnerable to fraying and bark stripping during this time. Stock fencing may be required permanently.

8.2 Direct seeding

While natural regeneration may result from massive seed falls, delivering millions of seed per hectare in the case of some tree species, it would be uneconomic to sow such quantities artificially. Nevertheless, establishing trees by direct seeding is, on the face of it, a cheap and attractive proposition, capable of being mechanised in a farm forestry project. High densities of seed can be broadcast, giving rapid canopy closure while allowing greater potential for selecting individuals well suited to the site, as well as good forestry specimens. Seed may also be collected locally as part of the operation. In practice, however, there are a number of problems to be overcome: some of these constraints, together with the opportunities, are outlined in Table 8.1.

Tree seeds are usually drilled in lines or broadcast randomly. Large seeds such as acorns are drilled as they need to sown to a depth of about 10 cm, after which the site is rolled. If other species are to be sown afterwards, the site would be harrowed. Smaller seeds are broadcast-sown after larger seeds, to a depth of around 2 cm and incorporated using a light roller. On lighter soils, seed will need to be sown deeper than on heavier soils as moisture retention in the former will be much less and this is a critical factor in seedling development.

Tree seeding can take place either in the autumn using untreated seed, or in the spring using treated seed. Untreated autumn sown seed will receive a natural pre-treatment from winter weather whilst buried in the soil. Seeds of some species require weeks of artificial pre-treatments while imbibed at full moisture content, using a regime of warm temperatures (around 15°C), followed by cold temperatures (1–4°C) in order to break dormancy. Even then, low moisture levels or temperature-induced secondary dormancy may occur after sowing. Autumn sowings are likely to be more successful as the seed germinates earlier and is less likely to suffer from heat damage and spring drought, but it may suffer more from predation (Willoughby *et al.*, 2004a). Wet sites should not be sown in autumn, to prevent rotting over the winter.

The proportion of viable tree seed that will become established varies greatly: even under favourable conditions, the percentage of seed surviving to form seedlings at the end of the first year can range from 0% to 50% (Willoughby *et al.*, 2004a). This implies sowing up to 200,000 viable seeds per hectare (of all species combined) in order to produce 10,000 reasonably evenly-spaced and vigorous trees by year 10 (i.e. 5% survival). Where biodiversity objectives are important, lower stocking levels may offer more diversity within the newly stocked area. Watson (1996) has advocated the sowing of 'nurse' crops, such as short-strawed wheat or barley, to

Table 8.1 Opportunities and constraints influencing the choice of direct seeding

Issues	Opportunities	Constraints
Site selection – soils	Appropriate for only quite specific lowland situations: good quality agricultural soils or restored brownfield sites	Heavy clay soils which are wet during the winter months result in seed rotting
Site selection – seed predation	Predation may be a minor issue if the planting site is distant from established woodland	Sites close to existing woodland are likely to suffer high levels of predation by small mammals such as mice, voles and squirrels
Species selection	Forestry Commission trials have been successful with a small range of trees and shrubs	Forestry Commission currently recommends that ash, oak and sycamore may be used to form a minimum of 75% of the planting mix; far less is known about other trees and shrubs but there has been some success with wild cherry, hawthorn, field maple, dogwood and birch
Sowing rates and germination	Seed pre-treated to break dormancy best purchased from seed merchant	Germination may be poor if sowing depth is incorrect
Weed control	Faster canopy closure than conventional planting should reduce the time for which herbicides are required	Weed control is essential in the first year
Time to canopy closure	Canopy closure can occur much quicker than conventional planting, thus shading out arable weeds and creating an environment more conducive to colonisation by woodland plants	Even if germination is successful, stem density may be uneven, so dense stands will require thinning, which adds further expense
Woodland structure	The structure of the developing wood may have a more 'natural' appearance, in terms of the variety of tree heights, density and open spaces, if well designed, and species germinate and establish as planned	Although 'naturalistic', the tree community may well differ from that envisaged in species diversity and frequency; consequently it may not closely resemble the woodland community upon which the design was based – even with thinning – and not fit the local landscape character
Costs compared to conventional planting	Direct seeding may be competitive if the initial seeding is successful; conventional agricultural machinery could be used for preparation and sowing; weed control required for fewer years than conventional planting; no need for guards, but fencing may be necessary	Failure to germinate or establish would require repeat seeding, thus increasing costs; oak seed, a major component of many woodlands, and wild cherry, are very expensive

accompany the tree seeds. In theory, a nurse crop will suppress competition from weeds, reduce seed predation by birds and provide some protection to the emerging tree seedlings. In practice, experiments using cover crops of spring wheat and linseed have generally proved disappointing, yielding lower tree seedling survival than in unaccompanied sowings. Nonetheless, in biodiversity terms, nurse crops can reduce herbicide applications during the establishment phase.

Seed predation by field mice, voles, grey squirrels and birds on directly sown sites can be a major problem as they cannot be fenced against effectively. The problem is particularly acute where the site is adjacent to or within existing woodlands, and in such situations direct seeding is not recommended. On ex-pasture or arable sites there is a better chance of successful germination, but in all cases the dangers of browsing of seedlings by deer, hares or rabbits means that fencing will often be needed. Following sowing, weed control is the next major issue, especially on ex-arable land. Pre-emergent herbicide mixes can be used initially, followed by end-of-season applications when the trees are fully dormant. Some in-season treatment may also be necessary, depending on the type of weed infestation and the tolerance of the young tree seedlings; full details are given in Willoughby *et al.*, (2004a). Thereafter the routine can be repeated annually until the trees are established at 2–4 years.

In summary, advice on direct seeding is currently restricted to a fairly narrow range of species which have been extensively tested by Forestry Commission, including: oak, ash, wild cherry, hawthorn, field maple, dogwood, birch and sycamore. Even with these species, complete success is not guaranteed, and it is difficult to be certain how the woodland will develop. On the other hand, in a wood designed for wildlife, patchy failures on parts of the site are not a disaster and will allow some natural development to occur. Seed costs vary with species, leading to a temptation to plant ash, birch and sycamore, which are cheaper and more readily available. Furthermore, cost comparisons of establishment show that seeding some species such as oak or wild cherry is more expensive than using nursery transplants. Sowing new native woodlands as mixed species stands risks creating management problems associated with random intimate mixtures (Box 7.3); but a compromise, where the more expensive components are sown as pure species groups within a matrix of cheaper, more reliable species, may offer a solution leading to a greater overall diversity.

PART TWO WOODLAND CREATION PRACTICE – **ESTABLISHING A NEW NATIVE WOODLAND**

This woodland was created in 1990; parts of the site were planted (top) and other areas were direct seeded with a range of species (bottom); note the difference in stem density.

8.3 Taking care of trees and shrubs after planting

Aftercare of newly created woodland is vital. Irrespective of the amount of care and attention that has been invested prior to, and including planting, if the site is not managed properly, all may be lost within a year or two. Weed control and protection are essential elements of aftercare, determining whether trees establish well and grow quickly towards canopy closure and site capture; or whether they die back and achieve little growth, buried under long grass or weeds. In lowland plantations on fertile sites, weeding may be needed for 3–5 years, but elsewhere will depend on the site conditions, the tree species mix, the vegetation into which the trees are planted, and the type of weed control treatments applied.

This site was sown with a commercial grass seed mix prior to planting with sessile oaks; no weed control was undertaken. By the fifth season, most trees were still alive, but their growth was severely retarded by the competition from a sward dominated by fescues and soft-brome, with a few herbs.

8.3.1 Weed control

Current policies of the UK Government and the European Union seek not only to regulate, but also to minimise or eliminate pesticide use wherever possible, endorsed in voluntary certification schemes such as the UK Woodland Assurance Standard. Herbicides are therefore likely to be restricted at sites with nature conservation designations such as Sites of Special Scientific Interest, and sites subject to Biodiversity and Habitat Action Plans. Recommendations for reducing herbicide use are given in the Forestry Commission Practice Guide *Reducing pesticide use in forestry* (Willoughby *et al.*, 2004b). The need for weed control, and hence cost, is directly related to the fertility and former use of the site.

Weeds compete for light, moisture and nutrients, and must be controlled if the trees are to survive. Until the root system of a young tree becomes well established, uptake of moisture and nutrients from the surface soil layers is in direct competition with the surrounding vegetation. Tall vegetation can also smother young trees, depriving them of light. Although the means of control is important (i.e. whether using cutting, mulches or herbicides), the method is less important than its actual performance in controlling vegetation around trees. Weed control increases not only survival, but also growth rates – sometimes spectacularly, depending upon:

- the timing of weed control treatments
- the area of weed control maintained
- the spatial pattern of control applications.

Timing, both within a single growing season and between successive seasons, is critical. To be most effective, weed control must be maintained for the part of the growing season when plant growth is most active. Work in fruit orchards has shown reductions in shoot extension of up to 60% in un-weeded control plots during a single season, whereas allowing weed growth to continue until mid-May caused only 10% reductions. This emphasises that there is only a short optimum period for weed control, mid-May to early June, contrary to the popular perception that the weeds can be allowed to grow before being removed: by then the damage will already have been done.

The results of ineffective weeding in the first season frequently carry over into subsequent seasons, even if bare-ground conditions are then maintained: these trees will not catch up those weeded properly from the start. Tree establishment experiments on motorway verges have shown that, over a three-year growth period, those weeded in year one and at least one subsequent year performed best (Buckley and Insley, 1984). Thus, any remission from sward competition at an early stage established a positive growth potential; later weeding treatments allowed the growth initiative to be lost.

Tiny, weed-free spots around trees can be effective, but areas up to 1 m diameter are frequently specified in tree establishment manuals. At 2 m spacing or 2,500 trees per ha, this would cover almost 20% of the planting area, or 50% if applied as 0.5 m strips along the tree rows; an important consideration if ground vegetation needs to be protected for conservation reasons or to prevent erosion. Larger spots avoid the sward collapsing on to young trees when lodging occurs in mid-season, and numerous studies have found a strong positive relationship between tree performance and the area of weed control: height, shoot diameter and shoot weight are all increased by larger diameter spots. Importantly, survival is also increased as competition in small weeded areas is greater and reinvasion more rapid. Provided the weed-free area is maintained in subsequent years, the roots are able to ramify within it and will continue to respond to larger weed-free treatments over a number of years (Insley and Buckley, 1986; Davies, 1987).

The spatial pattern of control applications is also important. Good relationships between the radius of weed-free spot-treatments and tree performance indicate that root spread is able to capitalise on the linear weed-free (radial) distance, which is optimum in circular weeding treatments centred on the tree: the perimeter/area ratios are less effective in strips. In spots, roots can develop in any direction and are only hindered when they reach the perimeter of the treatment.

Herbicides, mulches, mowing and surface cultivation are all in current use. Each method affects water conservation, soil temperature and nutrient mineralisation rate differently, so even if total weed control is achieved, the responses of trees to different surface treatments will vary. However, machine cutting is relatively ineffective as the rooted vegetation left behind can continue to transpire freely, sometimes to even a greater extent than in an uncut sward, where the dead vegetation forms an insulating layer. The need for tractor maintenance also necessitates wide spacing between rows of trees, which may not always be desirable in a naturalistic planting matrix (Section 7.4).

The most popular method of weed control in establishing plantations is currently herbicide application. In theory, either soil-acting residual herbicides, foliar-acting herbicides, or a combination of both can be used. In practice, foliar-acting herbicides (which operate either through direct contact, or are translocated to the roots, rhizomes and unsprayed stems) may offer sufficient control, although some local authorities do not allow the use of residual herbicides because their persistence in the soil may affect subsequent attempts to establish ground flora. Residual herbicides have been used in the past as they tend to be simpler and cheaper to apply, but many only control weeds prior to emergence and must therefore be applied to bare earth. As a result they have been used in the pre-planting phase, with foliar acting herbicides being used subsequently.

BOTTOM LEFT **Straw mulches used to suppress weed growth around planted oaks were still effective after the third growing season.**

BOTTOM RIGHT **Planted oaks five years after planting benefitting from a woven sheet mulch, despite vigorous weed growth in the inter-row spaces.**

The main alternatives to herbicides, apart from machine cutting (which is often ineffective) and cultivation (which is expensive), are mulches. Some mulch materials are inert, such as bituminous roofing felt and extruded polyethylene, and some are biodegradable, such as woodchips, composted bark, cardboard and specifically manufactured jute or fibre mats. In high-carbon materials such as straw and woodchips the elevated carbon:nitrogen ratio of the material may be important as it can cause nitrogen deficiency symptoms in trees on infertile soils. There are also possible interactions between mulches and fertiliser or herbicide additions: surface roots are encouraged by mulches, which may be affected by losses of nitrogen as ammonium. However, mulches also conserve nitrogen and prevent it from being lost to the same extent by diffusion (Armstrong and Moffat, 1996). On waterlogged sites, there is a danger that a covering of mulch may prevent surface evaporation, exacerbating anaerobic conditions. On the whole, however, mulches benefit tree growth by conserving moisture and enhancing the mineralisation of nutrients, particularly nitrogen, within the rooting zone.

Mulches should be effective for at least three growing seasons, and so obviate the need for repeat applications of herbicide. Some plastic mulches are thin and can rip easily, which can make planting much more difficult and restrict inter-row access if mowing is required. Ripping can be caused naturally by animals (including voles) and wind, but also deliberately by people in areas with good public access. Ideally, all plastic sheet material should be removed once the trees are established. Loose materials such as composted bark are widely used in urban landscaping, and if sufficient depth is applied (approximately 10–20 cm) they should be effective against weed growth for at least one year, before any repeat application is necessary. Composted wood chips or other chipped tree waste may have an added advantage of introducing a possible substrate for fungi and habitat for some invertebrates.

Other weed control techniques include topsoil stripping, soil inversion and the application of proprietary hot water-based organic foams. Soil inversion is achieved with a deep plough which inverts up to 1 m of soil, or by mounding with a mechanical bucket to create individual planting centres, but should only be undertaken if the site is known to have no below-ground archaeological features (Section 6.1). Inversion has the advantage that the weed seed bank should be buried beneath the surface, allowing trees to be planted in a relatively weed-free, but less fertile substrate. Trees should establish quicker, with less need for herbicides. However, if the soil inversion is not deep enough, vigorous ruderal communities may develop which are difficult to control.

Vigorous weed growth in this soil inversion plot looks unsightly (left), but five years after planting the sessile oaks had established well (right).

Plant communities that develop in the non-treated areas can be beneficial for wildlife, offering some structural diversity; providing seed for birds during the winter period; and nectar and pollen for insects in the summer. If the structure of the vegetation is suitable, they can in some circumstances provide temporary habitat for ground nesting birds such as the grey partridge and corn bunting in the lowlands, and twite and whinchat in the uplands. An alternative strategy on lowland arable land would be to sow a grass mix to exclude pernicious weeds such as ragworts and thistles, or a simple wildflower mix based on that devised for ride areas. This would help the development of open ground communities on the site, and its visual appearance, provided that the area around the trees was kept free of vegetation which would compete with the young trees.

8.3.2 Replacing dead trees

'Beating up' is the process of replacing trees that die after planting or the initial part of the establishment phase. Where woodland is created for wildlife, these losses are much less critical and may even have the advantage of creating variable spacing and differential rates of canopy closure that will add to the overall diversity. However, forestry grants may require trees to be replaced to meet the specified success criteria e.g. densities of 1,100–2,250 trees per ha, depending on the objectives of the planting. The necessity to replace trees increases progressively with wider spacing, so that at 3–3.5 m spacing, failures would create large gaps of 6–9 m between trees. Replacement plants will be at a comparative disadvantage and sometimes larger plants are used to compensate for the size disparity that will develop after a season's growth. There is no point in replacing trees beyond the end of the first growing season, as the established trees will by then have developed a competitive advantage, condemning the slower-growing replacements to be thinned early.

9 POST-ESTABLISHMENT MANAGEMENT

9.1 Post-establishment operations

Once the trees are established, an important objective when managing for wildlife is to achieve a varied canopy structure as quickly as possible. To some extent this will have already been built into the original design for a varied planting matrix, with different species developing at different rates, differential spacing and open space in the form of rides and glades. Further refinements and adjustments are possible during the period up to canopy closure (usually ranging from 5–15 years) using techniques such as re-spacing, pruning, premature thinning and coppicing. In some cases a more uniform closed canopy may be desirable, for example when creating non-intervention areas or Atlantic upland oakwood types which have little understorey. Later on the thinning and felling regimes determined by the choice of silvicultural system(s) will become important, but descriptions of these are beyond the scope of this book.

9.1.1 Respacing and cleaning

As the trees grow, some re-spacing to adjust final numbers may be desirable, particularly if uniformly dense thickets have been produced by natural regeneration or direct seeding, although this can be an expensive operation unless the material is saleable. For forestry purposes, thinning 2–4 m tall thickets to an average spacing of 1 m between trees may be done initially, followed by conventional thinning to normal stocking levels after a further 2–3 years. This is particularly important in the case of oak and beech, which tend to stagnate if they are not given sufficient crown space to develop (Willoughby et al., 2004a). Where the trees have been planted at close spacing for insurance, re-spacing to achieve lower and varying densities can also be applied retrospectively. For conservation purposes, non-intervention may be perfectly acceptable in some areas, allowing close canopy competition and heavy shading and the development of a high forest structure.

A normal practice in forestry is to carry out 'cleaning' of unwanted, volunteer woody species from the crop at the thicket stage, which can dramatically reduce the eventual species diversity of the stand. For woodland creation for wildlife, it is quite likely that these very species will be desirable additions within the developing stand, so cleaning would be inappropriate. However, there are cases where natural regeneration of one or two species, such as willows and birches, can threaten to overwhelm the planted species. To maintain the overall diversity, it may be necessary to clean some areas to prevent this happening.

Typically, the seedling densities delivered by natural regeneration are far from uniform and are the result of the intensity of the seed rain across the site, soil conditions, predation by animals and the presence of competing vegetation. In some patches individuals may be densely packed together, almost resembling an herbaceous sward at germination, while elsewhere the ground may be devoid of any seedlings. Attempts to reproduce this variability and unevenness in the canopy structure by altering the pattern of spacing between trees has been discussed earlier in Section 7.4. In contrast, a uniform 2 m spacing (2,500 trees per ha) is standard in commercial forestry, but for conservation purposes wider spacings of 2.5–4.5 m, equivalent to densities of 500–1,600 trees per ha within planting groups are generally recommended, allowing for natural colonisation of woody plants and ground flora. These lower densities, plus the provision of additional open space and shrubs, are widely accepted in grant schemes for native woodland.

9.1.2 Pruning young trees

To maximise its value for wildlife, woodland should be allowed to develop naturally during the establishment phase (5–15 years), without pruning the trees and shrubs. If pruning is necessary during this period, for example where timber production is an objective, it need not be too detrimental to wildlife. For example, if the wood has been well designed for wildlife, with areas of understorey trees and shrub planting along the woodland margins and rides, then the pruning should be of some benefit to the woodland as a whole; the accelerated height growth of the pruned trees themselves will provide greater structural diversity and allow more light at ground level, potentially encouraging field layer vegetation and shrub growth. Unpruned trees can be retained along the woodland edges, or in clumps alternating with pruned trees.

Ten-year old woodland pruned several times to ease mowing (left) and not pruned (below); note the lack of understorey in the unpruned woodland.

If necessary for commercial reasons, prune only selected trees judged to be the most likely to be felled, which should be just 10–15% of the initial number planted. This is generally carried out in the late summer or early autumn, avoiding the period of early spring growth and the bird-nesting season. Oak responds best to pruning in early winter; wild cherry is best pruned in July in order to minimise the risks of infection through the cut branch surfaces.

9.1.3 Thinning

Thinning is required as the tree canopy closes in order to prevent competition and to aid tree growth and development. For wildlife, thinning can enhance structure in the stand through development of an understorey and through improved crown development. There are several approaches to thinning: which is most appropriate will depend on how the wood was established. Flexibility in thinning frequency, proportion of trees harvested and thinning pattern helps to increase biodiversity. Whilst thinning is an accepted forestry practice, there is little guidance relating to new native woodland where wildlife is an important consideration. In this case, guidance needs to be more subjective, and visual assessment of new woodland is critical. Thinning is not usually considered until the trees are closing canopy, and then only if it is likely to have a positive impact on structural diversity within the wood as a whole. Where it is necessary, heavy thinning might be undertaken to reduce shading and allow the development of an understorey, but perhaps in relatively small areas of the wood, and on a rotational basis. In practice this will mean removing significantly more wood per harvest than would be the case in conventional thinnings, resulting in an overall loss in timber yield. However in some silvicultural treatments where timber is the objective, 'free growth' may be allowed, where individual tree crowns are allowed free development in order to maximise diameter growth for eventual sawlogs (Kerr, 1996).

The thinning pattern can also be critical. Selective thinning – in which each tree to be removed is individually selected and marked – gives most choice and can be used to remove trees that would become suppressed anyway, leaving the dominants, or the opposite, removing dominant trees to break up the canopy; as well as many other intermediate strategies. It is most likely to be applied where tree densities are highly variable – as in group plantings, naturally regenerated and other irregularly-spaced stands. However it requires skilled management and is therefore more costly than other options. Systematic thinning, on the other hand, requires less skill and can be applied where trees have been planted in regular rows or grids. The removal of complete rows will allow the crowns of adjacent trees to develop and spread, while at the same time maintaining some open ground species and shrub growth to be retained in the less shaded, thinned 'racks' for longer periods, until lighter conditions prevail later in the rotation. With some forms of line thinning, the miniature glades formed at the junctions of the thinning 'racks' and with the main rides provide even larger canopy gaps (Anderson, 1989). Obviously there is a limit to the process, as lines of trees cannot continue to be removed, and at some point selective thinning will take over.

With successive thinnings, and as the trees mature and their growth rates slow, more light penetrates to the understorey. This provides the opportunity for previously suppressed species to spread from existing depauperate plants, to germinate from buried seed, or colonise from the edges of the stand. Late-rotation conditions also encourage a true multi-storied forest structure as ground flora, shrubs and young trees respond to gaps beneath the main crop. After thinning, some of the wood should be left *in situ*, to create some deadwood in the new woodland (see Section 9.2).

9.1.4 Coppicing and group felling

Depending on the long term objective for the wood, derived in part from the typical landscape character of woodland in the locality, another way of developing a range of age structures relatively rapidly with value for wildlife is to fell areas (known as coupes) soon after they have been established: group felling or coppicing. Coppice is the traditional form of woodland management across much of Britain, but has largely died out. However, new markets are beginning to become viable again; woodfuel, a low-carbon, sustainable source of heat or power is gaining ground. Typically, coupes are cut on a rotation of e.g. 15 to 25 years, depending on the tree growth and wood product desired, providing wildlife with a continuity of the full range of growth stages within the wood from bare ground to immature high forest. It is usually beneficial to wildlife to keep a significant area of the woodland back from the coppice cycle to develop into high forest – as a range of species require mature features. How much will depend on the scale of the wood and the character of neighbouring woods; somewhere around or above a quarter will usually provide habitat for many species' needs in medium to large woods.

The areas to be felled can be based on the dimensions of the planted groups, but are better if done on a larger scale, in units up to 0.25 ha (50x50 m). Thus, in a woodland area of 3 ha (excluding rides and open space) there would be up to 12 felling units available. In one scenario, from year 5 onwards, when the trees have established, one unit could be felled each year until the whole area had been cut over at 16 years. Having created a growth differential from scrub cover to the late thicket stage, subsequent rotations can be extended to suit different wood markets or particular species of conservation interest, with some felling units reserved for longer to allow the development of mature woodland features. Some coppice wood products need short rotations, e.g. thatching spars and fencing hurdles at 6–8 years, while woodfuel and stakes may require more than 20 years. There are many permutations and combinations which can be designed to generate particular growth stages for wildlife, while taking account of markets and management costs. Cutting of the units (coupes) can be contiguous – so species with low mobility, such as some butterflies, can colonise suitable adjacent structures. By planning the coupes and timetable with care it is possible to accentuate structural complexity by contrasting edges between older and younger stands at the same time as providing areas of contiguous structure.

With increasing size of woodland the coupes can be correspondingly bigger (a good optimum for butterflies and birds is c.0.5 ha), when it becomes easier to accommodate longer rotations and areas of non-intervention, or even have more than one rotation. A 20-ha wood could accommodate two simultaneous rotations of 25 and 8 years, each of 0.5 ha, with a quarter of the wood set aside for maturation.

It is important to note that the yield of wood products from the first coppice rotation of any duration is likely to be minimal, until the root system has captured the full resources of the site in subsequent rotations. Also, it is crucial to ensure that browsing by deer and other animals is kept to a minimum, or the new coppice shoots will suffer or fail.

Group fells are similar in principle to coppicing, but rely on natural regeneration of the cleared areas rather than vegetative re-growth. They consist of small-scale, temporary clearings, cut to encourage stands of even-aged and often straight timber, usually on long cycles of 40–100 years, depending on growth rates. Group felling is the typical way of regenerating slow-growing upland oak woods, ensuring a continuity of age classes in the wood, including areas of thicket in otherwise closed canopy high forest. The diversity created is good for wildlife using immature stages of the woodland, from butterflies in the open glades to birds at the pole stage. Group felling can be introduced to new woodland usually quite early in its life to start the process before the whole wood needs thinning (see above).

9.2 Providing additional resources for wildlife

In this book we have talked at length about planting and managing trees and shrubs, and sowing grasses and herbs; not only to create naturalistic vegetation communities, but also to attract wildlife into the developing habitats. Other resources for wildlife such as artificial nestboxes and deadwood can also be valuable to wildlife, and here we discuss the merits of some of these.

9.2.1 Deadwood

Deadwood provides an important habitat niche for a wide range of wildlife; mammals such as wood mice and hedgehogs make use of log piles; birds such as willow tit may nest in holes in deadwood; lizards and other reptiles use deadwood along ride edges for basking; and amphibians such as great crested newt, common toad and common frog hibernate within piles of logs. Deadwood also supports invertebrates such as ground and rove beetles, and the larvae of the globally threatened stag beetles, lichens, saproxylic fungi and bryophytes. In mature woodland, especially in old growth which has not been managed for 60 years or more, there may be considerable volumes of deadwood of many species, offering a diverse range of microhabitats. This is in sharp contrast to new native woodland thickets which have very little deadwood, comprising mainly small branches and twigs, often heavily shaded.

Decaying wood can support a host of insects, mosses and fungi (sulphur tuft).

In new native woodland, any dead trees or brash should generally be left *in situ*. Brash piles will provide temporary shelter for some invertebrates. However, some small logs arising from pre-thinning or coppicing may be collected and placed in piles. These will be more valuable if actually lashed together into a 'Waterhouse' log pile (Read, 1999). This will provide an important habitat niche for some species that would naturally use deadwood in more mature woodland, although ancient woodland specialists are unlikely to colonise unless the new wood is actually adjacent to ancient woodland. The log piles should comprise a mix of species, preferably those planted in the new wood, and are best placed in damp, shady environments. Once in place, they should be left alone to ensure that the inhabitants are undisturbed. Log piles and deadwood in general are especially important habitats because decaying wood is far less common in the British countryside than it used to be, and is often removed during overzealous management.

9.2.2 Bat boxes

Bats have lost many of their natural roosting sites, such as veteran trees and old trees lost to Dutch elm disease. Storms such as that in 1987 in South East England have also destroyed some roosting sites, whilst creating others in snapped trees and boughs. Bats have adapted to use man-made structures, but many of these are also being lost, for example by the sealing of cavities in buildings, barn conversions, and timber treatment in buildings. Specially designed boxes are known to be used by bats in summer for roosting, mating roosts, and breeding; and in winter for hibernation. Consequently the provision of boxes can be important for local bat populations, but young woods at the thicket stage are not usually the best place for them. Young stems may not be strong enough to support the boxes, but more importantly, bat boxes require a serious commitment in terms of inspection and cleaning, particularly if they have sealed bottoms. Even if local bat groups can be persuaded to help with a bat box project in young woodland, there is no guarantee that volunteers will be able to maintain the boxes over a long period of time, which is essential to a successful programme. Where new woodland has been planted on nature reserves or sites with a high level of conservation management, then boxes may be attached to wooden posts at least 3 m above the ground, at the thicket stage or even earlier. Bats should be given the opportunity to choose between boxes facing in a variety of aspects, south being the warmest, with others being cooler, depending on shading.

9.2.3 Boxes for other mammals

Boxes are also available for other mammals such as dormouse and red squirrel. Although dormice favour extensive areas of ancient woodland with hazel coppice and a diverse range of shrubs, they also use a range of scrub types, hedgerows and young plantations, and may be attracted to new native woodland habitat, providing it is not isolated by open ground. If there is a continuity of thicket and dense understorey, then new woodland will have the potential to support dormice. Nestboxes can provide valuable breeding sites for dormice when natural holes are in short supply, which is likely to be the case in new native woodland. They are unlikely to be used for hibernation.

Dormice use nest boxes which are similar in appearance to bird boxes, but the entrance hole is at the back, facing the tree, and the box should be about 2.5 m above the ground. As dormice are easily disturbed by approaching people, the boxes should be sited well away from public areas, ideally near a routeway which dormice might be using. Boxes can be relatively easily constructed, or purchased from specialist suppliers. Like bats, dormice are a protected species, so should not be disturbed, unless a special licence has been obtained from Natural England. If dormice are known to be present, or suspected in the vicinity of the new wood, more detailed advice can be found in Natural England's *Dormouse Conservation Handbook* (Bright et al., 2006).

9.2.4 Bird nestboxes

Everyone is familiar with nestboxes, in particularly their use in gardens and more degraded habitats. Hole-nesting birds such as blue tit and great tit which are likely to use nestboxes are relatively common, and would not naturally nest in young woodland. Whether nestboxes should be put up in this habitat at the thicket stage is open to discussion, because it has been suggested that they might compete for food with young woodland specialists such as nightingale and willow warbler. In mature woodland, blue tit and great tit tend to feed in the tree canopy, whereas as willow warbler and nightingale forage in the denser understorey. While there is yet no firm evidence of competition in young woodlands, it is an area currently being considered by researchers. If new native woodland is being created today, better advice might be available by the time that it reaches the thicket stage.

Earlier in the life of the wood, barn owl boxes may be erected 3–5 m above the ground on a solitary mature tree or pole, as soon as the trees have been planted. These may also attract other species such as kestrel and stock dove. Long-eared owls might also benefit from the provision of basket nests at the thicket stage, in areas where the owls are known to breed. Factsheets on all nestboxes are available from conservation organisations such as the RSPB, and describe their construction and siting in detail.

9.2.5 Woodland ponds

Ponds provide excellent value for wildlife, and are now classified as a UK BAP priority habitat. Pond creation can be particularly valuable because new ponds can act as stepping stones to improve ecological connectivity, increase the diversity of ponds in an area, and strengthen local populations of uncommon species such as great crested newts and mud snails. The terrestrial habitat around a pond is also an important component of a well-balanced wildlife pond.

Existing pond incorporated into a new native woodland creation scheme.

Woodland pond construction on the site of a new native woodland creation scheme.

The time and effort involved in pond construction should not be underestimated. Pre-site checks need to be undertaken, for example to ensure that the pond does not damage nearby protected habitat or species; will not adversely impact on drainage or water courses; not be at risk from pollution; and will not require planning permission. There are many different designs and features which must be considered at the planning stage, such as size, depth, the relationship of the proposed pond to the surrounding habitat and land use, and most importantly, ensuring that the pond will hold water. Drawings and plans are essential for those involved, including contractors and if required, for planning officers. The construction phase will require careful planning, including access for machinery to deal with topsoil and spoil. Critically, the pond may need managing for some time after construction, particularly if it is being managed for particular species. Factsheets which cover these, and many more issues related to pond design, construction and management are available from Pond Conservation and other conservation organisations.

9.3 Introducing a woodland ground flora

Creating new native woodlands involves mass planting or encouraging natural regeneration of trees and shrubs, usually with little attention paid to the field layer. The priority is to establish a canopy cover in the hope that, in due course, a ground flora will develop and look after itself. In practice, on fertile soils, rank growth of tall ruderal herbs such as nettle, docks and cow parsley, together with grasses and woody plants such as bramble and ivy may develop rapidly (see Section 2.2.1), preventing or delaying the ingress of other woodland plants. Furthermore, in a dense planting matrix, this phase is often followed by long periods of canopy closure, shading out or impoverishing the volunteer field layer until lighter conditions prevail. In Chapter 2 we considered some characteristics of ancient woodland plants – namely their weak dispersal mechanisms, low rates of viable seed production and often strong reliance on vegetative spread. Consequently, their spread to, or within, new sites is very slow: in fragmented landscapes it is unrealistic to expect, in the medium term at least, many such species to find their way into new native woodland of their own accord. Even where dispersal is effective, competition with fast-colonising and shade-tolerant 'weeds' may also limit establishment on nutrient-rich soils.

9.3.1 Arguments for and against introducing a woodland ground flora

Given the long timescale of natural colonisation, there is a case for accelerating the introduction of a ground flora into new and recently planted woods. However, this can be a controversial area. As Table 9.1 shows, sown or planted field layers can potentially obscure natural biogeographical boundaries and may hybridise with local populations, reducing their subsequent fitness. The argument for using locally collected material may also be stronger in the case of herbaceous populations with poor dispersal characteristics, as any chance gene flow from introductions to surrounding wild populations would then be less likely to cause outbreeding depression. However, there are risks that bottlenecks caused by limited collections, or selection pressures arising during propagation, may result in reduced genetic diversity.

In Britain it is illegal to intentionally uproot any wild plant without the permission of the landowner. Even where that permission is obtained, it is an offence to pick, uproot, trade in, or possess (for the purposes of trade) certain species under Schedule 8 of the Wildlife and Countryside Act (1981, as amended in 1998). Native bluebell is a nominated species and a special licence is required from Natural England if the seed is to be sold. In a position statement, Plantlife (2003) warns potential purchasers to check that bulbs have not been sourced illegally from the wild, and point out the dangers of inadvertently introducing the fertile hybrid of native and Spanish bluebell or Spanish bluebell itself into the wider countryside. Similar dangers may arise with other woodland species that are also garden plants, such as the wild daffodil.

9.3.2 Procuring woodland plants

The 'shade', 'hedgerow' and 'woodland' wildflower seed mixes available from commercial suppliers contain species with widely ranging strategies. There is a high premium on cosmopolitan, colourful and reliably-germinating subjects requiring no special pre-treatments, such as red campion and foxglove, which grow well in moderate shade and moderately fertile soils. Most are more properly classed as shade-tolerant plants which are equally at home in open habitats; and relatively few true woodland species are included that can survive deep shade (Table 9.2). General purpose mixes also contain some redundant species which may survive for a short while but will not adapt to the conditions prevailing at the sowing site.

Table 9.1 Arguments for and against introducing field layer species into woodlands

Arguments for introductions	Arguments against introductions
Wildflower introductions: • make woods look attractive • overcome slow dispersal • increase biodiversity in new woodland • colonisation of other woods unlikely • Biological Records Centres and associated conservation bodies record introductions for future reference	Introductions obscure natural biogeographical boundaries of plant distribution: recent woods may begin to resemble ancient woods
Small, wide-ranging local collections: • maximise genetic diversity • avoid over harvesting • reduce selection pressures • reduce collateral damage to other species • accompanied by bulking up in plant nurseries	Artificial selection pressures imposed by small collections of plant material, or arising during nursery propagation, may narrow the genetic diversity of introduced material
Local collections reduce risks to co-evolved species, such as insect feeders and pollinators	Non-local ecotypes may be detrimental to other members of the woodland community, such as co-evolved phytophagous invertebrates
Nursery propagated material – regularly replenished from the field – maintains wild population characteristics	The process of collecting and harvesting of seed in the field may cause physical damage to non-target species, especially invertebrates
Habitat creation opportunities in urban and derelict land arguably have fewer constraints relating to the use of native species and cultural genotypes; species are more likely to be selected with ecological traits able to tolerate fertile and partially open environments	Habitat creation in the wider countryside poses potentially greater risks to nearby ancient woodlands, raising issues of gene transfer between wild and introduced populations and the ingress of invasive species.
The limited scale of most introductions is unlikely to 'swamp' local populations, especially in urban woods where gene flows to native populations are limited. However introduced genes may also increase genetic diversity in native populations and potentially increase their fitness: there is little evidence either way	Genetic patterns of native ecotypes may be degraded through hybridisation with introduced species, reducing their fitness through outbreeding depression. Interspecies hybrids between wild and cultivated plants are another potential danger with some native species such as bluebell and wild daffodil

Most mixes contain 80% by weight of grass seed (often 85% or more of actual propagule numbers) to provide a so-called 'nurse' crop to the developing wild flowers. Too often these contain mainly non-woodland turf grasses, which, in open to moderately shaded conditions, can quickly out-compete the herbs. Some companies recognise this by omitting the grasses, or offering the option of herbs alone. This is a far safer policy, perhaps supplemented with a low density of the local woodland grasses such as false brome or wood meadow-grass.

Another approach is to collect one's own seed, based on a careful selection of species present in neighbouring woods. This avoids buying redundant species and gets around the issue of using non-local material, but may not be cost-effective for larger woodland creation schemes that will require a plant nursery input and considerable bulking up of supplies. Some seed companies will make up customised mixtures to a client's specification, although the cost compared with standard commercial mixes is likely to be more, unless fewer species are requested.

An alternative to seeding, although again more costly, is to consider planting 'plugs', or module-grown individual plants of more difficult subjects, including ancient woodland species which produce little seed or have poor

Table 9.2 Common components of commercial woodland wildflower seed mixes

Species associated with ancient woodland	Ramsons Nettle-leaved bellflower Pignut Bluebell Primrose
Faster colonising woodland herbs	Garlic mustard Foxglove Wood avens Red campion Hedge woundwort Greater stitchwort Upright hedge-parsley Wood sage
Shade-tolerant herbs	Yarrow Agrimony Hedge bedstraw Meadowsweet Perforate St John's-wort Ragged-Robin Cowslip Selfheal Betony Tufted vetch
Grasses a) woodland edge species	False brome Tufted hair-grass Wood meadow-grass Wood millet
b) 'turf' species	Common bent Sheep's-fescue Red fescue Smooth meadow-grass

Wild daffodils could be introduced, but it is important to check that bulbs have not been illegally wild-collected.

germination. A more limited range of species is available from nurseries, but among them are the following:

	Propagation method
Bugle	Stolons, rhizomes
Wood anemone	Rhizomes
Woodruff	Seeds, rhizomes
Bluebell	Bulbs
Yellow archangel	Stolons
Primrose	Seeds, rhizomes
Wild daffodil	Bulbs
Sweet violet	Seeds, stolons
Common dog-violet	Seeds, plant division

There is experimental evidence that because of their more advanced developmental state, plugs usually withstand competition better than seedlings of the same species and will also flower sooner: an important advantage considering that flowering from the seedling stage can take up to 5–10 years for bluebell and wood anemone, respectively.

9.3.3 Introducing woodland plants

Various recommendations detailing methods, species choice, sowing rates, soil manipulation, weed control, and optimal shade levels have been reported for woodland flora introductions. The recurring theme is how to deal with the 'weed' populations that will inevitably compete with the target species until woodland conditions are achieved. Pre-treatment with herbicide and mulches (woodchips, bark or compost) or surface rotovation may be effective in providing a regeneration gap for field layer introductions, particularly when applied at a critical stage of tree canopy closure, say at 6–12 years (depending on original spacing), when light levels are beginning to fall below 25% of open values. In longer-established woodland, it may not even be necessary to carry out any ground preparation if the existing ground vegetation is sparse.

As many woodland species need chilling to promote germination, sowing is best done in the autumn (September–November) or early spring (February–April). Some, such as foxglove and red campion, also require light prior to germination and therefore respond better to surface broadcasting than burying under layers of soil or mulch, although some light scarification may be effective. Sowing rates depend on which species are being sown, but seed suppliers' rates (typically 4 g per m² for grass/herb mixes and 1–1.5 g per m² for herbs alone) can probably be

Primrose (left) and ramsons (right) are ancient woodland species often included in commercial wildflower seed mixes.

reduced by up to a tenth without appreciable loss of cover. The herb species in standard woodland mixes will initially be dominated by fast-germinating woodland edge species: unless a much higher proportion of interior woodland species such as bluebell, primrose and ramsons is specified, it will be two or three years before these become prominent in the field layer.

Plug planting densities are largely dictated by economics; in trials, Francis *et al.*, (1992) found that 6–9 plants per m^2 gave good results, reducing to 3–4 per m^2 for species exhibiting good vegetative spread. However, even at these lower densities the material cost could easily exceed £10,000 per ha compared with £1,000–£3,000 per ha for standard woodland seed mixes supplied at the recommended rate. A compromise solution is to introduce a few species with poor germination as plugs, with the remainder sown as a seed mix. Plugs are best planted as groups in early spring.

There is no need to plant a field layer everywhere in a wood; if confined to well-located patches dispersed through the site, these will act as centres for colonisation and spread to other parts. In sunnier microsites more rapid growth and flowering is likely to occur, while the number of visits made by pollinators in these areas will also increase seed viability. The margins of rides and glades are likely to fulfil these conditions, providing gradients where a balance between shade species and species of open habitats can be achieved. From an aesthetic point of view, these are also places where the results of habitat enhancement are likely to be seen.

Management, once the field layer is established should be minimal, but a varied light environment will maintain a range of species best, especially the more light-demanding subjects. The latter will benefit from periodic canopy thinning, group felling or coppicing, providing that the level of disturbance is not so great as to allow weed growth to become competitive.

9.4   Monitoring tree establishment and growth

Growth and establishment of planted and naturally regenerating trees and shrubs should be monitored during the establishment phase at least, as this will inform the need for gapping (beating) up. Monitoring beyond this phase will provide a record of the development of the wood, which can be considered in conjunction with data on colonisation by woodland species.

Photography is one of the simplest and most effective ways of assessing woodland creation in the longer term. Photographs immediately convey the effectiveness of tree establishment and growth, without the need to undertake detailed measurements and perform complicated statistics. Photographs need to be taken from strategic 'photo points', located throughout the woodland, mapped and identified with permanent markers such as metal poles or pegs. Landmarks such as a tree stump may also be used, with caution, as these may not be permanent.

For more quantitative data on the performance of species planted, including establishment and growth rates, measurements should be made annually at the end of the summer growing season in designated plots. The first measurements should be made at the start of the first growing season, to establish a baseline upon which future comparisons can be made. Measurements should include survival after the first growing season which will identify any replanting necessary, height and girth. Suppression of weed competition is another useful parameter which could be assessed as the trees begin to close canopy, by scoring the diversity and cover of ground vegetation.

9.5   Monitoring biodiversity change

The ultimate aim of creating new native woodland for wildlife and people is a wood which is well integrated into the local landscape, with biodiversity levels eventually similar to nearby ancient woodland. However, many woodland creation schemes which have been implemented to date have not incorporated biodiversity monitoring of any kind, and there is certainly no consistent approach adopted for defining monitoring programmes. Monitoring of woodland creation schemes can be justified on a scientific basis, but more than this, woodland owners may derive considerable satisfaction from discovering the plants and animals which have colonised their new woodlands. Monitoring of new woods will provide:

- a measure of how successful the planting has been
- an indication of the rate of ecosystem recovery
- evidence of the use of the new habitat by target species such as woodland birds

TOP LEFT **Migrant hawkers are frequent visitors to established new native woodland rides in late summer.**

TOP RIGHT **Fly agaric in a new woodland ride.**

- opportunities for management intervention to enhance the developing woodland ecosystem, and to mitigate any adverse impacts
- information for subsequent habitat creation and restoration efforts.

Depending on whether the prime purpose of a new woodland is for forestry, amenity or conservation, the composition of woods may be decidedly different in terms of their size, layout and complexity, and also therefore in their monitoring requirements. Nevertheless, it would be advantageous to implement standardised monitoring programmes which would constitute a basis for comparison between many sites. Of course, the ability to monitor depends on the available budget, but monitoring need not be too onerous, as the improvements in biodiversity year-on-year may be relatively small. If there is no formal requirement for monitoring, then the most cost-effective method is likely to be used.

Monitoring tree and shrub establishment and growth will yield immediate results, and in the first year will identify any need for planting replacements. Other groups such as birds and butterflies may also be monitored from the outset to provide baseline data on species present, and subsequently to inform ongoing management decisions. Bird communities in particular will change as the woodland moves towards the thicket stage. Insects and wildflowers will colonise rides and glades once the sward has become established. Colonisation by shade-tolerant plants will be a longer-term process, and monitoring may not start until the canopy closes, and the weed flora has been shaded out.

A basic level of monitoring might consider the success of tree and shrub planting in forest areas; the establishment of grass and wildflower seed mixes in rides and glades; and of particular importance, the colonisation of the developing woodland habitat by plants, birds, and insects such as butterflies, beetles and hoverflies. Surveys may be carried out annually initially, but thereafter once every three years may be sufficient. It may be necessary to employ the services of specialist ecological practitioners for some of this work.

9.5.1 Monitoring ground flora

Where open areas have been seeded with wildflowers, these should be carefully monitored over the first two growing seasons to gauge the success of the operation, and identify any areas which might require repeat sowing. A minimalist approach can be employed (as described in Section 6.2.3); essentially by setting up a minimum of three 2 x 2 m quadrats in homogeneous areas within the site, and recording the abundance of each species using percentage cover or the Domin scale, noting any other species present in the environs. Thereafter they may be monitored every two to three years, recording basic parameters such as species survival and abundance.

9.5.2 Monitoring birds

Birds are one of the most visible groups in woodland, and also easy to monitor. Initially species of more open country such as meadow pipit may be present, augmented by species such as yellowhammer and whitethroat as the tree and shrub layer develops. Then as canopy closes, other warblers, thrushes etc. move in. Structural and species diversity will have significant impact on colonisation, and birds present will give an indication of the state of the developing ecosystem – for example the presence of insectivorous birds. Some of these species may be birds of conservation concern, such as bullfinch or twite, so it is important to identify these, and to ensure that management decisions support these species.

Surveys based on the British Trust for Ornithology's (BTO) Breeding Bird Survey (Hill *et al.*, 2005) would be most suitable for new native woodland (see Section 6.2.3). The survey involves just two visits during the breeding season and yields information on species diversity and abundance. Further details can be obtained from the BTO website. Ideally bird surveys would be carried out annually, but this could be extended to every three to five years if necessary, particularly once the canopy closes.

9.5.3 Monitoring mammals

Mammal surveys are most likely to be undertaken in special circumstances, for example where dormouse habitat is being created. For such projects, specialist ecological practitioners with the necessary licences should be employed, who will probably deploy boxes or tubes. However, surveyors recording birds or other species can also be asked to record sightings or signs of mammals. It is not unusual to encounter deer and foxes during early morning bird surveys for example. Records may include live animals seen and counted; dead animals recorded; and signs such as trees which have been browsed, droppings and tracks. Any information is valuable for assessing the wildlife present in a new wood, and implementing management plans. Where deer are likely to cause damage to young trees, monitoring of their population densities might be useful to decide whether any control measures are necessary. Estimates can be made by counting faecal pellets in sample plots, either at a single visit (the standing crop method) or by clearing the plots at repeat intervals and measuring accumulation over time (the accumulation rate method). A recent Forestry Commission Bulletin describes a combination plot technique, combining both methods, to estimate deer numbers (Swanson *et al.,* 2008).

9.5.4 Monitoring butterflies

Butterflies are frequently recorded in habitat creation and restoration schemes. This is because most are readily identifiable; they benefit from habitat creation; they are known to respond rapidly and sensitively to subtle changes in habitat and climate; and are representative of the diversity and responses of other wildlife, particularly nectar feeding insects. Consequently, they are very well placed to act as general indicators of the state of health of an ecosystem, as well as informing management decisions.

The intensity of surveys will depend to some extent on the quality of the habitat created, and the proximity to potential donor sites. Colonisation rates will be influenced by the diversity of butterflies in the local landscape. In small woods, monitoring could be based on four, evenly spaced walks through the site during the flight season: i.e. in early to mid-May; the first two weeks of June; mid- to late July; and mid-August, noting species and numbers.

Monitoring ground flora along the perimeter of new native woodland.

LEFT **Common blue butterflies are frequently found in new woodland with good quality rides and glades.**

RIGHT **Peacock butterfly larvae feeding on common nettle along the margins of a new wood.**

Freshly emerged six-spot burnet moth in a woodland glade.

For larger woods with more substantial open areas, or those close to existing butterfly-rich habitat, it would be worthwhile monitoring butterflies annually whilst the new habitat is developing. A formal transect should be walked, with at least four visits as outlined above. Better data will be obtained if, during the period of peak activity from late June to mid-August, recording is carried out every two weeks. If practical, this would provide more accurate data and allow trends in abundance to be calculated year-on-year, although this involves more complicated analysis, and hence may require the services of a specialist ecological practitioner. For more details on butterfly monitoring, see Section 6.2.

GLOSSARY

accumulated temperatures	a measure of the degree of warmth or heat energy available during the growing season (usually calculated as the number of degree-days above a certain threshold, e.g. 5.6°C). It is strongly (inversely) related to elevation and distance from the sea and is one of the best predictors of forest yield in a UK context.
adaptive genetic diversity	genetic variation responsible for the ability of an individual to survive, reproduce and respond to environmental changes
advance(d) regeneration	regeneration of tree or shrub species already present on site, usually prior to any treatments designed to encourage natural regeneration
alleles	alternative forms of a gene locus or nucleotide sequence along a chromosome
ancient countryside	districts whose fields, woods, roads etc. date predominantly before AD 1700 and the Enclosure Acts of the 18th and 19th centuries
ancient woodland	a site continuously wooded for at least the past 400 years, since 1600 AD (taken as 250 years or 1750 AD in Scotland)
ancient woodland (indicator) species	plants or other species groups associated with continuously wooded sites, usually having weak dispersal. Considered to be 'indicators' of ancient woods, depending on regional affinities.
Ancient Woodland Inventory (AWI)	a survey originally carried out in the 1980s by the Nature Conservancy Council (now Natural England), using maps, historic documents and field surveys to locate ancient woodland sites and record losses over time
Ancient Woodland Priority Areas	core areas of ancient woodland networks where landscape connectivity and permeability criteria indicate good opportunities to link and extend ancient woodlands, either through new native woodland planting or through managing or creating other semi-natural habitats
ancient, semi-natural woodland	see ancient woodland above; the point here being that these woods are not only on ancient sites, but still retain largely intact canopies of native species
anionic resins	anion exchange resins used in soil analysis to determine availability to plants of nutrients such as nitrate and phosphate
base-rich	soils rich in base elements, such as calcium, potassium and magnesium
Biodiversity Action Plans (BAP)	plans initiated under the UK Biodiversity Action Plan (UKBAP) in 1994 as a response to the United Nations Convention on Biological Diversity in 1992, identifying and prioritising actions to protect threatened and nationally important species and habitats
Biodiversity Broad Habitat types	a broad habitat classification used in Biodiversity Action Plans; e.g. broadleaved, mixed and yew woodland, and coniferous woodland
Birds of Conservation Concern	a long-term wild bird surveillance programme, using population and trends against established criteria to assess conservation priorities, recording status as a 'traffic-light' scheme of red, amber and green
boreal elements; boreal zone	floristic elements or plant species associated with high northern latitudes between the tundra and temperate forest, covering Siberia, Scandinavia, Canada and Alaska, including the Scottish Highlands
box junction	an enlargement of the area where two rides intersect, creating a small glade
Breeding Bird Survey	a national monitoring project recording changes in breeding populations of widespread bird species across the UK
Broadleaves (Broadleaved Woodlands) Policy	1985 Government forestry policy encouraging 'greater use of broadleaved woodlands generally for conservation, recreation, sport and landscape', and aiming to ensure that 'the special interest of ancient semi-natural woodlands is recognised and maintained'
brown earth soils	mineral soils, brownish or reddish in colour, with free drainage, good aeration and well-incorporated organic matter
calcareous	substrates or soil with an alkaline reaction, i.e. pH 7 or above
Caledonian Pinewood Inventory	Forestry Commission inventory of native Scottish pinewoods, including 84 separate woods of various sizes and covering nearly 18,000 hectares
Caledonian pinewoods	the ancient native pinewoods of Scotland, remnants of post-glacial natural forests, now confined to poor, acid soils, usually in association with birch woods. A recognised Priority Habitat under the UK Biodiversity Action Plan.
Challenge Funds	grant funding for planting or management for specialist projects, such as coppicing for butterfly conservation or encouraging regeneration in specific regions, such as National Parks
chronosequence studies	studies in which measurements on individual stands are compared to others differing in age (but not necessarily on the same site type, a flaw in the method)
cleptoparasite	an animal, bird or insect that steals prey or food caught or collected by another
climate space	current or future distributions of a species, matched to its optimum requirements, depending on different climate change scenarios
closed population species	species (especially butterflies) breeding in discrete colonies, often sedentary in habit
coarse woody debris	dead woody material, in various stages of decomposition, located above the soil, larger than 7.5 cm in diameter (or equivalent cross-section)
community forest	forests designed for informal recreation by local communities, located near urban areas
composite provenancing	mixing different provenances of plant material together to introduce a wider range of genetic variation – for example in order to increase adaptability and fitness in a changing climate

connectivity	see habitat connectivity
continental influences	species typical of parts of mainland Europe which experience a continental (less oceanic) climate, with warmer summers and colder winters
coppice	the cutting of stems of young trees or shrubs close to the ground, causing them to re-sprout and to re-establish the canopy: or an area so treated
core networks	ecological networks defined by the characteristics of particular species, usually poorly-dispersing species (e.g. <1 km) with relatively large area requirements (e.g. 10 ha) of a specific habitat
coupe	a felled or coppiced area or compartment of woodland
Dedication Schemes	grant-aid schemes in which participating landowners agree to dedicate planted areas of their land to timber production 'in perpetuity'
dispersal limitation	colonisation of habitats limited by distance ; e.g. plants with seeds poorly adapted for wind or animal dispersal
District Wildlife Sites	see Sites of Nature Conservation Interest
ecological cost	see least-cost pathway
ecological networks	networks of a habitat or habitats that contain core areas, buffer zones and dispersal routes, facilitating species movement and gene flow through the wider landscape
Estate Duty	taxation on property, for example levying death duties on woodlands, or living transfers between owners
European Protected Species; EU Habitats Directive	species protected under Annex IV of the EC Directive on the Conservation of Natural Habitats and Wild Fauna and Flora (92/43/EEC) and the Wildlife and Countryside Act 1981
focal networks	ecological networks defined by the dispersal ability and area requirements of one or a group of species. For example, the target species may be deemed to have medium dispersal ability (<5 km) and moderate area (2 ha) requirements
focal species	species selected to be representative of the wider elements of ecological communities and key ecological processes
Forest Habitat Networks	see ecological networks: designed primarily for forest biodiversity enhancement
forwarder	a six- or eight-wheel articulated machine equipped with a hydraulic loader and timber grapple, used to transport logs from the forest floor to stacking areas at ride-side
gene flow	genes introduced from one local population to another by pollen or seed dispersal
generalist species	species able to utilise a range of different habitat types and food sources
generic species	a 'virtual' species, used to represent different habitat requirements and dispersal preferences of groups of real species, allowing models of functional ecological connectivity to be constructed
genes	a sequence of DNA along a chromosome, containing coding instructions responsible for the development and functioning of all living things
gleyed horizons	permanently, or more commonly seasonally waterlogged soils, causing iron to be reduced to its green/grey state. Where the water table is transient, aeration causes mottling of the profile (with red/orange oxidised iron compounds)
gregarious species	tree species that tend to occur in close proximity to each other; in pure stands, large groups or clusters
group felling	the felling of small groups of trees (e.g. 0.1–0.5 ha in extent) at varying time intervals, creating an uneven-aged forest structure
habitat connectivity	a functional attribute of the landscape related to ecological processes
habitat networks	see ecological networks
Habitats and Species Directive	an EU Directive protecting wild plants, animals and habitats making up the natural environment, creating a network of protected areas around the European Union of national and international importance (Natura 2000 sites). These sites include Special Areas of Conservation (SACs) supporting rare, endangered or vulnerable natural habitats, plants and animals and Special Protection Areas (SPAs), protecting important wild bird species and their habitats
high forest	a forest management system allowing trees to grow to at least two-thirds of their full potential height: woodland not managed as coppice or pollards
Higher Level Stewardship (HLS)	an agri-environment scheme providing funding to farmers and other land managers in England delivering effective environmental management on their land
humus	soil organic matter, consisting of various states of raw and decomposed litter of plant and animal remains
inbreeding depression	depression in fitness, reproductive ability or survival in a population due to inbreeding and loss of genetic diversity
indigenous	a species originating from and living in a particular region or environment, where it is self-perpetuating
IUCN Red List	a comprehensive inventory or List of Threatened Species created in 1963 by the International Union for the Conservation of Nature and Natural Resources (IUCN), indicating the critical conservation status of plant and animal species
Land Cover Map	a comprehensive survey of UK broad habitats for use within a GIS system
Landscape Character	a distinct and recognisable pattern of elements that occurs consistently in a particular type of landscape
least-cost pathway	a route offering the greatest ease of movement (*permeability*), of a species navigating through different land cover types

loamy soils	soils containing a balanced texture of sand, silt and clay particles
local provenance	populations of a species comprised of genetically similar individuals related by common descent, and occupying a particular biogeographic area to which it has usually become adapted and has not been introduced by humans
MAGIC	a web-based interactive map containing Multi-Agency Geographic Information for the Countryside, indicating key environmental schemes and designations, both statutory and non-statutory
mast years	years in which favourable climatic conditions encourage the production of exceptionally large quantities of seed
metapopulation	literally a 'population of populations', linked by occasional immigration, emigration and gene flow from one sub-population to another
mineralisation	a process in which plant (and animal) material is broken down and converted from an organic to an inorganic state, becoming available as nutrients for uptake by living organisms
modern plantations	closely spaced trees planted on open land, ranging from large, even-aged blocks of conifers in the uplands grown for production purposes, to small, mixed broadleaved woodlands on farmland planted for landscape and wildlife conservation
mor, mull and moder humus	Litter at the soil surface in various states of decomposition. In acid soils, mor humus forms a thick mat of litter (L), not significantly incorporated into the mineral soil, with little or no fermentation (F) or humus (H) layers. This contrasts with mull humus on base-rich soils where only thin litter (L) layers remain from recent litter fall; the decomposed organic matter is mixed deeply into the mineral soil. Moder humus is intermediate, with recognisable L, F and H layers, but is only shallowly incorporated into the mineral soil
mottling	see gleyed horizons
mutualists	organisms interacting in a way that is mutually beneficial to both
National Biodiversity Network	charitable company making species data available through its gateway to anyone interested in the UK's biodiversity
National Character Areas (NCAs)	English landscape types with distinctive characteristics, recognising landscape character, physical influences; historical and cultural influences; land cover; changing countryside and shaping the future
National Forest	a major reforestation initiative in central England beginning in the early 1990s and now extending over more than 500 km^2. Multiple objectives include public access, recreation and biodiversity aims.
National Inventory of Woods and Trees	an inventory providing information about the size, distribution, composition and condition of Britain's woodlands, surveyed between 1994 and 2000.
National Landscape Character Map for Wales	Welsh landscape types essentially achieve the same landscape management objectives as the English National Character Areas
National Vegetation Classification (NVC)	British vegetation classification system describing semi-natural plant communities in Britain, broken down into five volumes: 1) woodlands and scrub; 2) mires and heaths; 3) grasslands and montane communities; 4) aquatic communities, swamps and tall herb fens; and 5) marine communities and vegetation of open habitats
Natural Areas, Natural Area Profiles	regions designated by English Nature (now Natural England) describing the wildlife and natural features of an area and their interaction with land use, geology and human history. Important habitats, species and physical features are detailed in Natural Area Profiles (NAPs)
Natural Heritage Futures programme	describes the distinctive identities of 21 natural heritage areas covering the whole of Scotland
natural succession	spontaneous ecosystem development, beginning either from a bare mineral substrate or water (primary succession), or on existing soil profile after disturbance (secondary succession)
oceanicity	regions with a mild climate, having a small annual range of temperature, a long growing season, high relative humidity and low accumulated frost values
old growth	woodland that has been undisturbed for long periods, sometimes centuries, containing large old trees, a wide range of tree ages, and large quantities of fallen and standing dead wood in various stages of decay
origin	the natural range from which a species was originally derived or collected
outbreeding depression	crossing of two populations, resulting in reduced reproductive fitness and the disruption of evolutionary adaptation to one environment or the other
outcrossing	species usually with wide pollen dispersal, or other mechanisms to avoid self-fertilisation
parasitoid	organism that is parasitic on its host, but ultimately causes its death
Phase 1/Extended Phase 1 habitat survey	a rapid survey technique to record semi-natural vegetation and wildlife habitats over large areas. Based principally on vegetation structure, plus topographic and substrate features, it gives a broad picture of areas that might be of conservation importance, which can be followed up in more detailed extended surveys, for example on protected species such as bats and reptiles
phenology	the scientific study of periodic biological phenomena, such as flowering, breeding, and migration, in relation to climatic conditions
phenotypic	observable physical or biochemical characteristics of an organism, determined both by its genetic makeup and environmental influences
phytophagous	feeding, or utilising a particular plant species
Plantations on Ancient Woodland Sites (PAWS)	forestry plantations of conifers such as spruce and pine, or occasionally broadleaved species, replacing the original semi-natural canopy species on an ancient woodland site

podzolic soils	soils that develop as a result of acid weathering, producing separated horizons: the upper rich in organic matter, often with a bleached layer, due to downward transport of oxides and humus, forming further distinctive layers below
pollard	a tree whose shoots are repeatedly cut back on short rotations at 2–3 metres above ground, avoiding browsing damage, as in wood pasture
primary succession	see natural succession
Priority (BAP) Habitats	habitats of high conservation status prioritised in Biodiversity Action Plans which outline threats, set management targets and objectives and propose actions necessary to achieve recovery
provenance	the location from which seeds or plants were collected, not necessarily the origin of the parent trees
recent, semi-natural woodland	post-1600AD woodlands that have regenerated naturally on open land such as abandoned heaths, moors and grasslands
recruitment limitation	plant colonisation limited by conditions on site, such as suitable germination conditions, or predation and competition
reference communities or sites	semi-natural communities present in the local landscape, used as a guide to species selection for new woodland creation projects
residual herbicide	a herbicide that remains active in the soil and continues to destroy weeds for an extended period after it has been applied
Riparian and Wet Woodland Indicator	plant, insect or other species group associated with riparian woods, usually on established or ancient, semi-natural sites
riparian woodland	woods associated with fresh water; beside rivers, streams and lakes
saproxylic	species associated with dead wood, either fallen or standing, and especially in veteran trees; ranging from fungi, insects, epiphytes, hole-nesting birds and bats
scallop	semi-circular or rectangular excisions ('lay-bys') made into the canopy at the edges of a ride, effectively extending ride width and increasing light gradients; typically up to 20 m long and 20–50 m deep
scarification	any treatment which disrupts or reduces surface vegetation and litter and disturbs the upper layer of the mineral soil, creating a seedbed
secondary succession	see natural succession
seed bank	buried, viable seed present in the soil profile and litter layers, available for germination
seed zones	pre-designated zones for seed collection, usually based on major climatic, geological and landform divisions
seral stage	a series of stages in the development of ecosystem structure and composition over time: normally during primary or secondary succession
Sites of Nature Conservation Interest/Importance (SNCI) Sites of Interest/Importance for Nature Conservation (SINC)	designations at a county scale made by local planning authorities in order to protect areas of importance for wildlife from development. Designations are non-statutory, unlike SSSIs and NNRs
Soil Association	a mapping unit, usually consisting of two or more soils (a principal soil and associated soils) formed from the same parent material and associated with the landscape in a particular pattern
Soil Series	soils classified or grouped together because of their similar formation mode, soil chemistry and physical properties
source-sink effect	a dynamic where large patches or 'reserves' of suitable habitat contain populations that provide 'sources' of individuals dispersing into smaller, less secure patches, or 'sinks', replenishing extinctions as they occur. On their own, the 'sinks' are unlikely to maintain viable populations, but some limited reverse traffic to the sources may occur
Special Areas of Conservation (SACs)	areas defined in the EU Habitats and Species Directive (see above), designed to protect important habitats and species of European interest
specialist species	species having particular or specific habitat requirements or food sources
sub-Atlantic species	species widely distributed in the Atlantic province of Europe, but well represented in parts of central Europe and frequently in southern Fennoscandia. Some species occur widely around the Mediterranean, and a few reach Asia Minor
Target Area Statements (HLS)	describe priorities for HLS schemes in 'target areas'
Theme Statements (HLS)	describe priorities for HLS schemes outside 'target areas'
thicket	a dense, young-growth stage of new or existing woodland, in which the individual crowns coalesce to form a closed canopy, while still maintaining most of their lower branches
UK BAP priority species	the equivalent of Priority Habitats (see above) covering 1,150 species listed in the UK BAP
UK Biodiversity Action Plan (UK BAP)	see Biodiversity Action Plans
veteran trees	trees in late maturity that are of interest biologically, culturally or aesthetically because of their age, size or condition
wood pasture	management system in which the woodland area is permanently used for pasture, with open-grown trees usually pollarded to prevent browsing damage
Wild Bird Indicator	one of the Government's key indicators for sustainable development in the UK

LIST OF SPECIES MENTIONED IN THE TEXT

Mammals

Badger	*Meles meles*
Bank vole	*Clethrionomys glareolus*
Barbastelle	*Barbastella barbastellus*
Bechstein's bat	*Myotis bechsteinii*
Brandt's bat	*Myotis brandtii*
Brown hare	*Lepus capensis*
Brown long-eared bat	*Plecotus auritus*
Common pipistrelle	*Pipistrellus pipistrellus*
Daubenton's bat	*Myotis daubentonii*
Dormouse	*Muscardinus avellanarius*
Fallow deer	*Dama dama*
Field mouse	*Apodemus sylvaticus*
Field vole	*Microtus agrestis*
Fox	*Vulpes vulpes*
Greater horseshoe bat	*Rhinolophus ferrumequinum*
Grey long-eared bat	*Plecotus austriacus*
Grey squirrel	*Sciurus carolinensis*
Hedgehog	*Erinaceus europaeus*
Leisler's bat	*Nyctalus leisleri*
Lesser horseshoe bat	*Rhinolophus hipposideros*
Muntjac	*Muntiacus reevesi*
Nathusius' pipistrelle	*Pipistrellus nathusii*
Natterer's bat	*Myotis nattereri*
Noctule	*Nyctalus noctula*
Otter	*Lutra lutra*
Rabbit	*Oryctolagus cuniculus*
Red deer	*Cervus elaphus*
Red squirrel	*Sciurus vulgaris*
Roe deer	*Capreolus capreolus*
Serotine bat	*Eptesicus serotinus*
Sika deer	*Cervus nippon*
Soprano pipistrelle	*Pipistrellus pygmaeus*
Whiskered bat	*Myotis mystacinus*
Wild cat	*Felis silvestris*
Wood mouse	*Apodemus sylvaticus*

Birds

Barn owl	*Tyto alba*
Black grouse	*Lyrurus tetrix*
Blackcap	*Sylvia atricapilla*
Blue tit	*Cyanistes caeruleus*
Brambling	*Fringilla montifringilla*
Bullfinch	*Pyrrhula pyrrhula*
Capercaillie	*Tetrao urogallus*
Carrion crow	*Corvus corone*
Chaffinch	*Fringilla coelebs*
Cirl bunting	*Emberiza cirlus*
Coal tit	*Periparus ater*
Collared dove	*Streptopelia decaocto*
Common crossbill	*Loxia curvirostra*
Common redstart	*Phoenicurus phoenicurus*
Common whitethroat	*Sylvia communis*
Corn bunting	*Miliaria calandra*
Crested tit	*Lophophanes cristatus*
Cuckoo	*Cuculus canorus*
Dunnock	*Prunella modularis*
Eurasian jay	*Garrulus glandarius*
Fieldfare	*Turdus pilaris*
Firecrest	*Regulus ignicapillus*
Garden warbler	*Sylvia borin*
Golden oriole	*Oriolus oriolus*
Goshawk	*Accipiter gentilis*
Grasshopper warbler	*Locustella naevia*
Great spotted woodpecker	*Dendrocopos major*
Great tit	*Parus major*
Greenfinch	*Carduelis chloris*
Green woodpecker	*Picus viridis*
Grey partridge	*Perdix perdix*
Hawfinch	*Coccothraustes coccothraustes*
Hen harrier	*Circus cyaneus*
Kestrel	*Falco tinnunculus*
Lapwing	*Vanellus vanellus*
Lesser redpoll	*Carduelis flammea*
Lesser spotted woodpecker	*Dendrocopos minor*
Lesser whitethroat	*Sylvia curruca*
Linnet	*Carduelis cannabina*
Long-tailed tit	*Aegithalos caudatus*
Magpie	*Pica pica*
Marsh tit	*Poecile palustris*
Meadow pipit	*Anthus pratensis*
Merlin	*Falco columbarius*
Mistle thrush	*Turdus viscivorus*
Montagu's harrier	*Circus pygargus*
Moorhen	*Gallinula chloropus*
Nightingale	*Luscinia megarhynchos*
Nightjar	*Caprimulgus europaeus*
Osprey	*Pandion haliaetus*
Parrot crossbill	*Loxia pytyopsittacus*
Pheasant	*Phasianus colchicus*
Pied flycatcher	*Ficedula hypoleuca*
Pied wagtail	*Motacilla alba*
Red kite	*Milvus milvus*
Redshank	*Tringa totanus*
Redwing	*Turdus iliacus*
Reed bunting	*Emberiza schoeniclus*
Ring ouzel	*Turdus torquatus*
Robin	*Erithacus rubecula*
Scottish crossbill	*Loxia scotica*
Short eared owl	*Asio flammeus*
Siskin	*Carduelis spinus*
Skylark	*Alauda arvensis*
Song thrush	*Turdus philomelos*
Spotted flycatcher	*Muscicapa striata*
Starling	*Sturnus vulgaris*
Stock dove	*Columba oenas*
Stonechat	*Saxicola torquatus*
Treecreeper	*Certhia familiaris*
Tree pipit	*Anthus trivialis*
Tree sparrow	*Passer montanus*
Turtle dove	*Streptopelia turtur*
Twite	*Carduelis flavirostris*
Waxwing	*Bombycilla garrulus*
Whinchat	*Saxicola rubetra*
Willow tit	*Poecile montanus*
Willow warbler	*Phylloscopus trochilus*
Wood pigeon	*Columba palumbus*
Wood warbler	*Phylloscopus sibilatrix*
Woodcock	*Scolopax rusticola*
Woodlark	*Lullula arborea*
Wren	*Troglodytes troglodytes*
Yellowhammer	*Emberiza citrinella*

Amphibians and reptiles

Adder	*Vipera berus*	Natterjack toad	*Bufo calamita*
Common frog	*Rana temporaria*	Sand lizard	*Lacerta agilis*
Common toad	*Bufo bufo*	Slow worm	*Anguis fragilis*
Grass snake	*Natrix natrix*	Smooth snake	*Coronella austriaca*
Great crested newt	*Triturus cristatus*	Viviparous lizard	*Lacerta vivipara*

Insects

Asian longhorn beetle	*Anoplophora glabripennis*	Migrant hawker	*Aeshna mixta*
Azure damselfly	*Coenagrion puella*	Mountain ringlet	*Erebia epiphron*
Black hairstreak	*Satyrium pruni*	Northern brown argus	*Aricia atraxerxes*
Brimstone	*Gonepteryx rhamni*	Orange tip	*Anthocharis cardamines*
Brown argus	*Aricia agestis*	Painted lady	*Vanessa cardui*
Brown hairstreak	*Thecla betulae*	Peacock	*Inachis io*
Chequered skipper	*Carterocephalus palaemon*	Pearl-bordered fritillary	*Boloria euphrosyne*
Comma	*Polygonia c-album*	Purple emperor	*Apatura iris*
Common blue	*Polyommatus icarus*	Purple hairstreak	*Neozephyrus quercus*
Common emerald	*Hemithea aestivaria*	Red admiral	*Vanessa atalanta*
Cream-spot tiger	*Arctia villica*	Ringlet	*Aphantopus hyperantus*
Dingy skipper	*Erynnis tages*	Scotch argus	*Erebia aethiops*
Duke of Burgundy	*Hamearis lucina*	Silver-spotted skipper	*Hesperia comma*
Essex skipper	*Thymelicis lineoloa*	Silver washed fritillary	*Argynnis paphia*
Gatekeeper	*Pyronia tithonus*	Six-spot burnet	*Zygaena filipendulae*
Gipsy moth	*Lymantria dispar*	Small blue	*Cupido minimus*
Green tiger beetle	*Cicindela campestris*	Small copper	*Lycaena phlaeas*
Golden-ringed dragonfly	*Cordulegaster boltonii*	Small heath	*Coenonymphya pamphilus*
Green hairstreak	*Callophrys rubi*	Small pearl-bordered fritillary	*Boloria selene*
Green-veined white	*Pieris napi*	Small skipper	*Thymelicus sylvestris*
Grizzled skipper	*Pyrgus malvae*	Small tortoiseshell	*Aglais urticae*
Heath fritillary	*Melitaea athalia*	Small white	*Pieris rapae*
High brown fritillary	*Argynnis adippe*	Southern wood ant	*Formica rufa*
Holly blue	*Celastrina argiolus*	Speckled wood	*Pararge aegeria*
Large blue	*Maculinea arion*	Spotted longhorn beetle	*Rutpela maculata*
Large skipper	*Ochlodes sylvanus*	Treble bar	*Aplocera plagiata plagiata*
Large white	*Pieris brassicae*	White admiral	*Limenitis camilla*
Marbled white	*Melanargia galathea*	White-letter hairstreak	*Satyrium w-album*
Meadow brown	*Maniola jurtina*	Wood white	*Leptidea sinapis*

Plants

Agrimony	*Agimonia eupatoria*	Box	*Buxus sempervirens*
Alder buckthorn	*Frangula alnus*	Bracken	*Pteridium aquilinum*
Alder	*Alnus glutinosa*	Bramble	*Rubus fruticosus*
Almond willow	*Salix triandra*	Bristly oxtongue	*Picris echioides*
Annual meadow-grass	*Poa annua*	Broad bean	*Vicia faba*
Ash	*Fraxinus excelsior*	Broad buckler-fern	*Dryopteris dilitata*
Aspen	*Populus tremula*	Broad-leaved dock	*Rumex obtusifolius*
Autumn hawkbit	*Leontodon autumnalis*	Broad-leaved willowherb	*Epilobium montanum*
Barren strawberry	*Potentilla sterilis*	Broom	*Cytisus scoparius*
Bastard balm	*Melittis melissophyllum*	Buckthorn	*Rhamnus cathartica*
Bay willow	*Salix pentandra*	Bugle	*Ajuga reptans*
Beech	*Fagus sylvatica*	Bulbous buttercup	*Ranunculus bulbosus*
Betony	*Stachys officinalis*	Burnet-saxifrage	*Pimpinella saxifraga*
Bilberry	*Vaccinium myrtillus*	Butcher's-broom	*Ruscus aculeatus*
Bird cherry	*Prunus padus*	Cat's-ear	*Hypochaeris radicata*
Bird's-nest orchid	*Neottia nidus-avis*	Charlock	*Sinapis arvensis*
Bittersweet	*Solanum dulcamara*	Cleavers	*Galium aparine*
Black bryony	*Tamus communis*	Clematis	*Clematis vitable*
Black-grass	*Alopercurus myosuroides*	Climbing corydalis	*Ceratocapnos claviculata*
Black medick	*Medicago lupulina*	Cock's-foot	*Dactylis glomerata*
Black-poplar	*Populus nigra*	Colt's-foot	*Tussilago farfara*
Blackthorn	*Prunus spinosa*	Common bent	*Agrostis capillaris*
Blue moor-grass	*Sesleria caerulea*	Common bird's-foot-trefoil	*Lotus corniculatus*
Bluebell	*Hyacinthoides non-scripta*	Common chickweed	*Stellaria media*
Bog-myrtle	*Myrica gale*	Common couch	*Elytrigia repens*
Bottle sedge	*Carex rostrata*	Common cow-wheat	*Melampyrum pratense*

Plants, continued

Common name	Scientific name	Common name	Scientific name
Common dog-violet	Viola riviniana	Glaucous sedge	Carex flacca
Common fleabane	Pulicaria dysenterica	Globeflower	Trollius europaeus
Common hemp-nettle	Galeopsis tetrahit	Goat willow	Salix caprea
Common juniper	Juniperus communis	Golden-rod	Solidago virgaurea
Common knapweed	Centaurea nigra	Goldilocks buttercup	Ranunculus auricomus
Common mouse-ear	Cerastium fontanum	Gorse	Ulex europaeus
Common nettle	Urtica dioica	Great willowherb	Epilobium hirsutem
Common ragwort	Senecio jacobaea	Greater bird's-foot-trefoil	Lotus pedunculatus
Common reed	Phragmites australis	Greater plantain	Plantago major
Common restharrow	Ononis repens	Greater stitchwort	Stellaria holostea
Common rock-rose	Helianthemum nummularium	Greater tussock-sedge	Carex paniculata
Common sorrel	Rumex acetosa	Grey willow	Salix cinerea
Common spotted-orchid	Dactylorhiza fuchsii	Ground-elder	Aegopodium podagraria
Common stork's-bill	Erodium cicutarium	Ground ivy	Glechoma hederacea
Common twayblade	Listera ovata	Hairy wood-rush	Luzula pilosa
Common vetch	Vicia sativa	Hairy rock-cress	Arabis hirsuta
Common whitebeam	Sorbus aria	Hairy-brome	Bromus ramosus
Common valerian	Valeriana officinalis	Hard-fern	Blechnum spicant
Compact rush	Juncus conglomeratus	Harebell	Campanula rotundifolia
Coralroot bitter-cress	Cardamine bulbifera	Hawthorn	Crataegus monogyna
Corsican pine	Pinus nigra ssp. laricio	Hay-scented buckler fern	Dryopteris aemula
Cow parsley	Anthriscus sylvestris	Hazel	Corylus avellana
Cowberry	Vaccinium vitis-idaea	Heath bedstraw	Galium saxatile
Cowslip	Primula veris	Heath wood-rush	Luzula multiflora
Crab apple	Malus sylvestris	Heather	Calluna vulgaris
Crack willow	Salix fragilis	Hedge bedstraw	Galium mollugo
Creeping bent	Agrostis stolonifera	Hedge mustard	Sisymbrium officinale
Creeping buttercup	Ranunculus repens	Hedge woundwort	Stachys sylvatica
Creeping cinquefoil	Potentilla reptans	Hemp-agrimony	Eupatorium cannabinum
Creeping lady's-tresses	Goodyera repens	Herb Paris	Paris quadrifolia
Creeping soft-grass	Holcus mollis	Herb Robert	Geranium robertianum
Creeping thistle	Cirsium arvense	Hoary ragwort	Senecio erucifolius
Creeping willow	Salix repens	Hoary willowherb	Epilobium parviflorum
Crested dog's-tail	Cynosurus cristatus	Hogweed	Heracleum sphondylium
Cuckooflower	Cardamine pratensis	Holly	Ilex aquifolium
Curled dock	Rumex crispus	Honeysuckle	Lonicera periclymenum
Cut-leaved crane's-bill	Geranium dissectum	Hop	Humulus lupulus
Daisy	Bellis perennis	Hornbeam	Carpinus betulus
Dandelion	Taraxacum officinale	Horseshoe vetch	Hippocrepis comosa
Devil's-bit scabious	Succisa pratensis	Italian rye-grass	Lolium multiflorum
Dewberry	Rubus caesius	Ivy	Hedera helix
Dog's mercury	Mercurialis perennis	Ivy-leaved speedwell	Veronica hederifolia
Dog-rose	Rosa canina	Kidney vetch	Anthyllis vulneraria
Dogwood	Cornus sanguinea	Killarney fern	Trichomanes speciosum
Douglas fir	Pseudotsuga menziesii	Lady's bedstraw	Galium verum
Dove's-foot crane's-bill	Geranium molle	Lady-fern	Athyrium filix-femina
Downy birch	Betula pubescens	Large bitter-cress	Cardamine amara
Downy oat-grass	Helictotrichon pubescens	Large-leaved lime	Tilia platyphyllos
Downy willow	Salix lapponum	Lesser burdock	Arctium minus
Dropwort	Filipendula vulgaris	Lesser celandine	Ranunculus ficaria
Dwarf thistle	Cirsium acaule	Lesser pond-sedge	Carex acutiformis
Dyer's greenweed	Genista tinctoria	Lesser stitchwort	Stellaria graminea
Early gentian	Gentianella anglica	Lesser trefoil	Trifolium dubium
Early-purple orchid	Orchis mascula	Lesser twayblade	Listera cordata
Elder	Sambucus nigra	Lime	Tilia x europaea
Enchanter's-nightshade	Circea lutetiana	Lodgepole pine	Pinus contorta
English elm	Ulmus procera	Lords-and-ladies	Arum maculatum
European larch	Larix decidua	Male-fern	Dryopteris filix-mas
Eyebright	Euphrasia officinalis	Marsh bedstraw	Galium palustre
Fairy flax	Linum catharticum	Marsh fern	Thelypteris palustris
False brome	Brachypodium sylvaticum	Marsh hawk's-beard	Crepis paludosa
False oat-grass	Arrhenatherum elatius	Marsh saxifrage	Saxifraga hirculus
Field forget-me-not	Myosotis arvensis	Marsh thistle	Cirsium palustre
Field horsetail	Equisetum arvense	Marsh valerian	Valeriana dioica
Field maple	Acer campestre	Marsh violet	Viola palustris
Field-rose	Rosa arvensis	Meadow buttercup	Ranunculus acris
Foxglove	Digitalis purpurea	Meadow fescue	Festuca pratensis
Garlic mustard	Alliaria petiolata	Meadow foxtail	Alopecurus pratensis
Giant fescue	Festuca gigantea	Meadow oat-grass	Helictotrichon pratense

Plants, continued

Common name	Scientific name
Meadow vetchling	*Lathyrus pratensis*
Meadowsweet	*Filipendula ulmaria*
Melancholy thistle	*Cirsium heterophyllum*
Midland hawthorn	*Crataegus laevigata*
Moschatel	*Adoxa moschatellina*
Mouse-ear-hawkweed	*Pilosella officinarum*
Narrow buckler-fern	*Dryopteris carthusiana*
Narrow-leaved meadow-grass	*Poa angustifolia*
Nettle-leaved bellflower	*Campanula trachelium*
Nipplewort	*Lapsana communis*
Norway spruce	*Picea abies*
Opposite-leaved golden-saxifrage	*Chrysosplenium oppositifolium*
Osier	*Salix viminalis*
Oxeye daisy	*Leucanthemum vulgare*
Oxlip	*Primula elatior*
Pedunculate oak	*Quercus robur*
Pendulous sedge	*Carex pendula*
Perennial rye-grass	*Lolium perenne*
Perforate St John's-wort	*Hypericum perforatum*
Pignut	*Conopodium majus*
Primrose	*Primula vulgaris*
Purple moor-grass	*Molinia caerulea*
Purple willow	*Salix purpurea*
Quaking-grass	*Briza media*
Ragged-Robin	*Lychnis flos-cuculi*
Ramsons	*Allium ursinum*
Raspberry	*Rubus ideaus*
Red campion	*Silene dioica*
Red clover	*Trifolium pratense*
Red valerian	*Centranthus ruber*
Remote sedge	*Carex remota*
Rhododendron	*Rhododendron ponticum*
Ribwort plantain	*Plantago lanceolata*
Rosebay willowherb	*Chamerion angustifolium*
Rough hawkbit	*Leontodon hispidus*
Rough meadow-grass	*Poa trivialis*
Rowan	*Sorbus aucuparia*
Salad burnet	*Sanguisorba minor* ssp. *minor*
Sanicle	*Sanicula europaea*
Scots pine	*Pinus sylvestris*
Selfheal	*Prunella vulgaris*
Sessile oak	*Quercus petraea*
Sheep's sorrel	*Rumex acetosella*
Sheep's-fescue	*Festuca ovina*
Silver birch	*Betula pendula*
Silverweed	*Potentilla anserina*
Sitka spruce	*Picea sitchensis*
Small nettle	*Urtica urens*
Small scabious	*Scabiosa columbaria*
Small-leaved elm	*Ulmus minor* ssp. *minor*
Small-leaved lime	*Tilia cordata*
Smooth meadow-grass	*Poa pratensis*
Soft-rush	*Juncus effusus*
Soft-brome	*Bromus hordeaceus*
Solomon's seal	*Polygonatum multiflorum*
Spanish bluebell	*Hyacinthoides hispanica*
Spear thistle	*Cirsium vulgare*
Spindle	*Euonymus europaeus*
Spreading meadow-grass	*Poa humilis*
Spurge laurel	*Daphne laureola*
Squinancywort	*Asperula cynanchica*
Stone bramble	*Rubus saxatilis*
Sweet chestnut	*Castanea sativa*
Sweet vernal-grass	*Anthoxanthum odoratum*
Sweet violet	*Viola odorata*
Sycamore	*Acer pseudoplatanus*
Tall fescue	*Festuca arundinacea*
Three-nerved sandwort	*Moehringia trinervia*
Thyme-leaved speedwell	*Veronica serpyllifolia*
Timothy	*Phleum pratense*
Tor-grass	*Brachypodium pinnatum*
Tormentil	*Potentilla erecta*
Traveller's-joy	*Clematis vitalba*
Tufted hair-grass	*Deschampsia cespitosa*
Tufted vetch	*Vicia cracca*
Turnip	*Brassica rapa*
Twinflower	*Linnaea borealis*
Upright brome	*Bromopsis erecta*
Upright hedge-parsley	*Torilis japonica*
Velvet bent	*Agrostis canina*
Violet helleborine	*Epipactis purpurata*
Viper's-bugloss	*Echium vulgare*
Water avens	*Geum rivale*
Water horsetail	*Equisetum fluviatile*
Water mint	*Mentha aquatica*
Wavy hair-grass	*Deschampsia flexuosa*
Wayfaring-tree	*Viburnum lantana*
Western gorse	*Ulex gallii*
White bryony	*Bryonia dioica*
White clover	*Trifolium repens*
White dead-nettle	*Lamium album*
White helleborine	*Cephalanthera damasonium*
White poplar	*Populus alba*
Wild angelica	*Angelica sylvestris*
Wild cabbage	*Brassica oleracea* var. *oleracea*
Wild carrot	*Daucus carota* ssp. *carota*
Wild cherry	*Prunus avium*
Wild daffodil	*Narcissus pseudonarcissus* ssp. *pseudonarcissus*
Wild madder	*Rubia peregrina*
Wild marjoram	*Origanum vulgare*
Wild mignonette	*Reseda lutea*
Wild privet	*Ligustrum vulgare*
Wild service-tree	*Sorbus torminalis*
Wild teasel	*Dipsacus fullonum*
Wild thyme	*Thymus polytrichus*
Winter-cress	*Barbarea vulgaris*
Wood anemone	*Anemone nemorosa*
Wood avens	*Geum urbanum*
Wood club-rush	*Scirpus sylvaticus*
Wood dock	*Rumex sanguineus*
Wood meadow-grass	*Poa nemoralis*
Wood melick	*Melica uniflora*
Wood millet	*Milium effusum*
Wood sage	*Teucrium scorodonia*
Wood sorrel	*Oxalis acetosella*
Wood speedwell	*Veronica montana*
Wood spurge	*Euphorbia amygdaloides*
Woodruff	*Galium odoratum*
Wood-sedge	*Carex sylvatica*
Wych elm	*Ulmus glabra*
Yarrow	*Achillea millefolium*
Yellow archangel	*Lamiastrum galeobdolon*
Yellow oat-grass	*Trisetum flavescens*
Yellow pimpernel	*Lysimachia nemorum*
Yew	*Taxus baccata*
Yorkshire-fog	*Holcus lanatus*

Mosses

Common name	Scientific name
Greater fork-moss	*Dicranum majus*

Fungi

Common name	Scientific name
Fly agaric	*Amanita muscaria*
Sulphur tuft	*Hypholoma fasciculare*

ACRONYMS

ADHD	Attention Deficit Hyperactivity Disorder	LCA	Landscape Character Assessment
AONB	Area of Outstanding Natural Beauty	MAGIC	Multi Agency Geographic Information for the Countryside
BBC	British Broadcasting Corporation	MOHC	Meteorological Office Hadley Centre
BEETLE	Biological and Environmental Evaluation Tools for Landscape Ecology	MONARCH	Modelling Natural Resource Responses to Climate Change
BRANCH	Biodiversity Requires Adaptation in Northwest Europe under a Changing Climate	NAP	Natural Area Profile
		NBN	National Biodiversity Network's Gateway
BTCV	British Trust for Conservation Volunteers	NCA	National Character Area
BTO	British Trust for Ornithology	NFC	The National Forest Company
CCW	Countryside Council for Wales	NGO	Non-governmental organisation
CORINE	Coordination of Information on the Environment	NH Futures	Natural Heritage Futures
		NHS	National Health Service
Defra	Department for Environment, Food and Rural Affairs	NNR	National Nature Reserve
		NVC	National Vegetation Classification
EC	European Community	OS	Ordnance Survey
ESC	Ecological Site Classification	PAWS	Plantations on Ancient Woodland Sites
EU	European Union	RSPB	Royal Society for the Protection of Birds
EUNIS	European Nature Information System	SAC	Special Areas of Conservation
FHN	Forest Habitat Network	SNCI	Sites of Interest/Importance for Nature Conservation
FWPS	Farm Woodland Premium Scheme		
FWS	Farm Woodland Scheme	SNH	Scottish Natural Heritage
GIS	Geographical Information Systems	SPECIES	Spatial Estimator of the Climate Impacts on the Envelope of Species
HAP	Habitat Action Plan		
HLS	Higher Level Stewardship	SRDP	Scottish Rural Development Programme
IEA	Institute of Environmental Assessment (now the Institute of Environmental Management and Assessment)	SSSI	Sites of Special Scientific Interest
		UK BAP	UK Biodiversity Action Plan
		UKCP09	UK Climate Projections
IPCC	Intergovernmental Panel on Climate Change	WGS	Woodland Grant Scheme
JNCC	Joint Nature Conservation Committee	WHO	World Health Organisation
K-LIS	Kent Landscape Information System	WRME	Wood Raw Material Equivalent

REFERENCES

Agate, E. (ed.) 2000. *Tree planting and aftercare a practical handbook.* BTCV, Wallingford.

Agate, E. (ed.) 2002. *Woodlands a practical handbook.* BTCV, Wallingford.

Altringham, J. 2003. *British Bats.* The New Naturalist Library. HarperCollins Publishers, London.

Amar, A, Hewson, CM, Thewlis, RM, Smith, KW, Fuller, RJ, Lindsell J, Conway G, Butler S and MacDonald, MA. 2006. *What's happening to our woodland birds? Long-term changes in the populations of woodland birds.* RSPB Research Report No 19, RSPB, Sandy.

Anderson, MA. 1989. *Opportunities for habitat enhancement in commercial forestry practice.* In Buckley, GP (ed). *Biological habitat reconstruction.* Belhaven Press, London. Pp. 129–146.

Armstrong, AT and Moffat, AJ. 1996. How compatible are different weed control methods with the application of nitrogenous fertilisers during tree establishment? *Arboricultural Journal* 20, 411–423.

Asher, J, Warren, M, Fox, R Harding, P Jeffcoate, G and Jeffcoate, S. 2001. *The Millennium Atlas of Butterflies in Britain and Ireland.* Oxford University Press, Oxford.

Ashmole, M and Ashmole, P. 2009. *The Carrifran wildwood story.* Borders Forest Trust, Jedburgh.

Bacles, CFE, Lowe, AJ and Ennos, RA. 2004. Genetic effects of chronic habitat fragmentation on tree species: the case of *Sorbus aucuparia* in a deforested Scottish landscape. *Molecular Ecology* 13, 573–584.

Bacles, CFE, Lowe, AJ and Ennos, RA. 2006. Efficient seed dispersal across a fragmented landscape. *Science* 311, 628.

Berry, PM, Dawson, TP, Harrison, PA and Pearson, RG. 2002. *Impacts on native woodland dynamics and distribution.* In Broadmeadow, MSG (ed). *Climate change and UK forests.* Forestry Commission Bulletin 124, Forestry Commission, Edinburgh. Pp.169–180.

Berry, PM, Harrison, PA, Dawson, TP and Walmsley, CA (eds.) 2005. *Modelling Natural Resource Responses to Climate Change (MONARCH): A Local Approach.* UKCIP Technical Report, Oxford.

Bird, W. 2004. *Natural fit. Can green space and biodiversity increase levels of physical activity?* RSPB, Sandy.

Bird, W. 2007a. *Natural thinking. Investigating the links between the natural environment, biodiversity and mental health.* RSPB, Sandy.

Bird, W. 2007b. *Natural health.* RSPB, Sandy.

Bossuyt, B, Heyn, M and Hermy, M. 2002. Seed bank and vegetation composition of forest stands of varying ages in central Belgium: consequences for regeneration of ancient forest vegetation. *Plant Ecology* 162, 33–48.

Bourn, N, Thomas, J, Stewart, K and Clarke, R. 2002. Importance of habitat quality and isolation. Implications for the management of butterflies in fragmented landscapes. *British Wildlife* 13, 398–403.

Brenchley, WE and Adam, H. 1915. Recolonisation of cultivated land allowed to revert to natural conditions. *Journal of Ecology* 3, 193–210.

Briggs, J. 2008. Landscape character map for Wales. *Landscape Character Network News* 27, 16–18.

Bright, P, Morris, P and Mitchell-Jones, T. 2006. *The dormouse conservation handbook.* English Nature, Peterborough.

Broadhurst, LM. 2007. *Managing Genetic Diversity in Remnant Vegetation: Implications for Local Provenance Seed Selection and Landscape Restoration*. Technical Note 01/2007, Land and Water Australia, ACT.

Broadhurst LM, Lowe A, Coates DJ, Cunningham SA, McDonald M, Vesk, PA and Yates, C. 2008. Seed supply for broadscale restoration: maximising evolutionary potential. *Evolutionary Applications* 1, 587–597.

Broadmeadow, MSG and Ray, D. 2005. *Climate change and British woodland.* Forestry Commission Information Note 69. Forestry Commission, Edinburgh.

Broadmeadow, MSJ, Ray, D and Samuel, CJS. 2005. Climate change and the future for broadleaved tree species in Britain. *Forestry* 78, 145–161.

Brown, AFH and Warr, SJ. 1992. *The effects of changing management on seed banks in ancient coppices.* In Buckley, GP (ed.) *Ecology and Management of Coppice Woodlands.* Chapman and Hall, London. Pp. 147–166.

Buckley, GP and Insley, H. 1984. Sward control strategies for young trees. *Aspects of Applied Biology* 5, 97–107.

Buckley, GP and Knight, DG. 1989. *The feasibility of woodland reconstruction.* In Buckley, GP (ed) *Biological Habitat Reconstruction.* Belhaven Press, London. Pp. 171–188.

Buckley, GP, Howell, R and Anderson, MA. 1997. Vegetation succession following ride edge management in lowland plantations and woods – 2. The seed bank resource. *Biological Conservation* 82, 305–316.

Cannell, MGR, Palutikof, JP and Sparks, TH. (eds.) 1999. *Indicators of Climate Change in the UK.* DETR, London.

Central Science Laboratory. 2000. *Interactions between mammals and farm woodlands during establishment and maturation.* MAFF Final Project Report WD0126.

Central Science Laboratory. 2003. *Maximising the biodiversity value of farm woodlands to the agri-environment.* Defra Final Project Report WD0129.

Cohn, EVJ, Trueman, IC and Packham, JR. 2000. More than just trees. *Aspects of Applied Biology* 58, 93–100.

Collinson, N. 2007. *Space for People: woodland creation for public access.* In: *New woods, new lives, new landscapes. A conference on creating woodland for our future.* The Woodland Trust, Grantham.

Collinson, N and Sparks, T. 2008. Phenology – nature's calendar: an overview of results from the UK Phenology Network. *Arboricultural Journal* 30, 271–278.

Cooke, RJ. 1992. *Phase 2 woodland NVC surveys 1988–1991 in England and Wales.* English Nature, Peterborough.

Corney, PM, Smithers, RJ, Kirby, JS, Peterken, GF, Le Duc, MG and Marrs, RH. 2008. *Impacts of nearby development on the ecology of ancient woodland.* Woodland Trust, Grantham.

PART TWO WOODLAND CREATION PRACTICE – REFERENCES

Crafer, T. 2005. *Foodplant List for the Caterpillars of Britain's Butterflies and Larger Moths*. Atropos Publishing, Holmfirth.

Crawford, CL. 2009. Ancient woodland indicator plants in Scotland. *Scottish Forestry* 63, 6–19.

Davies, RJ. 1987. *Trees and weeds: weed control for successful establishment*. Forestry Commission Handbook 2, HMSO, London.

Day, J, Symes, N and Robertson, P. 2003. *The Scrub Management Handbook: Guidance on the management of scrub on nature conservation sites*. Natural England, Peterborough.

De Groot, RS, Wilson, MA and Boumans, RMJ. 2002. A typology for the classification, description and valuation of ecosystem functions, goods and services. *Ecological Economics* 41, 393–408.

De Keersmaeker, L, Martens, L, Verheyen, K, Hermy, M, de Schrijver, A and Lust, N. 2004 Impact of soil fertility and insolation on diversity of herbaceous woodland species colonising afforestation in Muizen forest (Belgium). *Forest Ecology and Management* 188, 291–304.

Defra. 2006. *Food security and the UK: an evidence and analysis paper*. Defra, London.

Defra. 2007a. *A Strategy for England's Trees, Woods and Forests*. Defra, London.

Defra. 2007b. *Hedgerow Survey Handbook*. Defra, London.

Defra. 2010. *Defra's climate change plan*. Defra, London.

Defra and Forestry Commission. 2005. *Keepers of time: A statement of policy for England's ancient and native woodland*. Defra and the Forestry Commission, Cambridge.

Department of Health. 2004. *Choosing Health: A White Paper*. The Stationery Office, London.

Devillers, P, Devillers-Terschuren, J and Ledant, J-P. 1991. *CORINE Biotopes Manual: Habitats of the European Community*. Commission of the European Communities, Brussels.

Dudley, N. 2001. *A Midsummer Night's Nightmare? The future of UK woodland in the face of climate change*. The Woodland Trust, Grantham.

Eden Project. 2008. *Annual Review 2007/08*. Eden Project, Cornwall.

Edwards, D, Morris, J, O'Brien, L, Sarajevs, V and Valatin, G. 2008. *The economic and social contribution of forestry for people in Scotland*. Research Note FCRN102. Forestry Commission, Edinburgh.

Elton, CS. 1966. *The Pattern of Animal Communities*. Methuen, London.

English Heritage. 2007. *Understanding the archaeology of landscapes – a guide to good recording practice*. English Heritage.

English Nature. 2004. *Reptiles: guidelines for developers*. English Nature, Peterborough.

EUNIS. 2007. *European Nature Information System (EUNIS)*. European Environment Agency, Copenhagen.

Eycott, A, Watts, K, Moseley, SD and Ray, D. 2007. *Evaluating biodiversity in fragmented landscapes: the use of focal species*. Forestry Commission Information Note 89. Forestry Commission, Edinburgh.

Eycott, AE, Watts, K, Brandt, G, Buyung-Ali, LM, Bowler, DE, Stewart, GB and Pullin, AS. 2008. *What is the evidence for the development of connectivity to improve species movement, as an adaptation to climate change?* – Unpublished contract report to Defra (Defra Contract CR0389). Forest Research, Farnham, Surrey and Centre for Evidence-Based Conservation, Bangor.

Faber Taylor, A and Kuo, FE. 2009. Children with attention deficits concentrate better after a walk in the park. *Journal of Attention Disorders* 12, 402–409.

Faber Taylor, A, Wiley, A, Kuo, FE and Sullivan, WC. 2001. Trees for children: helping inner city children get a better start in life. *Technology Bulletin No. 7*. USDA Forest Service, Northeastern Area, Pennsylvania.

FAO. 2006. *Global forest resources assessment 2005: progress towards sustainable forest management*. FAO Forestry Paper 147, Food and Agriculture Organisation of the United Nations, Rome.

Ferris, R and Carter, C. 2000. *Managing rides, roadsides and edge habitats in lowland forests*. Bulletin 123, Forestry Commission, Edinburgh.

Forest Service, Northern Ireland. 2008. *Native woodland. Definitions and guidance*. Northern Ireland Native Woodland Group. Forest Service, Northern Ireland.

Forestry Commission. 2001. *Ecological Site Classification: a PC-based decision support system for British forests*. Forestry Commission, Edinburgh.

Forestry Commission. 2003a. *National inventory of woodland and trees: Great Britain*. Forestry Commission, Edinburgh.

Forestry Commission. 2003b. *Forest and water guidelines: fourth edition*. Forestry Commission, Edinburgh.

Forestry Commission. 2007. *A woodfuel strategy for England*. Forestry Commission, Edinburgh.

Forestry Commission. 2008. *English Woodland Grant Scheme: Operations Note 4: National Vegetation Classification*. Forestry Commission, England.

Forestry Commission. 2009a. *Forestry statistics: a compendium of statistics about woodland, forestry and primary wood processing in the United Kingdom*. Forestry Commission, Edinburgh.

Forestry Commission. 2009b. *Forestry statistics: a compendium of statistics about woodland, forestry and primary wood processing in the United Kingdom*. Forestry Commission, Edinburgh.

Forestry Commission. 2009c. *Environmental impact assessment of forestry projects*. Forestry Commission, Edinburgh.

Forestry Commission and Natural England. 2008. *England's Trees, Woods and Forests – Delivery Plan 2008–2012*. Forestry Commission, Edinburgh.

Forestry Commission Scotland. 2003. *Forest habitat networks and Scottish Forestry Grant Scheme expansion grants*. Guidance Note 20, Forestry Commission, Edinburgh.

Forestry Commission Scotland. 2006. *Seed sources for planting native trees and shrubs in Scotland*. Guidance note, Forestry Commission, Edinburgh.

Forestry Commission Scotland. 2008. *All Forests Visitor Monitoring Survey (2004–2007)*. Final Report. Forestry Commission, Edinburgh.

Fox, R, Asher, J, Brereton, T, Roy, D and Warren, M. 2006. *The state of butterflies in Britain and Ireland*. Butterfly Conservation and the Centre for Ecology and Hydrology.

Fox, R, Warren, MS and Brereton, TM. 2010. A new Red List of British butterflies. *Species Status* 12, 1–32. Joint Nature Conservation Committee, Peterborough.

Francis, JL, Morton, AJ and Boorman, LA. 1992. The establishment of ground flora species in recently planted woodland. *Aspects of Applied Biology* 29, 171–178.

Francis, J and Morton, A. 2001. Enhancement of amenity-woodland field layers in Milton Keynes. *British Wildlife* 12, 244–251.

Franco, AMA, Hill, JK, Kitschke, C, Collingham YC, Roy, DB, Fox, R, Huntley, B and Thomas, CD. 2006. Impacts of climate warming and habitat loss on extinctions at species' low altitude range boundaries. *Global Change Biology* 12, 1545–1553.

Fraser, S and Buckley, GP. 2000. *The Farm Woodland Premium Scheme in England, with particular reference to participants in Kent and East Sussex*. In A. Yoshimoto (ed). *Optimal Management in Farm Woodlands*. Miyazaki University, Japan.

Fuller, RJ. 1995. *Bird life of woodland and forest*. Cambridge University Press, Cambridge.

Garrod, G and Willis, K. 1992. Valuing goods' characteristics: An application of the Hedonic Price Method to Environmental Attributes. *Journal of Environmental Management* 34, 59–76.

Gent, T and Gibson, S. 2003 *Herpetofauna Workers Manual*. Joint Nature Conservation Committee, Peterborough.

Good, JEG, Norris, D, McNally, S and Radford, GL. 1997. *Developing new native woodland in the English Uplands*. Research Report 230, English Nature, Peterborough.

Gould, SJ. 1997. *An evolutionary perspective on strengths, fallacies, and confusions on the concept of native plants*. In Wolsche-Bulmahn, J (ed). *Nature and Ideology: Natural Garden Design in the Twentieth Century*. Oaks Research Library and Collection, Washington DC. Pp. 11–19.

Gove, B, Power, SA, Buckley, GP and Ghazoul, J. 2007. Effects of herbicide spray drift and fertilizer overspread on selected species of woodland ground flora: comparison between short-term and long-term impact assessments and field surveys. *Journal of Applied Ecology* 44, 374–384.

Government Report. 1995. *Biodiversity: the UK Steering Group Report*. Volume II. Action Plans. HMSO, London.

Gregory, RD, Wilkinson, NI, Noble, DG, Robinson, JA, Brown, AF, Hughes, J, Gibbons, DW and Galbraith, CA. 2002. The population status of birds in the United Kingdom, Channel Islands and the Isle of Man: an analysis of conservation concern 2002–2007. *British Birds* 95, 410–450.

Grime, JP, Hodgson, JG and Hunt, R. 1990. *The abridged comparative plant ecology*. Unwin Hyman Ltd., London.

Hall, JE, Kirby, KJ and Whitbread, AM. 2004. *National Vegetation Classification: Field guide to woodland*. Joint Nature Conservation Committee, Peterborough.

Harmer, R. 1999a. *Using natural colonisation to create or expand new woodlands*. Forestry Commission Information Note 23, Forestry Commission, Edinburgh.

Harmer, R. 1999b. *Creating new native woods: turning ideas into reality*. Forestry Commission Information Note 15, Forestry Commission, Edinburgh.

Harmer, R, Kerr, G and Boswell, R. 1997. Characteristics of lowland broadleaved woodland being restocked by natural regeneration. *Forestry* 70, 199–210.

Harmer, R, Peterken, G, Kerr, G and Poulton, P. 2001. Vegetation changes during 100 years of development of two secondary woodlands on abandoned arable land. *Biological Conservation* 101, 291–304.

Harris, S, Morris, P, Wray, S and Yalden, DW. 1995. *A review of British Mammals: population estimates and conservation status of British mammals other than cetaceans*. Joint Nature Conservation Committee, Peterborough.

Harrison, PA, Berry, PM and Dawson, TP (eds.) 2001. *Climate change and nature conservation in Britain and Ireland: modelling natural resource responses to climate change (the MONARCH project)*. UKIP Technical Report, Oxford.

Henwood, K. 2001. *Exploring linkages between environment and health: is there a role for environmental and countryside agencies in promoting benefits to health?* Unpublished report to the Forestry Commission.

Herbert, R, Samuel, S and Patterson, G. 1999. *Using local stock for planting native trees and shrubs*. Forestry Commission Practice Note 8. Forestry Commission, Edinburgh.

Hermy, M, Honnay, O, Firbank, L, Grashof-Bokdam, CJ and Lawesson, JE. 1999. An ecological comparison between ancient and other forest plant species of Europe, and the implications for forest conservation. *Biological Conservation* 91, 9–22.

Hill, D, Fasham, M, Tucker, G, Shewry, M and Shaw, P (eds.) 2005. *Handbook of biodiversity methods: survey, evaluation and monitoring*. Cambridge University Press, Cambridge.

Hill, DA and Greenaway, F. 2008. Conservation of bats in British woodlands. *British Wildlife* 19, 161–169.

Hill, JK, Thomas, CD, Fox, R, Telfer, MG, Willis, SG, Asher, J and Huntley, B. 2002. Responses of butterflies to 20th century climate warming: implications for future ranges. *Proceedings of the Royal Society B* 269, 2163–2171.

Hill, MO. 1996. *TABLEFIT Version 1.0, For Identification of Vegetation Types*. Institute of Terrestrial Ecology, Huntingdon.

Hill, MO, Mountford, JO, Roy, DB and Bunce, RGH. 1999. *Ellenberg's indicator values for British plants*. ECOFACT Volume 2A, Technical Annex. ITE Monkswood, Huntingdon.

Hipps, NA, Davies, MJ, Dodds, P and Buckley, GP. 2005. Effects of phosphorus nutrition and soil pH on the growth of ancient woodland indicator species and their competitors. *Plant and Soil* 271, 131–141.

HM Government. 2009. *The UK low carbon transition plan: national strategy for climate and energy*. The Stationery Office, Norwich.

Hodge, S. 1995. *Creating and managing woodlands around towns*. Forestry Commission Handbook 11. HMSO, London.

Hodge, SJ and Harmer, R. 1996. Woody colonisation on unmanaged urban and ex-industrial sites. *Forestry* 69, 245–261.

Honnay, O, Hermy, M and Coppin, P. 1999. Impact of habitat quality on forest plant species colonisation. *Forest Ecology and Management* 115, 157–170.

Hopkins, J. 2007. British wildlife and climate change 2. Adapting to climate change. *British Wildlife* 18, 381–387.

Hopkins, JJ, Allison, HM, Walmsley, CA, Gaywood, M and Thurgate G. 2007. *Conserving biodiversity in a changing climate: guidance on building capacity to act*. Published by Defra on behalf of the UK

Biodiversity Partnership, Department of Food and Rural Affairs, London.

Hossell, JE, Ellis, NE, Harley, MJ and Hepburn, IR. 2003. Climate change and nature conservation: implications for policy and practice in Britain and Ireland. *Journal for Nature Conservation* 11, 67–73.

Hubert, J and Cottrell, J. 2007. *The role of forest genetic resources in helping British forests respond to climate change.* Forestry Commission Information Note 86, Forestry Commission, Edinburgh.

Hubert, J and Cundall, E. 2006. *Choosing provenance in broadleaved trees.* Forestry Commission Information Note 82. Forestry Commission, Edinburgh.

Hutson, AM. 1993. *Action plan for the conservation of bats in the United Kingdom.* Bat Conservation Trust, London.

Insley, H and Buckley, GP. 1986. *Causes and prevention of establishment failure in amenity trees.* In Bradshaw, AD, Goode, DA and Thorp, E (eds.) *Ecology and Design in Landscape.* Blackwell Scientific Publications, Oxford. Pp 127–141.

Institute of Environmental Assessment 1995. *Guidelines for baseline ecological assessment.* Institute of Environmental Assessment. E and F Spon, An Imprint of Chapman and Hall, London.

Intergovernmental Panel on Climate Change. 2007. *Climate Change 2007: The physical science basis.* Contribution of Working Group 1 to the Fourth Assessment Report of IPCC.

Joint Council for Landscape Industries. 2002. *Specifying seed source for trees for large scale amenity and forestry planting: recommendations for best practice.* Landscape Institute, London.

Joint Nature Conservation Committee. 2004. *Common standards monitoring guidance for birds.* Joint Nature Conservation Committee, Peterborough.

Joint Nature Conservation Committee. 2007a. *Report on the species and habitat Review.* Biodiversity reporting and information group, UK Biodiversity Partnership.

Joint Nature Conservation Committee. 2007b. *Handbook for Phase 1 habitat survey – a technique for environmental audit.* Joint Nature Conservation Committee, Peterborough.

Jones, AT. 1999. The Caledonian pinewood inventory of Scotland's native Scots pine woodlands. *Scottish Forestry* 53, 237–242.

Kaplan, S. 1995. The restorative benefits of nature: toward an integrative framework. *Journal of Environmental Psychology* 15, 169–182.

Kennedy, F. 2002. *The Identification of Soils for Forest Management.* Forestry Commission Field Guide, Forestry Commission, Edinburgh.

Kent County Council. 2004. *The Landscape Assessment of Kent.*

Kerr, G. 1995. *The use of treeshelters: 1992 survey.* Technical Paper 11, Forestry Commission, Edinburgh.

Kerr, G. 1996. The effect of heavy or 'free growth' thinning on oak (*Quercus petraea* and *Q. robur*). *Forestry* 69, 303–317.

Key, R. 2000. Bare ground and the conservation of invertebrates. *British Wildlife* 11, 183–191.

Kirby, KJ. 1992. *Woodland and wildlife.* Whittet Books Ltd., London.

Kirby, KJ. 1993. Assessing nature conservation values in British woodland – a review of recent practice. *Arboricultural Journal* 17, 253–276.

Kirby, KJ. 2009. *Where would be the best places to put new woodland from a biodiversity perspective: Oxfordshire as a case study?* In Catchpole, R, Smithers, R, Baarda, P and Eycott, A. (eds.). *Ecological networks: science and practice.* IALE UK, Edinburgh.

Kirby, P. 1992. *Habitat management for invertebrates: a practical handbook.* RSPB, Sandy.

Laitakari, J, Vuori, I and Oja, P. 1996. Is long term maintenance of health related physical activity possible? An analysis of concepts and evidence. *Health Education Research* 4, 463–477.

Latham, J, Blackstock, TH and Howe, EA. 2008. *Ecological connectivity in Wales: planning action to help terrestrial biodiversity respond to habitat fragmentation and climate change.* CCW Staff Science Report No. 08/7/1., Bangor.

MAFF (Ministry of Agriculture, Fisheries and Food). 1986. *The Analysis of Agricultural Materials.* Reference Book 427, HMSO, London.

Martin, J and Swanwick, C. 2003. *Overview of Scotland's National Programme of Landscape Character Assessment.* Scottish Natural Heritage Commissioned Report F03 AA307.

Matlack, GR. 1994. Plant species migration in a mixed-history forest landscape in eastern North America. *Ecology* 75, 1491–1502.

Millennium Ecosystem Assessment. 2005. *Ecosystems and Human Well-being: Synthesis.* Island Press, Washington D.C.

Ministry of Agriculture, Nature and Food Quality (Netherlands). 2004. *Ecological networks: experiences in the Netherlands.*

Moseley, D, Ray, D, Watts, K and Humphrey, J. 2008. *Forest Habitat Networks Scotland.* Unpublished contract report to Forestry Commission Scotland, Forestry Commission GB and Scottish Natural Heritage. Forest Research, Edinburgh.

Mountford, E, Peterken, GF, Edwards, PJ and Manners, JG. 1999. Long-term change in growth, mortality and regeneration of trees in Denny Wood, an old-growth wood-pasture in the New Forest (UK). *Perspectives in Plant Ecology, Evolution and Systematics* 2, 223–272.

Murphy, JM, Sexton, DMH, Jenkins, GJ, Boorman, PM, Booth, BBB, Bown CC, Clark, RT, Collins, M, Harris, GR, Kendon, EJ, Betts, RA, Brown, SJ, Howard, TP, Humphrey, KA, McCarthy, MP, McDonald, RE, Stephens, A, Wallace, C, Warren, R, Wilby, R and Wood, RA. 2009. *UK Climate Projections Science Report: Climate change projections.* Met Office Hadley Centre, Exeter.

Murray, R. 2003. *Forest School Evaluation Project: a study in Wales.* Report to the Forestry Commission by nef (new economics foundation), London.

Nail, S. 2008. *Forest policies and social change in England.* Springer, New York.

Natural England. 2006. *England Leisure Visits – Report of the 2005 Survey.* Research International Ltd, London.

Natural England. 2008. *Farm Environment Plan Features Manual.* Natural England, Peterborough.

Newton, N and Ashmole, P. (eds.) 1999. *Cariffran Wildwood Project: native woodland restoration in the Southern Uplands of Scotland. Management Plan.* Borders Forest Trust, Jedburgh.

Oates, M. 2004. The ecology of the Pearl-bordered Fritillary in woodland. *British Wildlife* 15, 229–236.

O'Brien, E. 2005a. *Trees and woodlands: Nature's health service.* Forest Research, Farnham.

O'Brien, E. 2005b. Social and cultural values of trees and woodlands in northwest and southeast England. *Forest, Snow and Landscape Research* 79, 169–184.

O'Brien, E, Townsend, M and Ebden, M. 2008. *Environmental volunteering: motivations, barriers and benefits.* Summary Report to Scottish Forestry Trust and Forestry Commission.

Oliver, CD. 1981. Forest development in North America following major disturbances. *Forest Ecology and Management* 3, 153–168.

Pepper, H. 1999. *Recommendations for fallow, roe and muntjac deer fencing: new proposals for temporary and reusable fencing.* Forestry Commission Practice Note 9. Forestry Commission, Edinburgh.

Peterken, GF. 1974. A method for assessing woodland flora for conservation using indicator species, *Biological Conservation* 6, 239–245.

Peterken, GF. 1981. *Woodland Conservation and Management.* Chapman and Hall, London.

Peterken, GF. 2000a. Rebuilding networks of forest habitats in lowland England. *Landscape Research* 25, 291–303.

Peterken, GF. 2000b. Identifying ancient woodland using vascular plant indicators. *British Wildlife* 11, 153–158.

Peterken, GF. 2009. Woodland origins of meadows. *British Wildlife* 20, 161–170.

Peterken, GF and Francis, JL. 1999. Open space as habitats for vascular ground flora species in the woods of central Lincolnshire, UK. *Biological Conservation* 91, 55–72.

Peterken, GF and Hughes, MR. 1995. Restoration of floodplain forests in Britain. *Forestry* 68, 187–202.

Peterken, GF and Mountford, EP. 1995. Lady Park Wood: the first fifty years. *British Wildlife* 6, 206–213.

Peters, RL. 1990. Effects of global warming on forests. *Forest Ecology and Management* 35, 13–33.

Plantlife. 2003. Position statement on sale of bluebells in the UK. Plantlife International, Salisbury.

Potter, MJ. 1991. *Treeshelters.* Forestry Commission Handbook 7, HMSO, London.

Pottie, S, Finlow-Bates, KS, Parrott, D, Moore NP, Langton, SD and Hutson, AM. 1997. *Use of farm woodlands and young forest plantations by bats.* Report to the conservation and Rural Development Division, MAFF.

Pretty, J, Griffin, M, Peacock, J, Hine, R, Sellens, M and South, N. 2005. *A countryside for health and wellbeing: the physical and mental health benefits of green exercise.* Report for the Countryside Recreation Network.

Pryor, SN and Smith, S. 2002. *The area and composition of plantations on ancient woodland sites.* The Woodland Trust, Grantham.

Pyatt, DG. 1982. *Soil Classification.* Forestry Commission Research Information Note 68/82/SSN. Forestry Commission, Edinburgh.

Pyatt, DG, Ray, D and Fletcher, J. 2001. *An ecological site classification for forestry in Great Britain.* Bulletin 124. Forestry Commission, Edinburgh.

Rackham, O. 1992. *Mixtures, mosaics and clones: the distribution of trees within European woods and forests.* In Cannell, MGR, Malcolm, DC and Robertson, PA (eds.). *The ecology of mixed-species stands of trees.* British Ecological Society special publication 11, Blackwell Scientific Publications, Oxford. Pp 1–20.

Rackham, O. 1986. *The history of the countryside.* Dent, London.

Ray, D. 2008a. *Impacts of climate change on forestry in Wales.* Forestry Commission Research Note 301. Forestry Commission Wales.

Ray, D. 2008b. *Impacts of climate change on forestry in Scotland – a synopsis of spatial modelling research.* Forestry Commission Research Note 101. Forestry Commission Scotland.

Read, DJ, Freer-Smith, PH, Morison, JIL, Hanley, N, West, CC and Snowdon, P. (eds.) 2009. *Combating climate change – a role for UK forests. An assessment of the potential of the UK's trees and woodlands to mitigate and adapt to climate change.* The Stationery Office, Edinburgh.

Read, HJ. 1999. *Veteran trees: a guide to good management.* English Nature, Peterborough.

Rodwell, JS. (ed.) (1991 et seq.) *British Plant Communities*, Volume 1 (*Woodlands and Scrub* (1991)); Volume 2 (*Heaths and Mires* (1991)); Volume 3 (*Grasslands and Montane Communities* (1992)); Volume 4 (*Aquatic Communities, Swamps and Tall-herb Fens* (1995)); Volume 5 (*Maritime and Weed Communities and Vegetation of Open Habitats* (2000)). Cambridge University Press, Cambridge.

Rodwell, J and Dring, J. 2001. *European significance of British vegetation types.* English Nature Research Reports 460, English Nature, Peterborough.

Rodwell, J and Patterson, G. 1994. *Creating new native woodlands.* Forestry Commission Bulletin 112, HMSO, London.

Rose, F. 1999. Indicators of ancient woodland – the use of vascular plants in evaluating ancient woods for conservation. *British Wildlife* 10, 241–251.

Rose, F. 2006. *The Wildflower Key.* Penguin Books, England.

Scott, A. 2004. *Woodland wildflowers: assessing the effects and success of species introduction.* MSc thesis, University of Liverpool.

Scottish Natural Heritage. 2002. *Natural heritage Futures: An Overview.* Scottish Natural Heritage.

Scottish Natural Heritage. 2004. *Community woodlands in or near settlements.* Information Note Series, Scottish Natural Heritage.

Smith, RM and Roy, DB. 2008. Revealing the foundations of biodiversity: the Database of British Insects and their Foodplants. *British Wildlife* 20, 17–25.

Smithers, RJ, O'Hanley, JR, Harrison, PA and Berry, PM. 2007. *Appendix 2: Limits to climate space modelling.* In Walmsley, CA, Smithers, RJ, Berry, PM, Harley, M, Stevenson, MJ, Catchpole, R (eds.). *MONARCH (Modelling Natural Resource Responses to Climate Change): a synthesis for biodiversity conservation.* UK Climate Impacts Programme, Oxford.

Soutar, RG and Peterken, GF. 1989. The conservation of genetic variation in Britain's native trees. *Arboricultural Journal* 13, 33–43.

Spencer, J and Kirby, K. 1992. An inventory of ancient woodland for England and Wales. *Biological Conservation* 62, 77–93.

Stebbings, RE. 1988. *Conservation of European Bats.* Christopher Helm Publishers Ltd., London.

Stiven, R and Smith, M. 2005. *Lessons learned from tree planting on Rùm National Nature Reserve, 1957–2004.* Commissioned Report F02LD08, Scottish Natural Heritage.

Swanson, G, Armstrong, H and Campbell, D. 2008. *Estimating deer* abundance in woodlands: the combination plot techniques. Forestry Commission Bulletin 128, Forestry Commission, Edinburgh.

Swanwick, C. 2002. *Landscape Character Assessment. Guidance for England and Scotland.* Countryside Agency and Scottish Natural Heritage.

Swetnam, RD, Ragou, P, Firbank, LG, Hinsley, SA and Bellamy, PE. 1998. Applying ecological models to altered landscapes: scenario-testing with GIS. *Landscape and Urban Planning* 41, 3–18.

Tabbush, P. 2005. *Consultation and community involvement in forest planning: Research in Cranborne Chase and North Dorset.* Forest Research, Farnham.

Tabbush, P and O'Brien, E. 2003. *Health and well-being: Trees, woodlands and natural spaces.* Forest Research, Farnham.

Tansley, AG. 1939. *The British Isles and their Vegetation.* Cambridge University Press, Cambridge.

The National Forest Company. 2005. *The Forest Strategy 2004–2014.* The National Forest, Swadlincote.

Thompson, R. 2004. *Predicting site suitability for natural colonization: upland birchwoods and native pinewoods in northern Scotland.* Forestry Commission Information Note 54, Forestry Commission, Edinburgh.

Thompson, RN, Humphrey, JW, Harmer, R and Ferris, R. 2003. *Restoration of native woodland on ancient woodland sites.* Forestry Commission Practice Guide. Forestry Commission, Edinburgh.

Van Calster, H, Chevalier, R, Van Wyngene, B, Archaux, F, Verheyen, K and Hermy, M. 2008. Long-term seed bank dynamics in a temperate forest under conversion from coppice-with-standards to high forest management. *Applied Vegetation Science* 11, 251–268.

Van Lerberghe, P and Balleux, P. 2001. *Afforesting agricultural land.* Institut pour le Développement Forestier, Paris.

Vera, FWM. 2000. *Grazing Ecology and Forest History.* CABI Publishing, UK.

Verheyen, V and Hermy, M. 2001. The relative importance of dispersal limitation of vascular plants in secondary forest succession in Muizen Forest, Belgium. *Journal of Ecology* 89, 829–840.

Walmsley, CA, Smithers, RJ, Berry, PM, Harley, M, Stevenson, MJ and Catchpole, R. 2007. *Monarch (Modelling Natural Resources to Climate Change): a synthesis for biodiversity conservation.* UKCIP, Oxford.

Ward Thompson, C. 2007. *Woodland and a healthy society. New woods, new lives, new landscapes.* In: Proceedings of a conference on creating woodland for our future. The Woodland Trust, Grantham.

Ward, LK and Spalding, DF. 1993. Phytophagous British insects and mites and their food-plant families: total numbers and polyphagy. *Biological Journal of the Linnean Society* 49, 257–276.

Warren, MS and Fuller, RJ. 1993. *Woodland rides and glades: their management for wildlife.* Joint Nature Conservation Committee, Peterborough.

Watson, JW. 1996. Establishment of broadleaf woodland by direct seeding with arable crops: ecology of the Temperate Taungya method. *Aspects of Applied Biology* 44, 117–119.

Watts, K, Griffiths, M, Quine, C, Ray, D and Humphrey, JW. 2005a. *Towards a woodland Habitat Network for Wales.* Contract Science Report, 686. Countryside Council for Wales, Bangor.

Watts, K, Humphrey, JW, Griffths, M, Quine, C and Ray, D. 2005b. *Evaluating biodiversity in fragmented landscapes: principles.* Forestry Commission Information Note 73. Forestry Commission, Edinburgh.

Watts, K, Ray, D, Quine, C, Humphrey, JW and Griffiths, M. 2007. *Evaluating biodiversity in fragmented landscapes: applications of landscape ecology tools.* Forestry Commission Information Note 85. Forestry Commission, Edinburgh.

Weldon, S, Bailey, C and O'Brien, E. 2007. *New pathways for health and well-being in Scotland: research to understand and overcome barriers to accessing woodlands.* Report to Forestry Commission Scotland.

Wesche, S, Kirby, K and Ghazoul, J. 2006. Plant assemblages in British beech woodlands within and beyond native range: Implications of future climate change for their conservation. *Forest Ecology and Management* 236, 385–392.

Whitbread, AM and Kirby, KJ. 1992. *Summary of National Vegetation Classification woodland descriptions.* UK Nature Conservation Report 4, Joint Nature Conservation Committee, Peterborough.

Wildlife Trusts. 2007. *Living landscapes. A call to restore the UK's battered ecosystems, for wildlife and people.* The Wildlife Trusts, UK.

Wildlife Trusts in the South East. 2006. *A living landscape for the South East. The ecological network approach to rebuilding biodiversity for the 21st century.* Wildlife Trusts for the South East, UK.

Williamson, DR. 1992. *Establishing Farm Woodlands.* Forestry Commission Handbook 8. HMSO, London.

Willoughby I, Evans H, Gibbs J, Pepper H, Gregory S, Dewar J, Nisbet T, Pratt J, McKay H, Siddons R, Mayle B, Heritage S, Ferris R and Trout, R. 2004b. *Reducing pesticide use in forestry.* Forestry Commission Practice Guide, Forestry Commission, Edinburgh.

Willoughby, I, Jinks, R, Gosling, P and Kerr, G. 2004a. *Creating new broadleaved woodland by direct seeding.* Forestry Commission Practice Guide. Forestry Commission, Edinburgh.

Woodland Trust. 2004a. *Making woodland count. Its contribution to our quality of life.* A report prepared by ERM, in collaboration with Professor Kenneth Willis for The Woodland Trust. www.woodlandtrust.org.uk

Woodland Trust. 2004b. *Space for People. Targeting action for woodland access.* Woodland Trust, Grantham.

Woodland Trust. 2009a. *Position statement: woodland creation.* www.woodlandtrust.org.uk

Woodland Trust. 2009b. An internal paper on food security and land use in the UK.

World Health Organisation. 2005. *Mental Health Declaration for Europe. Facing the challenges, building solutions.* WHO European Ministerial Conference on Mental Health. Helsinki, January 2005.